Zoos and Tourism

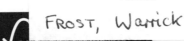

ASPECTS OF TOURISM
Series Editors: **Chris Cooper** *(Oxford Brookes University, UK)*, **C. Michael Hall** *(University of Canterbury, New Zealand)* and **Dallen J. Timothy** *(Arizona State University, USA)*

Aspects of Tourism is an innovative, multifaceted series, which comprises authoritative reference handbooks on global tourism regions, research volumes, texts and monographs. It is designed to provide readers with the latest thinking on tourism worldwide and push back the frontiers of tourism knowledge. The volumes are authoritative, readable and user-friendly, providing accessible sources for further research. Books in the series are commissioned to probe the relationship between tourism and cognate subject areas such as strategy, development, retailing, sport and environmental studies.

Full details of all the books in this series and of all our other publications can be found on http://www.channelviewpublications.com, or by writing to Channel View Publications, St Nicholas House, 31-34 High Street, Bristol BS1 2AW, UK.

ASPECTS OF TOURISM
Series Editors: Chris Cooper *(Oxford Brookes University, UK)*, C. Michael Hall *(University of Canterbury, New Zealand) and* Dallen J. Timothy *(Arizona State University, USA)*

Zoos and Tourism

Conservation, Education, Entertainment?

Edited by
Warwick Frost

CHANNEL VIEW PUBLICATIONS
Bristol • Buffalo • Toronto

Library of Congress Cataloging in Publication Data
A catalog record for this book is available from the Library of Congress.
Zoos and Tourism: Conservation, Education, Entertainment?/Edited by Warwick Frost.
Includes bibliographical references and index.
1. Zoos–Social aspects. 2. Wildlife conservation. 3. Tourism. I. Frost, Warwick.
QL76.Z754 2011
590.7'3–dc22 2010041489

British Library Cataloguing in Publication Data
A catalogue entry for this book is available from the British Library.

ISBN-13: 978-1-84541-164-0 (hbk)
ISBN-13: 978-1-84541-163-3 (pbk)

Channel View Publications
UK: St Nicholas House, 31–34 High Street, Bristol BS1 2AW, UK.
USA: UTP, 2250 Military Road, Tonawanda, NY 14150, USA.
Canada: UTP, 5201 Dufferin Street, North York, Ontario M3H 5T8, Canada.

The policy of Multilingual Matters/Channel View Publications is to use papers that are natural, renewable and recyclable products, made from wood grown in sustainable forests. In the manufacturing process of our books, and to further support our policy, preference is given to printers that have FSC and PEFC Chain of Custody certification. The FSC and/or PEFC logos will appear on those books where full certification has been granted to the printer concerned.

Typeset by Datapage International Ltd.
Printed and bound in Great Britain by Short Run Press Ltd.

Contents

Contributors

Philipp Boksberger, University of Applied Sciences Chur, Switzerland, philipp.boksberger@fh-htwchur.ch

Corazon Catibog-Sinha, University of Western Sydney, Australia, c.sinha@uws.edu.au

Gary Crilley, University of South Australia, Australia, gary.crilley@unisa.edu.au

Nancy Cushing, Newcastle University, Australia, nancy.cushing@newcastle.edu.au

John Dobson, University of Wales, Cymru, jdobson@uwic.ac.uk

Warwick Frost, La Trobe University, Australia, w.frost@latrobe.edu.au

Sam Ham, University of Idaho, USA, sham@uidaho.edu

Kevin Hannam, University of Sunderland, England, kevin.hannam@sunderland.ac.uk

Joan Henderson, Nanyang Technological University, Singapore, ahenderson@ntu.edu.sg

Kirsten Holmes, Curtin University, Australia, k.holmes@curtin.edu.au

Chantelle Jobberns, University of Technology Sydney, Australia

Jennifer Laing, Monash University, Australia, Jennifer.laing@buseco.monash.edu.au

Sharon Linke, La Trobe University, Australia,

Kevin Markwell, Southern Cross University, Australia, kevin.markwell@sc.edu.au

Peter Mason, Victoria University, Australia, peter.mason@vu.edu.au

Abraham Pizam, University of Central Florida, USA, apizam@mail.ucf.edu

Richard Robinson, University of Queensland, Australia, richard.robinson@uq.edu.au

Amir Shani, Ben-Gurion University, Israel, shaniam@bgu.ac.il

Markus Shuckert, University of Applied Sciences Chur, Switzerland, marcus.schuckert@fh-htwchur.ch

Karen Smith, Victoria University Wellington, New Zealand, karen.smith@vuw.ac.nz

Liam Smith, Monash University, Australia, liam.smith@buseco.monash.edu.au

Stephen Wearing, University of Technology Sydney, Australia, stephen.wearing@uts.edu.au

Betty Weiler, Monash University, Australia, betty.weiler@buseco.monash.edu.au

Leanne White, Victoria University, Australia, leannek.white@vu.edu.au

Caroline Winter, University of Ballarat, Australia, c.winter@ballarat.edu.au

Acknowledgements

The editor thanks the following for their assistance, encouragement and patience: Elinor Robertson and Sarah Williams at Channel View; Laura Lawton and Wes Roehl, editors of *Tourism Review International*, who encouraged me to co-edit a special issue on zoos and aquaria; Sue Broad and Liam Smith, whose offices were next to mine and got me thinking about zoos and tourism (and Liam for introducing me to *the Mighty Boosh*) and Michael Hall, who worked with me on editing a book on Tourism and National Parks, from which the idea to move onto zoos naturally grew. Finally, a special thanks to Sarah, Stephen and Alex.

Chapter 1

Rethinking Zoos and Tourism

WARWICK FROST

Zoos are important and popular tourist attractions. Spread around the world, they range from substantial operations in major cities, with visitation levels comparable to other top attractions, to small, regional, owner-operator ventures. Nature-based attractions constructed in artificial settings, they face the challenge of trying to balance the potentially conflicting aims of conservation, education and entertainment. The best zoos are continually developing fresh and effective techniques on visitor interpretation and animal management, the worst highlight the manipulation of animals for human gratification.

Modern zoos are dynamic institutions. In the 19th and early 20th centuries, they were seen as integral parts of a worldwide conservation movement. Advocates of national parks were often involved in zoos and vice versa. Zoos had a role in conserving and scientifically studying endangered species and this scientific interest often extended to seeing zoos as vehicles for acclimatising and introducing 'useful' exotic species (Hoage & Deiss, 1996). However, in the late 20th century, there were revolutionary changes in how zoos saw their role and the experiences they offer to visitors. This was primarily driven by major shifts in public attitudes to nature and conservation. There was widespread public concern for the protection of threatened ecosystems and species, and the sustainability of constant economic growth was questioned. These changes in society meant that zoos were increasingly viewed as anachronistic. Their ubiquitous cramped cages, with bare concrete floors, were symbolic of a bygone past that could no longer be tolerated in modern societies (Baratay & Hardouin-Fugier, 2002; Hancocks, 2001; Jamieson, 1985; Mazur, 2001; Tribe, 2004) (see Figure 1.1 and 1.2). The very future of individual zoos, and the institution in general, began to be seriously questioned. Indeed, one survey of zoo visitors found that 27% believed that zoos should be abolished (Shackley, 1996: 104).

Two examples of the pressure that modern zoos were being subjected to are worth highlighting. London Zoo, perhaps the most famous zoo in the world, seemed to plummet from grace after reaching peak attendances in the 1950s. In the 1970s, the editor of the *Ecologist* declared, 'London Zoo is a shameful establishment where wild animals [live] in totally inappropriate conditions', and a newspaper termed it the 'Beasts' Belsen' (both quoted in Hancocks, 2001: 52). In 1992, the combination of

1

Figure 1.1 Old fashioned exhibit, but still in use. The zebra enclosure at Rome Zoo. (Photo: Warwick Frost)

Figure 1.2 Old fashioned exhibit, but still in use. The Giraffe House at London Zoo. (Photo: Warwick Frost)

public concern and declining attendances led to the UK government withdrawing its annual grant and, for a time, it appeared that London Zoo would close (Shackley, 1996). In 1963, Melbourne's *Herald* newspaper ran an extensive campaign, highlighting the cruel and degrading conditions that animals were kept in at Melbourne Zoo. It posed the question that if the situation could not be improved, then perhaps it was time for the zoo to be closed (De Courcy, 1995).

Faced with such challenges, zoos began to radically change what they did and why they did it. Enclosures became larger and more naturalistic, with grass and plants replacing concrete, and metal bars giving way to moats and glass. Rather than simply gazing through bars, visitors were 'immersed' while walking through themed landscapes, often with freely ranging animals (Figure 1.3). The successes of the pioneers in these trends, such as Seattle's Woodland Park Zoo, were quickly copied by others (Hancocks, 2001). Through publicly embracing conservation as their key role, zoos repositioned themselves as relevant institutions within modern society (Tribe, 2004) (Figure 1.4).

Nonetheless, criticism of zoos continues. As Hancocks (2001: xv) argues, despite the changes 'we should not accept zoos as they currently are'. The recent case of Knut, the polar bear at Berlin Zoo, demonstrates this continuing conflict between animal welfare and financial impera-

Figure 1.3 Modern 'immersive' exhibit, in which visitors move through a more natural environment with free roaming animals, London Zoo. (Photo: Warwick Frost)

Figure 1.4 Display board of the roles of zoos at Rome Zoo. The emphasis is on research, conservation and education rather than entertainment or recreation. (Photo: Warwick Frost)

tives. Born in 2006, Knut was rejected by his mother and would normally have died. However, the zoo decided to raise him and he became the first polar bear to survive childhood at the zoo in 30 years. As a cute and charismatic baby animal, Knut became a zoo superstar, dramatically raising attendances and featuring heavily in the media (even gracing the cover of the glossy magazine *Vanity Fair*). However, there were also concerns about his increasingly aggressive behaviour and the long-term effects of his unnatural upbringing. An unseemly dispute over the ownership of Knut and his profits further highlighted the issues of his commodification.

Even zoos that have invested heavily in naturalistic enclosures and made commitments to conservation and environmental education campaigns, remain subject to heavy public and media scrutiny. In the 1960s, Melbourne Zoo reacted to press criticism by embarking on a major rebuilding programme based on advanced principles of display and animal husbandry. Yet, despite all its successes, recently it has once again been the subject of media complaints on two counts. The first is an increasing focus on commercial imperatives and the second is the ill-treatment of some of its 'star' animals (Dennis, 2008; Millar & Houston, 2008a, 2008b).

It is extraordinary to consider that among the wide range of entities catering for our leisure in the modern world, zoos stand alone as the only entity that is continually under critical scrutiny, to the extent of periodic and widespread calls for major changes and even their abolition. This striking situation is best understood by comparison with other leisure attractions. Museums occasionally attract claims of inappropriate displays, particularly human remains and culturally sensitive items. However, these controversies are about specific items and do not result in moves to shut or completely re-order museums. Similarly, from time to time, there are calls to ban certain works of art, but no one is running a campaign to shut down art galleries. In these cases, we are dealing with objects. Is it different if we consider living things? What about national parks? Like zoos, they seek to balance conservation with tourism and recreation. In many cases, this doesn't work too well, and there are complaints that they are being mismanaged. However, these critics don't call for the closure of national parks. This singling out of zoos is curious. Perhaps it is because zoos are widely seen as 'popular' rather than 'high' culture (Mullan & Marvin, 1987: 125).

Perhaps zoos suffer from a 'crisis of identity'; with managers, visitors and other stakeholders not sure whether zoos are protected areas for nature or visitor attractions or some sort of hybrid. The intensity, range and time span of the debate about their roles is not repeated for any other tourism operation. Of course, even attaching the descriptor of tourism to zoos may be seen as provocative. However, zoos do have a role in tourism. They operate as attractions and form part of the attributes of a destination. That this role tends to be ignored, downplayed or criticised is part of this crisis of identity.

Are zoos really tourist attractions? It could be argued that they are simply visitor attractions, mainly catering to local populations and having little economic impact on host communities. Taking such a view relegates zoos to the status of other recreational amusements, like shopping malls and cinemas (the analogy of cinemas is interesting given the ongoing campaigns to reduce Hollywood's use of live animals, see, e.g. Cheeta, 2008). From a public policy perspective (whether we like it or not), economic benefit justifies governments' support of tourism development, even if it consumes the natural environment. If zoos do not bestow an economic benefit from tourism, their case for existence becomes weaker.

Certainly, the literature often presents zoos as being mainly for local people, typically on no more than a family excursion or picnic just for the day. When visitor statistics are quoted, they seem to confirm a pattern that the majority are from the domestic market. Consider these examples. For London Zoo, 50% of visitors were from London and 87% from the UK (Tribe, 2004: 37). At Chester Zoo, 64% of visitors came from within a radius of 50 miles (80 km) (Swarbrooke, 1995: 343). The accessibility of zoos to local markets is also demonstrated by the high levels of repeat visitation. At Chester Zoo, 84% had been previously (Swarbrooke, 1995: 343), while in another UK study it was 91% (Shackley, 1996: 103). A study at Woodland Zoo in Seattle showed that 50% of visitors only had short visits, spending just two hours or less (Mullan & Marvin, 1987: 133). Such statistics suggest a 'typical' zoo visitor who is local, regular and recreational, rather than a tourist.

However, we need to take care. There is evidence that zoos are on the tourists' itineraries and they form a large market. While 87% of visitors to London Zoo are British, it is significant that the remaining 13% are from overseas. At 130,000 per year, that is a sizeable flow of tourists, one that many attractions would dream of. Similarly, while 64% of Chester Zoo's visitors are from within a radius of 80 km, 36% are from outside that local area. In Australia, there are about 8 million visitors to zoos, of which 5 million are domestic (Tribe, 2004: 37). However, that leaves an impressive 3 million international visits.

Rather than counting visitors, an alternative approach is to consider international visitors and their activities. For Australia, the 2008/2009 International Visitor Survey recorded that 53% visited wildlife parks, zoos or aquaria. This is a similar rate to a range of other attractions, including national parks, heritage buildings or museums and art galleries (and much higher than wineries or the performing arts). Furthermore, it is much higher than the 18% of domestic tourists who visit wildlife parks, zoos and aquaria (Tourism Australia, 2009). Such data indicate that visiting zoos and aquaria is a major activity among international tourists in Australia.

While many major urban zoos pick up a steady, though incidental flow of tourists, others are more directly targeted at tourists. Some major zoos utilise rare charismatic animals, such as polar bears and pandas, to attract tourists in a way similar to the 'blockbuster' exhibitions of museums or art galleries. Others, such as San Diego Zoo, Monterey Aquarium and Steve Irwin's Australia Zoo, appeal so directly to tourist markets that they become 'destination attractions', major operations that define the image and attributes of the destination. In popular destinations, there may be a 'clustering' of zoos and wildlife attractions, as in Miami, which has four such operations close together (Shackley, 1996).

Small specialised zoos may rely heavily on tourists. This is especially so where they have a bioregional focus, providing distinctive animals from a region. Examples include Montana Grizzly Encounter in Bozeman, USA; Crocosaurus in Darwin; Alice Springs Desert Park; and a number of small operations on the main tourist routes around Hobart, which features Tasmanian Devils.

Of all the tourism-orientated, zoo-type attractions, aquaria stand out. These have long been situated in areas with high tourism flows (Ford, 2009). In recent years, this trend has accelerated, with the developers of tourism precincts seeking to include aquaria as focal points (Judd, 1999; Shackley, 1996). Aquaria are utilised in this way as they are concentrated attractions, able to be established anywhere and requiring relatively little space. They also have a natural affinity with the trend of redeveloping former wharf areas as shopping/residential/tourism complexes. Examples include the Aquarium of the Bay located at the entrance to Fisherman's Wharf in San Francisco; the Sydney Aquarium in Darling Harbour; and the National Aquarium at Baltimore's Inner Harbour. The Vancouver Aquarium benefits from being in close proximity to recently developed harbour precincts, while Underwater World in Singapore is located on the resort island of Sentosa.

Zoos and aquaria cannot simply be seen as recreational attractions for local people. They also function as tourism attractions and there is a trend for that role to become increasingly important. Again, this highlights a crisis of identity. Entertainment (or recreation) – the third role of zoos – can be split between the activities and expectations of local visitors and tourists. This has implications for both the operators of zoos and aquaria and the tourism industry.

The aim of this book is to undertake a critical examination of the conflicting roles of zoos and current zoo practices through the lens of tourism studies. There have been quite a number of excellent studies of zoos and many of these have considered tourism and how that has an impact on zoos (e.g. Hancocks, 2001; Mullan & Marvin, 1987). However, these studies have not been by experts in tourism – Hancocks was a zoo designer and administrator and Mullan and Marvin are sociologists. Accordingly, their commentary on tourism has tended to be limited. By contrast, it is striking that so few research studies on zoos and aquaria have been published in the tourism literature. Mason (2000) found that there had only been a handful of studies specifically dealing with tourism and zoos. Eight years later, the introduction for the first special issue of a tourism journal on zoos argued that very little had changed (Frost & Roehl, 2008). This deficiency in the literature is even more striking if we contrast it with the hundreds of studies in other areas of nature-based tourism, such as ecotourism operators or national parks. This may be the result of zoos and aquaria being seen as mass market attractions. Taking our cue from Robert Frost, tourism researchers have tended to take the road less travelled, looking at niche and new developments. There is value in occasionally choosing to explore the road well travelled.

Taking a tourism perspective allows a fresh approach to the important debate about the role of zoos. If a major part of the problem is that zoos are too commercially focused, placing visitors above animals, then there is surely value in considering what those in tourism marketing think about the issue (if only – and my tongue is in my cheek – to know the enemy better). If zoos are becoming more like theme parks, then there is value in consulting the research literature on theme parks and other tourist attractions – and vice versa – studies in tourism attractions can learn a great deal from the experiences of zoos. Most importantly, a major component of tourism studies has been nature-based attractions, including protected areas such as national parks, the recent growth of ecotourism and the development of interpretation and other visitor services for nature-based tourists. To understand zoos better, we need to reach out to these studies as well.

This collection looks at an old problem with a fresh set of eyes. The broad perspective is tourism, but as is widely recognised, tourism is a multi-disciplinary field. Accordingly, underlying the authors' interest in tourism are background disciplines as diverse as marketing, geography, sociology, history, education, hospitality, biology and other environmental sciences. The result is not one 'standard tourism' focus, but a range of differing, even conflicting perspectives.

The chapters in the collection are grouped under four broad themes, each with a short introductory essay. The first group revisits the ongoing debate over the role of zoos in conservation. The second group considers new, often more commercial, directions being taken by zoos and aquaria. The third takes this further, exploring an increasing emphasis on the visitor experience. The final group examines the influence of media. These themes are overlapping and many of the chapters could easily have been placed under multiple headings. Within each theme, the chapters take different approaches and positions, highlighting that there are still some unresolved debates. The role of academic researchers is to tell stories that (hopefully) encourage people to think about and question the way things are. Our aim is to get people rethinking zoos and aquaria, questioning, reflecting and improving them and the way they operate.

Part 1

Conservation

Zoos are often presented as being like Noah's Ark, a place of last refuge for endangered animals, maintaining a breeding population that can be used for future restocking of the wild. It is a widely used metaphor, popularised by writers such as Gerald Durrell and embraced by many. It is also a view that has been increasingly questioned and debated.

While zoos are highly popular tourist attractions, it is often argued that this role of providing pleasure to visitors is not enough in itself to justify removing animals from the wild and placing them in artificial enclosures. The entertainment role would only be justified, it is argued, if it was *secondary* to a conservation role. However, it is also often argued that zoos generally have not devoted enough of their resources to this role and changes in public attitudes to animals and their confinement have led to a shrinking market and support for zoos (for examples of these arguments see Bostock, 1993; Hancocks, 2001; Jamieson, 1985; Mazur, 2001; Shackley, 1996).

Historically, zoos have performed relatively poorly in conserving species. Two unfortunate examples serve to illustrate this. The first is the Tasmanian Tiger or thylacine. In 1936, the last known thylacine died at Beaumaris Zoo, Hobart, on a severe winter's night after its keeper forgot to return it to its quarters (Figure T1.1). From the 1850s onwards, thylacines had been displayed in zoos in London, Washington, Vienna, Paris and Antwerp, as well as throughout Australia. They were popular due to their rarity, but no zoo engaged in a captive breeding programme or habitat conservation. Nor did they lobby the Tasmanian Government to remove their bounty (Paddle, 2000). It was only after the last in captivity had died that there were unsuccessful attempts to stock a breeding colony (Fleay-Thomson, 2007). The second example is a 1949 collecting expedition to the Cameroons in Africa by Durrell. His aim was to capture the rare Pygmy Flying Squirrel (Idiurus). Indeed, he collected over 30, but all died before he reached Britain (Botting, 1999).

Countering these failures are the successes of zoos in saving species, including the Mongolian Wild Horse, Père David's Deer, European Bison, Oryx and Golden Lion Tamarin. However, it is argued that the number is quite small and it has been more a case of good luck that these have been saved (Hancocks, 2001; Shackley, 1996). Indeed, it might seem that some zoos engage in a form of *greenwashing*, trumpeting their role in saving animals, when they are really doing very little. Hancocks (2001)

Figure T1.1 Dark tourism in zoos: Commemorative panel at the site of Beaumaris Zoo. (Photo: Jennifer Laing)

provides an example of a North American zoo that opened a 'Chimpanzee Conservation Center' with great fanfare, but which turned out to be no more than a new exhibit.

Perhaps the Ark metaphor is the wrong one and the debate needs to be shifted. In recent years, many zoos have demonstrated a much greater commitment to conservation through a wide range of programmes. There has been a realisation that just preserving a breeding population is not enough by itself. These newer conservation strategies comprise three components. The first is global collaborations, involving zoos, conservation bodies and protected area agencies. The second is working on conservation projects in the countries where the animals hail from, protecting habitat and preserving remaining populations. In this case, zoos become the public showcase for such programmes. The third (and newest) is zoos utilising their engagement with visitors to deliver persuasive messages as to how people can help conserve animals under threat. A good example of this is the current campaign for changes to food labelling laws so that consumers can see whether or not they include palm oil (the product responsible for rainforest clearing in southeast Asia). Zoos failed to save the Tasmanian Tiger, but by acting with collaborative partners, they may be part of the answer to saving the Tasmanian Devil and many other threatened species.

It is often argued that zoos are primarily for people (Mullan & Marvin, 1987; Rothfels, 2002). A large number of studies have consistently identified that people value zoos for the recreational experience more than conservation (see, e.g. Hancocks, 2001; Jiang *et al.*, 2008; Mullan & Marvin, 1987; Ryan & Saward, 2004; Shackley, 1996; Tribe, 2004; Turley, 1999). The consistency of these results may seem worrying, though we need to realise that those surveyed were not asked to choose *between* recreation and conservation. It could be that both are important. As zoos change how they approach conservation, the challenge may be in convincing visitors that what they do has relevance to both the animals and the paying customer.

There are five chapters under this general theme of conservation. The first, by Catibog-Sinha, examines collaborative programmes between various zoos and the Philippine government. Four endangered species are covered by these programmes: the Philippine Crocodile, the Philippine Spotted Deer, the Philippine Cockatoo and the Visayan Warty Hog. Rather than just protecting these species in an ark, these programmes aim to reintroduce them to parts of the Philippines in cooperation with local agencies and communities. Intriguingly in these partnerships between Western zoos and the government of a developing nation, it is the Philippines who retains ownership of the animals and a dominant role.

In the second chapter, Shani and Pizam propose a new typology for zoos and other captive wildlife settings. Past typologies have tended to focus on the level of freedom the animals enjoyed, but this, it is argued, is too simplistic and fails to examine the underlying motives and values of the organisations operating these settings. Instead, Shani and Pizam argue for a typology based on Kellert's nine basic wildlife values. Although these values represent general attitudes towards animals and nature, it is argued that they also best explain the various ways in which animals are displayed and exhibited in animal-based attractions.

The third and fourth chapters take a critical view of the conservation justification for zoos. Wearing and Jobberns argue that zoos, like much in ecotourism and nature-based tourism, do not stand up to scrutiny. While, they argue, there is often a rhetoric of conservation and nature-centeredness, the reality is that they are often primarily for the entertainment of tourists and achieve little for conservation. They present animal rescue and reintroduction centres as much more ethical attractions worthy of more promotion within tourism. Smith, Weiler and Ham argue the need for much more visitor research, particularly into motivations and how zoos can effectively communicate conservation messages to tourists.

The fifth chapter is an empirical study by Linke and Winter. Their interest was in applying the Theory of Planned Behaviour to zoos, searching for connections between attitudes and behaviour. Their study indicates that while visitors hold attitudes that zoos are equally important for their conservation, education and entertainment roles, the main reason for visiting tended to be to have an entertainment experience.

Chapter 2

Zoo Tourism and the Conservation of Threatened Species: A Collaborative Programme in the Philippines

CORAZON CATIBOG-SINHA

Introduction

Zoos worldwide are urged to address species conservation not only through long-term commitment to captive management and propagation, but also through environmental education, research, habitat conservation and reintroduction (WAZA, 2005; Zimmermann *et al.*, 2007). This chapter discusses the collaborative agreement between the Philippines and several leading zoos overseas on the conservation of certain zoo animals. It examines the salient features of these institutional agreements in the context of wildlife conservation and the sustainability of zoo tourism. Based on the results of interviews with key staff involved in these programmes as well as an in-depth analysis of government documents (i.e. memoranda of agreement, legislations, treaties, biodiversity country reports and zoo accomplishment reports), this chapter explores the role of collaborative partnerships in sustaining zoo tourism and species conservation. The discussion is placed in the broader context of sustainability, which is grounded in the basic principles of biodiversity conservation, precautionary principle, public education and awareness, and community involvement/participation.

Zoos and Zoo Tourism

Zoo tourism involves direct interaction of visitors with wildlife under captive or semi-captive conditions. Zoos include zoological gardens, biological parks, safari parks, public aquariums, bird parks, reptile parks and insectariums; there are approximately 10,000–12,000 zoos worldwide (WAZA, 2005). However, more than 90% of zoos have substandard management in the care of captive animals and a poor record of involvement in the conservation of wildlife (Armstrong *et al.*, 1993; Kelly, 1997; Van Linge, 1992). Nevertheless, there are some 1000 publicly or privately owned zoos worldwide, which are internationally recognised for their good practice in animal care and species conservation; they receive more than 600 million visitors annually (WAZA, 2005).

Zoos provide opportunities for visitors to view and interact directly with wildlife, despite the artificial or unnatural setting. According to Beardsworth and Bryman (2001), the zoo is very much part of the 'tourist trail'. A survey of international tourists in Cairns, Australia, revealed that a majority of the respondents preferred direct wildlife encounters in controlled setting, either in a zoo or a wildlife park (Coghlan & Prideaux, 2008). Zoo tourism usually involves a one-day visit; it is generally a family-orientated leisure activity (Ryan & Saward, 2004; Turley, 2001). For some tourists, zoos cannot be 'an effective substitute for viewing wildlife in their natural settings' (Ryan & Saward, 2004: 260). On the other hand, others greatly enjoy the zoo experience that encourages them to travel and see wild animals in their natural habitats.

Zoos can serve as an excellent tool for promoting and imparting conservation awareness and learning. Zoos can take direct action to conserve species through education and conservation programmes, and these programmes can be integrated into zoo tourism (Catibog-Sinha, 2008a). The visitors surveyed in three Malaysian zoos, perceived zoos as a place for conservation, education, research and recreation. Those surveyed in Hamilton Zoo (New Zealand) placed a high value on viewing the animals (Ryan & Saward, 2004). Hunter-Jones and Hayward (1998) found that visitors, mostly children, surveyed from 200 zoos in the UK, placed great importance on watching and learning about the exhibits. The study by Woods (2002) revealed that the best tourist experiences in zoos were associated with wildlife interaction as well as an opportunity not only to view a large number and a wide variety of animals, but also to learn about them. The motivating factors for visitors surveyed in the Cleveland Metropark Zoo (USA) included not only enjoyment, relaxation and family togetherness, but also education. A survey of visitors at three Indian zoos revealed that zoos can help protect wild animals, such as the Lion-tailed macaques, and provide excellent learning venues to convey messages about conservation (Mallapur *et al.*, 2008). A survey of visitors to Denver Zoo revealed that zoos are important for education (55%) and for conserving wildlife (29%) (Reading & Miller, 2007). Catibog-Sinha (2008b) reports that in the Philippines, visitors to a mini zoo within an urban park in Metro Manila benefited from their interaction with wildlife, discovering information previously unknown to them. Clearly, a well-planned interpretation programme will greatly enrich the recreational experience of zoo visitors and increase their appreciation of wildlife (Balmford *et al.*, 2007; Rhoads & Goldworthy, 1979).

To promote the roles of zoos in conservation, research and education, several zoo operators/authorities formed a global zoo network, known as the World Association of Zoos and Aquaria (WAZA), subsequently formulating the World Zoo and Aquariums Conservation Strategy (WZACS). The strategy is a response to the challenges put forward during the 2002 World Summit on Sustainable Development and UN Millennium Development Goals. The strategy reaffirms that zoos are not merely for entertainment. It emphasises that zoos should have a prominent role in the conservation of wildlife, particular those with small populations, both in captivity and in the wild. Zoos are also expected to undertake a wide range of basic research in animal welfare and wildlife management. The role of tourism research in zoo management was highlighted by Frost and Roehl (2008). The research data are used to enrich the interpretative and entertaining aspects of zoo tourism, as well as provide the bases for improving the zoos' educational and conservation management programmes (Mason, 2000; Mazur, 2001; Melfi, 2005; WAZA, 2005).

Zoo Animals: Threatened Species

Collectively, zoos maintain about 1 million living wild animals from various parts of the world. Half of these collections are mammals, birds, reptiles and amphibians (WCMC, 1992), the majority of which are large in body size, colourful and have interesting behavioural characteristics (Churchman & Bossler, 1990; Puan & Zakaria, 2007; Turley, 2001; Ward *et al.*, 1998). Unfortunately, many of these charismatic zoo animals are rare because they inhabit only certain geographical areas or they have restricted biological requirements or their populations have declined over the years due to habitat loss, over-exploitation or combinations of all these factors (Gaston & Blackburn, 1995; Miller & Lacy, 2003). Large animals, for example, are likely to become rare because they occur in low density and are often targeted by hunters for game and meat (Dobson & Yu, 1993). Because of their vulnerability and irreplaceability, many zoo visitors tend to sympathise with their situation. Hence, threatened species in zoo collections are used as flagships in fund raising and conservation campaigns.

To sustain zoo tourism, zoos need to acquire and maintain healthy animal collections. Zoos usually replenish their collections with animals trapped from the wild or those bred in captivity (Hanson, 2002; Holst & Dickie, 2007). However, acquiring threatened endemic species from the wild, especially from developing but biodiversity-rich countries, can be complex and even political. The global degradation and loss of natural habitats and over-exploitation of wildlife, coupled with tight government policies, have caused some difficulties in the acquisition and transport of zoo animals from the wild. Kelly (1997: 1) predicted that in the 21st century, the whole biota, 'may need to be assembled from remnant and/or reintroduced endemic species in habitats that have been preserved or reconstructed'. Nonetheless, even these habitats are being rapidly transformed to other land uses, leading either to the displacement or the disappearance of many native wildlife (Millennium Ecosystem Assessment, 2005).

Zoos may also replace or replenish their collections from in-house captive breeding programmes or purchase captive-born specimens from other zoos. However, merely propagating zoo animals as replenishments is both inadequate and unsustainable. Furthermore, there is no guarantee that reproduction will be successful under captive condition because not all founders breed successfully, and if they do, some breed less than others. Moreover, proper genetic management and behavioural studies are crucial in sustainable zoo management. However, not all zoos have the technical and financial capabilities to undertake these measures. For instance, genetic uniformity in captive animals resulting from inbreeding must be prevented by increasing the founder population (preferably collected from the wild) or by moving animals (or their genetic materials, gametes or embryos) to various breeding facilities within a country or around the world (Catibog-Sinha, 2008a; Ellis & Seal, 1996). As part of good practice in zoo management, the movement of animals, including their genetic resources, should be monitored to ensure that the genealogical records of these animals are properly maintained. The creation of hybrids, which often have morphological and health problems, is bad public relations that responsible zoos do not wish to support.

Conservation Measures: *In situ* and *Ex situ*

Many modern zoos undertake sustainable zoo tourism through integrated management approaches. Many of the leading zoos have already transformed some of their exhibits into 'experience centres', which offer specific thematic attractions (e.g. rainforest, cats, primates) and learning experiences (Rabb, 1996; Young, 2003). Zoos are engaged in the conservation of several threatened species both in their natural habitats (*in situ* conservation) and in captivity (*ex situ* conservation). Through their interpretation programme, zoos make the visitors aware of and responsive to the zoos' contribution to sustainable tourism and species conservation.

Ex situ conservation is considered by the Convention on Biological Diversity (CBD) (Article 9) as a complementary measure to *in situ* conservation. *In situ* conservation includes the maintenance of species in their natural environment through wildlife protection as well as habitat management and restoration. *Ex situ* conservation involves establishing back-up populations of threatened species through captive breeding, which is necessary only when their natural habitats are seriously degraded and/or the species themselves are over-exploited. When habitats are consistently destroyed by natural and/or man-made calamities, the probability of species surviving in captivity, with proper animal care protocol, would be much higher. Countries that have ratified the convention, such as the Philippines, are urged to rescue plants and animals from extinction by maintaining viable populations in captivity with the intention of reintroducing them into their natural habitats when conditions return to normal.

Modern zoos have a crucial role in contributing to the country's conservation efforts through the simultaneous implementation of *in situ* and *ex situ* measures. Linking both conservation measures is vital in zoo research and conservation science (Ryder & Feistner, 1995; WAZA, 2005; Zimmermann *et al.*, 2007). Mallinson and Hartley (2008: 488) state that long-term conservation efforts entail 'balancing ex-situ expertise with in-situ partnership endeavours'. The Species Survival Commission of the IUCN underscores the complementarity between *in situ* and *ex situ* programmes of zoos, which can be achieved through improved coopera-tion among zoos and various conservation organisations and govern-ment bodies.

Partnerships and Collaboration: Philippine Case Study

Partnerships for sustainability, wherein involved parties can share resources and technological know-how, can help promote institutional learning in sustainable development (Morse, 2008). Plummer *et al.* (2006) state that 'working together' in the form of partnerships and collabora-tion is vital in nature-based tourism. In particular, building partnerships in conservation among relevant stakeholders provides a significant foundation in overcoming the issues/problems associated with com-mon-pool resources, such as wildlife (Jones & Burgess, 2005). There is a need for organisations involved in wildlife conservation in general and wildlife breeding in particular, to cooperate at local, national and international levels in response to the accelerating rate of species extinction (Mallinson & Hartley, 2008; Prance, 1997; Westley & Miller, 2003).

In the Philippines, networking and collaboration among zoos are essential to initiate collective action for conservation and sustainable zoo tourism. The Philippines is considered one of the 'hottest of the hotspots' in the world in terms of high vulnerability and high irreplaceability of its endemic species (Brooks *et al.*, 2004; Mittermeier *et al.*, 2004). More than 50% of the endemic wildlife in the Philippines is gravely threatened because 97% of the country's lowland old-growth forest has already been destroyed (Myers *et al.*, 2000). Since the endemic species of the Philippines are not found anywhere else in the world, their extinction would mean a global loss (Catibog-Sinha & Heaney, 2006).

Even though zoos are possible places for *ex situ* conservation, many zoos in the Philippines are still keeping wild animals merely for public display and entertainment. Some of these zoos have not yet met the minimum animal welfare standards (Almazan *et al.*, 2005; Bagarinao, 1998), much less so in implementing long-term conservation measures to sustain the populations of even their prized collections. More than 100 animal facilities (mostly privately owned) have been accredited or issued permits by the government, but not all have appropriate breeding programmes because they are generally poorly funded and inadequately managed. As a result, the international zoo community has been helping the Philippines in establishing back-up populations of certain endangered endemic species in *ex situ* facilities. This is in response to the global call by WAZA (2005), which encourages zoos to help one another, especially those that have fewer resources and technical expertise. Such call for partnerships can facilitate not only the maintenance of live animals in captivity for public viewing, entertainment, education and research, but also the *ex situ* breeding of threatened species to sustain viable populations and possible reintroduction to their natural habitats.

Partnerships and collaborations among institutions are re-affirmed and formalised through written agreements. One such agreement is the Memorandum of Agreement (MOA), which articulates the objectives/ goals, responsibilities, financial obligations and expectations of participating institutions. The MOA integrates the views of the involved parties and ensures that the terms and conditions are consistent with existing national legislations, institutional protocols and international commitments. In the case of the Philippines, an MOA is forged between a foreign zoo (Second Party) and the government (First Party) through the Protected Areas and Wildlife Bureau of the Department of Environment and Natural Resources (PAWB-DENR), the body tasked to protect wild terrestrial animals and habitats. The MOA is notarised to establish the legitimacy of the agreed terms/conditions and commitments to specific conservation concerns.

The Philippines has entered into several memoranda of agreement with some prominent zoos in Australia, Denmark, France, the USA, etc. Before entering into any formal agreement, each potential foreign zoo partner may be assessed based on one or more of the following criteria: membership to WAZA or any of its regional chapters/branches, research and conservation expertise and previous records of institutional partnerships. Currently, 10–12 collaborative captive breeding programmes are in place in the country (A. Meniado, personal communication). This chapter focuses only on the programmes for the conservation of four endemic species, all of which are considered globally threatened (Table 2.1).

Table 2.1 Species under joint programmes on *ex situ* conservation

Species	Conservation status	Partnership initiatives
Philippine Crocodile	IUCN Red List: Critically Endangered (CITES: Appendix I)	The national and international breeding centres are managed collaboratively through the Philippine Crocodile Recovery Team, with Melbourne Zoo (Australia) as the designated international coordinator. In 2009, 50 crocodiles were released into the wild at Dicatian Lake in the northern Philippines.
		The Danish Crocodile Zoo maintains a founder group for some European zoos (Chester Zoo; London Zoo; Zurich Zoo; Cologne Zoo; Bergen Aquarium).
		The North American Cooperative for Conservation of the Philippine Crocodile is committed to assist with the captive rearing of offspring produced at Gladys Porter Zoo (Texas, USA).
		The Henry Doorly Zoo (Nebraska, USA) is conducting population genetics as a basis for captive management and reintroduction.
		Collaborative field studies in the Philippines showed that the crocodile population in the Northern Sierra Madre region of Luzon may be one of the last two viable populations of the species in the wild. The population situation on Mindanao Island is uncertain.
Philippine Spotted Deer	IUCN Red List: Endangered; recommended to be upgraded to Critically Endangered	The *ex situ* programme consists of two subspecies, which are treated separately in captive breeding initiatives.
		A studbook on the world herd of Philippine Spotted Deer is being maintained.
		The Philippine Spotted Deer Conservation Committee was set up.

Table 2.1 (*Continued*)

Species	Conservation status	Partnership initiatives
		The Durell Wildlife Conservation Trust sponsored overseas training courses of four Filipinos.
		Habitat rehabilitation and protection are the major *in situ* initiatives.
Philippine Cockatoo	IUCN Red List: Critically Endangered (CITES: Appendix I)	The European Association of Zoos and Aquaria (EAZA) runs the European StudBook (ESB) as part of its breeding programme, where a studkeeper is nominated to maintain the demographic and genetic data of the Philippine Cockatoo being kept in all EAZA zoos.
		Psittacine beak and feather disease is being monitored in the wild population.
		Espace Zoologique (France), in collaboration with national and local governments and NGOs (e.g. *Katala* Foundation), has conducted field surveys and public awareness campaigns, including habitat rehabilitation and protection, in Palawan and Mindanao.
Visayan Warty Pig	IUCN Red List: Critically Endangered	The *ex situ* programme consists of two populations. Habitat rehabilitation and protection are major *in situ* initiatives.

The Memorandum of Agreement

The statutory obligations of the Philippine government to biodiversity conservation are an important contextual factor in drafting MOAs. The international commitments of the Philippines under the CBD and the Convention on the Trade of Endangered Species of Flora and Fauna (CITES) as well as the National Integrated Protected Area System Act of 1992 and Wildlife Resources Conservation and Protection Act of 2001 are the legal backdrop of these agreements. Compliance with the constitutional and regulatory rules of the country of origin of the animals is a primary requirement of all official agreements entered into by the Philippine government.

Despite certain institutional and legal constraints, the signatories of the MOA are given some degree of flexibility to minimise bureaucratic impediments and to encourage practical and innovative actions dealing with species conservation and habitat protection. For example, technical/management committees composed of representatives from both Parties may be created to facilitate decision making and the collective implementation of various activities, such as captive breeding, habitat protection, capacity building and the promotion of public awareness and education. On-site partnerships with relevant local non-government organisations and local government units are encouraged and strongly supported by the government. Jones and Burgess (2005) state that incentive structures and mechanisms (e.g. the creation of steering committees, grassroots organisations, grants and fund raising) have to be developed to encourage social change (i.e. through public education and awareness campaigns, advocacy movements) in any collective action for the conservation of commonly owned resources.

Ownership and repatriation of zoo animals

The Philippines is the first country in South East Asia, if not in the world, to impose its sovereign right over the management of endemic species that are being maintained by foreign zoos and other breeding facilities.

In the past, the collection and export of wild-caught animals for zoo display were poorly regulated in the country. Many of the zoo animals were fraudulently collected, purchased and transported. The government records on the whereabouts and status of these exported animals were inadequately managed, and the absence of a clear policy on the matter had exacerbated the over-exploitation of Philippine wildlife. The administrative measures to address these problems were established during the early 1990s and have since been refined.

All foreign zoos have to enter into an MOA with the Philippine government on matters pertaining to the collection, transport and display of Philippine fauna. The MOA specifies that zoo animals being the property of the Philippine government, can neither be sold nor purchased. This means that foreign zoos may maintain and propagate these animals but only on a loan basis. Furthermore, none of the animals may be collected from the wild. A specified number of loaned specimens are to be supplied only by government-accredited captive breeding zoos/centres that are located either in the Philippines or overseas. When collection from the wild is technically justifiable, as when the genetic heterozygosity of the captive population has to be maintained, the zoo partner has to apply for a separate collection permit and comply with existing national legislations on wildlife collection. Since the MOA stipulates that the loaned animals are to be used only for conservation, research, education and/or public display, no pharmacological screening or extraction of genetic materials for commercial purposes will be allowed without the government's prior approval (M. Lim, personal communication).

Captive breeding and *ex situ* conservation

Developing a captive-breeding programme for highly threatened endemic species is undeniably a difficult as well as a controversial conservation measure. Captive breeding can contribute to species conservation only if the captive populations are scientifically managed by ensuring that the demography is stable and reproduction is self-sustaining (Russello & Amato, 2004; WAZA, 2005).

The Philippine Wildlife Resources Conservation and Protection Act of 2001 indicates that captive breeding of endemic species is a precautionary measure to ensure that species on the brink of extinction are not lost forever. Unfortunately, the breeding centres in the country have inadequate technical and resource capabilities for maintaining the genetic integrity of the captive population. Through partnerships with leading zoos overseas, which have captive breeding expertise and a long-term commitment to captive management of threatened species, the Philippines has moved forward to saving its wildlife resources. The technical guidance on the management of *ex situ* populations developed by the IUCN (2004) and the intermittent advice from some members of the IUCN-Species Survival Commission's Captive Breeding Specialist Group (many of whom are zoo members) have been useful in the implementation of the country's *ex situ* conservation initiatives.

As part of the partnerships agreement, in-country breeding facilities are to be established. Table 2.2 lists the breeding facilities located in the Philippines that are being maintained by Filipino counterparts and those located overseas being maintained by zoo partners. Subject to the

Table 2.2 Breeding facilities of threatened fauna covered by an MOA

Species	In-country breeding facilities and Philippine counterpart	Foreign-based facilities and foreign zoo counterparts	Location of in situ conservation projects (sanctuaries) in the Philippines
Philippine Crocodile	CENTROP (Center for Tropical Conservation, Silliman University, Dumaguete) Palawan Wildlife Rescue and Conservation Center (Puerto Princesa, Palawan)	Primary zoo partners – Melbourne Zoo (Australia) – Danish Crocodile Zoo/*Krokodille Zoo* (Eskilstrup, Denmark) – Gladys Porter Zoo (Texas, USA) Breeding Loan Breeding Agreement – Pittsburgh Zoo and Aquarium (Pennsylvania, USA) – Omaha's Henry Doorly Zoo (Nebraska, USA) – St. Augustine Alligator Farm (Florida, USA) – Crocodylus Park (Darwin, Australia) Wildlife Transfer Certificates (in progress) – Chester Zoo (UK)	Lake Dunoy, San Mariano, Isabela Dicatian Lake, Isabella (release/recovery site) Dalupiri Island (part of the Babuyan island groups, off north-west Luzon island) Oriental Mindoro Liguasan Marsh, Mindanao Davao Del Norte, Mindanao

Table 2.2 (*Continued*)

Species	In-country breeding facilities and Philippine counterpart	Foreign-based facilities and foreign zoo counterparts	Location of in situ conservation projects (sanctuaries) in the Philippines
Philippine Spotted Deer	Negros Forest and Ecological Foundation-Biodiversity Conservation Center (Bacolod) Mari-it Conservation Center, College of Forestry-West Visayas State University (Iloilo) CENTROP (Center for Tropical Conservation, Silliman University, Dumaguete) AY Reyes Zoological and Botanical Garden, Dumaguete, Negros Oriental	Mulhouse Zoo/*Parc Zoologique et Botanique de la Ville de Mulhouse* (France) White Oak Conservation Center (Florida)	Panay Island Negros Occidental
Philippine Cockatoo	Palawan Wildlife Rescue and Conservation Center (Puerto Princesa, Palawan)	*Espace Zoologique* (France)	Palawan Rasa Island (Narra, Palawan)

Table 2.2 (*Continued*)

Species	In-country breeding facilities and Philippine counterpart	Foreign-based facilities and foreign zoo counterparts	Location of in situ conservation projects (sanctuaries) in the Philippines
Philippine Warty Pig	Negros Forest and Ecological Foundation-Biodiversity Conservation Center (Bacolod) Mari-it Conservation Center, College of Forestry-West Visayas State University (Iloilo) CENTROP (Center for Tropical Conservation, Silliman University, Dumaguete) AY Reyes Zoological and Botanical Garden, Dumaguete, Negros Oriental	San Diego Zoo (California); for the Panay Warty Pig population Rotterdam Zoo (Netherlands); for the Negros Warty Pig population	Negros Occidental Panay Island

availability of resources, the exchange of technical staff between facilities is required.

In situ conservation

The Philippine National Integrated Protected Areas System Act (1992) has improved the policy direction of the country in the implementation of an integrated system of protected areas. The Act states that areas with high biodiversity value, such as wildlife habitats, are to be protected and managed. However, these areas cannot be fully protected all the time due to financial, political and security issues.

Recognising the value of *in situ* conservation to sustain *ex situ* populations, zoo partners have initiated several in-country programmes under the aegis of the MOAs (Table 2.2). For example, *Espace Zoologique* (France) has collaborated with the non-government *Katala* Foundation and the local government in the protection of the Philippine Cockatoo on Rasa Island (Palawan), as well as the promotion of this tiny island as an ecotourism destination. Another example is the establishment of the *in situ* programme for the Philippine Crocodile established in north-east Luzon Island by Melbourne Zoo in collaboration with the *Mabuwaya* Foundation and the local government. Community-managed crocodile sanctuaries were also established to protect the species and its wetland habitat, while at the same time maintaining subsistence fishing and possibly developing community-based wildlife tourism. The role of local partners in conservation, as acknowledged by the zoo partners, has been very valuable in these programmes.

Balmford *et al.* (1995) suggest that zoos can maximise their support to conservation by investing in well-managed *in situ* conservation initiatives rather than setting up additional *ex situ* breeding facilities. This may be the case because out of the 272 rare species kept in captivity, only 10% have an effective population size to sustain genetic variability (WCMC, 1992). Conway (2007: 18) argues that 'a clear direction for 21st century zoos is to aid the maintenance of wild populations in parks and reserves'. Tisdell and Wilson (2001: 233) suggest that 'in-situ ecotourism is likely to be a more powerful force for fostering pro-conservation attitudes and actions among visitors than ex-situ wildlife based tourism in aquaria and zoos'. Thus, the Philippines recognises the need to implement *ex situ* conservation measures to complement *in situ* conservation, but only as a last resort to conserve highly threatened species (Catibog-Sinha & Heaney, 2006; UNEP, 1992).

Reintroduction

The MOA states that some of the captive-born offspring may be returned and reintroduced to their original natural habitat sometime in the future, preferably in accordance with the IUCN (1995) guidelines. Reintroducing threatened species into the wild for tourism has been suggested (King & Higginbottom, 2008); however, its long-term sustainability as an effective conservation measure as well as an authentic wildlife tourist experience should be carefully assessed. Care is needed in order to ensure that conservation goals are not compromised by economic imperatives.

Reintroduction is not only very expensive but also very challenging and risky (Balmford *et al.*, 1996; Ellis & Seal, 1996; Germano & Bishop, 2009). Not all zoos, even those in developed countries, are ready or capable of undertaking the reintroduction of threatened species (R. Lacy, personal communication). In the Philippines, no reintroduction attempts made so far have been successful, including those (e.g. Philippine Eagle) that were carefully planned and financed (Catibog-Sinha, 2008a). The success of the 2009 release of captive-bred crocodiles at Dicatian Lake is yet to be determined. Globally, only 15–18 species out of 120 reintroduced species were able to establish self-sufficient populations in the wild (Baillie *et al.*, 2004).

Despite these problems, zoos stand to benefit if they incorporate captive breeding and reintroduction including pre- and post-release environmental enrichment, as part of their long-term conservation and zoo management strategies (Watters & Meehan, 2007). This is rightly so because species survival is closely linked to the sustainability of zoo tourism.

Community participation: Capacity building and conservation awareness

The MOA stipulates the need to involve the community in all aspects of species conservation and habitat protection. Community involvement includes participation in community-based projects, information and education campaigns (IECs), research and training. The integration of local knowledge and foreign expertise will greatly enhance the value of these initiatives (Catibog-Sinha & Heaney, 2006; Reed *et al.*, 2006).

Since participation of local communities in protected area management contributes to the success of many *in situ* conservation programmes in the Philippines (Catibog-Sinha & Heaney, 2006), zoo partners have initiated various community-based projects. For example, the local villagers of San Mariano (northern Philippines) were mobilised to set up a grassroots organisation to protect the Philippine crocodile. Another example is the empowerment of a locally based organisation in Palawan, which has been leading the national campaign for the establishment of Rasa Island as a protected sanctuary for the Philippine Cockatoo and as an ecotourism destination.

Public education and awareness is a long-term contribution of zoos to conservation. Public awareness campaigns, such as the publication of brochures/posters and radio broadcasts, have been sponsored by zoo partners. For example, a series of posters ('Only in the Philippines') drew national and global attention to the plight of the threatened endemic species of the country. The nomination of some zoo animals as flagship species for certain zoo projects has highlighted their charismatic value and has increased global conservation support, especially through zoo tourism.

The MOA also states that Filipino researchers should be involved/ trained in zoo management and captive breeding techniques. The training components, however, should not be limited to the routine/mundane aspects of the project. Researchers are empowered when they can enhance their technical competency and credibility, as well as cultivate their leadership, organisation and communication skills (Rockloff & Moore, 2006).

Those with leadership potential from among the local stakeholders can be encouraged and harnessed to participate actively in research and the decision-making process. Local leadership is more effective when developmental and legal processes are made clear to the participants. For example, technical and management committees have been created to collectively decide on matters pertaining to the conservation of the focal species (A. Manila, personal communication). The involvement of local communities in ecotourism planning is also crucial in sustaining tourism development (Cole, 2006). Active citizen participation in natural resource management is positively correlated with the existence of open communication among group members who have the assurance that they have enough technical support to achieve their goals (Koehler & Koontz, 2008).

Financial assistance

One of the articles of the MOA is the provision of financial assistance. While the Philippine national budget appropriated for wildlife conservation is supplemented by tourism income and donations, it is not adequate to fully support long-term species conservation. Partner zoos, from their own zoo income and fund-raising activities, have been instrumental in providing new and additional funds. For instance, Mulhouse Zoo and Berlin Zoo had been financing the captive breeding programmes of the Spotted Deer and Warty Pig in the Philippines (PAWB, 2008). It is crucial for zoos to develop partnerships with the private and public sectors as well as with non-governmental organisations to alleviate the financial constraints being experienced by less-able zoos (Smith *et al.*, 2007).

The public display of animals (especially the charismatic species) in zoos and appropriate interpretation programmes have been effective in raising funds from the public (Christie, 2007). Tisdell and Wilson (2001) have shown that tourists in Australia are willing to pay for wildlife conservation. The majority of the visitors surveyed in UK zoos suggested that 'giving money to a conservation organization' was the most practical way to support conservation (Balmford *et al.*, 2007: 125). Many zoos in the USA would like to display threatened Philippine endemic species, such as the Philippine Eagle, to promote deeper conservation awareness among visitors and raise research funds for conservation in the Philippines (T. Katzner, National Aviary in Pittsburgh, USA, personal communication). The Danish Crocodile Zoo allocates one Danish crown from each admission fee to their crocodilian conservation project overseas. Likewise, the breeding centres in the Philippines are also able to generate revenue directly from visitors' fees, concessions and donations (Josie de Leon, personal communication). For example, the Palawan Wildlife Rescue and Conservation Centre, which houses the Philippine Crocodile and Philippine Cockatoo, is a major tourist attraction on the island.

Information sharing

Sharing knowledge and ideas is crucial in creating institutional capabilities and effectiveness in pursuing sustainable tourism (Buckley, 1996; Ruhanen, 2008) and species conservation (WAZA, 2005). Research data and field experiences can help both Parties in project implementation and policy development. Zoo tourism will also benefit from this information because a network of zoo sponsors and visitors can be informed and mobilised to support conservation.

The MOA stipulates that all relevant information derived from the study of loaned animals by partner zoos should be shared freely with the Philippine government. The MOA also stipulates that relevant research publications should be submitted to the First Party and that the research contribution of the specific personnel and/or unit of the government agency should be appropriately acknowledged in these publications. Furthermore, research data, including any commercial benefits derived from biotechnologically generated research, shall be 'equitably shared' with the Philippine government in accordance with existing national legislation on bioprospecting.

The scientific data from zoological studies provide the technical bases in decision making pertaining to wildlife management. For instance, the *Recovery Plan for the Philippine Crocodile*, which was jointly prepared by Melbourne Zoo and the Philippine government, is now being used in the recovery programme for the species (Banks, 2005). Melbourne Zoo, as the nominated international coordinator of the Philippine Crocodile National Recovery Team, has facilitated information transfer through meetings, conferences and websites. Melbourne Zoo provides updates on *Crocodylus mindorensis* held at the zoo and at the Crocodylus Park (Darwin) to the Australasian Species Management Programme of the Australasian Regional Association of Zoological Parks and Aquaria (ARAZPA) and to the IUCN Crocodile Specialist Group (Banks, 2004; PAWB, 2008) to foster global conservation support for the world's most endangered crocodile.

Another source of information that has to be shared by zoos is the studbook. The studbook is a useful and reliable report on the genealogical history of each animal in captivity; access to information on the studbook is crucial in captive breeding research and zoo animal management (Glaston, 2001; Russello & Amato, 2004). In the case of the Philippine Cockatoo, the European Association of Zoos and Aquaria (EAZA) runs the European StudBook (ESB) as part of its breeding programme, in which a studkeeper from *Espace Zoologique* has been nominated to maintain the demographic and genetic data of all Philippine Cockatoo collections in EAZA zoos. Based on the studbook data, the viability of the captive populations can be assessed, and management actions at the global level can be seriously undertaken.

Field research data, while preliminary in some cases, have to be shared as well. The ecological/genetic studies of the Philippine Warty Pig have supported the Philippine decision to establish separate breeding facilities for the Panay and Negros populations to prevent hybridisation. Precautionary measures are necessary because adverse biological consequences are not always reversible. Scientifically based information can also enrich the interpretation materials for tourists and stimulate further research on zoo management and sustainable zoo tourism.

Monitoring and evaluation

The MOA incorporates the need for monitoring and evaluation to determine the performance of zoo partners in accordance with the agreement, as well as to assess the effectiveness of the institutional partnerships. The level of performance of the Parties for the duration of the agreement may vary depending on the prevailing economic, social and political circumstances. Since the Philippines does not have adequate funding to visit all breeding sites, especially those located overseas, the mandatory accomplishment reports submitted by the Second Party are, in most cases, accepted in good faith. Mutual trust and understanding among partners is crucial in successful collaborative networks (Parung & Bititci, 2008). The successful joint ventures in conservation among 75 AZA (Association of Zoos and Aquaria)-accredited institutions and related facilities in the USA, international government organisations and non-governmental organisations were attributed not only to effective leadership and clear and consistent communication, but also to mutual trust (Smith *et al.*, 2007).

Conclusion

Zoos provide opportunities for visitors to view and interact directly with wildlife, albeit in artificial conditions. Zoos are important recreational venues, but their role is not only to provide entertainment. As part of the integrated approach to zoo management, zoos are also engaged in the conservation of certain threatened species both in their natural habitats (*in situ* conservation) and in captivity (*ex situ* conservation). Zoos can take direct action to conserve species through education and conservation programmes, and these programmes can be integrated into zoo tourism. Zoos are expected to undertake a wide range of basic research in animal welfare and wildlife management. Zoo tourism can help generate funds to support the role of zoos in conservation, education and research. Through their interpretation programmes, zoos can make visitors aware of and responsive to the zoos' contribution to sustainable tourism and species conservation.

This chapter attempts to demonstrate the contribution of zoos to sustainable tourism by undertaking collective action for the conservation of threatened species. Countries, like the Philippines, are urged to rescue highly threatened animals by maintaining viable populations both in the wild and in captivity. In response to the global call by WAZA (2005), which encourages zoos to help one another, especially those that have fewer resources and technical expertise, the international zoo community has been helping the Philippines in establishing back-up populations of certain endangered endemic species in *ex situ* facilities as well as supporting *in situ* conservation initiatives.

Institutional partnerships and collaborations between the Philippines and a foreign zoo are formalised using an MOA. The MOA integrates the views of the involved parties and ensures that the terms and conditions are consistent with existing national legislations, institutional protocols and international commitments. Compliance with the constitutional and regulatory rules of the country of origin of the animals is a primary requirement of all official agreements entered into by the Philippine government with any zoological and/or captive breeding entities. Thus, MOAs establish the legitimacy of conservation concerns of and mutual trust between/among the Parties.

The salient provisions of the MOA are on matters pertaining to ownership and repatriation of zoo animals, captive breeding and *ex situ* conservation, *in situ* conservation, species reintroduction, community empowerment through capacity building and conservation awareness, provision of financial assistance, information sharing, and monitoring and evaluation. These provisions may be integrated in developing a specific implementing/operational policy or code of practice with respect to zoo tourism, animal collection, captive breeding, reintroduction and habitat rehabilitation.

Successful partnerships depend on effective leadership, clear and consistent communication and mutual trust. Zoos, through partnerships and collaboration, can serve as catalysts for social change. Zoos can work together and with the tourism industry to facilitate the proper management of zoos as well as to enhance the awareness of visitors about biodiversity conservation in general and species conservation in particular.

Acknowledgement

The author benefited from interviews with the key staff of the Protected Areas and Wildlife Bureau (Philippines), particularly Director Mundita Lim, Antonio Manila, Athea Lota, Josefina de Leon and Inocensio Castillo, and from several personal conversations with Director Todd Katzner of the National Aviary (Pittsburgh, Pennsylvania); Collete Adams of Gladys Porter Zoo (Texas); and Dr Robert Lacy, Chair of the IUCN-SSC Captive Breeding Specialist Group. Special thanks to the Protected Areas and Wildlife Bureau for providing the author with updated information and reports, especially to Angelita Meniado, Chief of the Wildlife Section, for her patience and cooperation.

Chapter 3
A Typology of Animal Displays in Captive Settings

AMIR SHANI AND ABRAHAM PIZAM

Introduction

Animals are incorporated into the tourism industry in various ways. Most tourist–wildlife interactions occur in environments with some degree of man-made elements, in which wildlife animals are displayed to visitors. In addition to observing wildlife in their natural environment, animals can be viewed for various purposes in captive settings. In fact, visiting captive animal sites has become the central – and for most people, the only – venue for observing and interacting with wildlife (Beardsworth & Bryman, 2001; Turley, 2001). The range of captive-based sites is very broad, as they constitute 'a series of visitor attractions based around animals kept in some kind of captivity, ranging from conventional zoos to open-air safari parks' (Shackley, 1996: 96). The wide variety of animal-based attractions, each with its own distinctive nature and characteristics, demands classification of these sites, especially in light of their considerable heterogeneity. Along with the growing attention placed on animal-based attractions in the tourism literature in recent years, a comprehensive typology of animal-based attractions can be useful in capturing their complexity and advancing this academic field.

Earlier attempts to classify animal-based attractions typically did so according to the level of captivity at the sites. Orams (1996, 2002) differentiates between wildlife interactions in wild settings, such as national parks, migratory routes and breeding sites; semi-captive attractions, such as wildlife parks and dolphin pens; and fully captive attractions, such as zoos, theme parks, aquariums and oceanariums. Shackley (1996) also offered a classification of animal-based attractions in captivity settings, based on the animals' 'mobility restriction' (ranging from 'complete confinement' to 'complete freedom') and on the motivation behind the attractions (ranging from 'conservation/education' to 'entertainment'). For example, in Shackley's model, circuses are characterised as having high mobility restriction and a dominant entertainment orientation; aquariums as having high mobility restriction and a dominant education/conservation orientation; horse racing as having medium mobility restriction and a dominant entertainment orientation;

and nature preserves as having very low mobility restriction and a dominant education/conservation orientation.

However, the accuracy and usefulness of this typology are questionable. First of all, it is difficult to measure the level of 'freedom' the animals enjoy, as this term and its meaning are vague and contentious (see Bostock, 1993). Secondly, even in a single attraction, the animal displays may not be homogenous. An attraction can include a wide variety of exhibits, which can each be distinguished based on different criteria, such as mobility restriction or the purpose factors described by Shackley (1996). Thus, the diversification within the attractions requires that more attention be paid to the nature of the wildlife exhibits themselves, rather than to the attraction as a whole.

Animal exhibits can be differentiated based on various factors. For example, in some exhibits, captivity is signalled by iron bars (as was common in traditional zoos), while in other exhibits, more modern practices are used, such as invisible barriers, sunken enclosures or enclosures surrounded by moats (Shelton & Tucker, 2008). Exhibits or areas within the attractions – just like an entire single attraction – can be categorised based on species emphasis (e.g. marine mammals, birds) or concentration on different ecosystems, region or habitat (e.g. rainforest, desert). Taking Disney's Animal Kingdom as a case study, Milman (2008) mentioned that, conceptually, the iconic theme park features three types of animals: real wildlife, extinct (e.g. dinosaurs) and mythical (e.g. dragons). Nevertheless, these and similar examples are either situation-based classifications of animal exhibits or are based on technical, biological and/or ecosystem taxonomies. Thus, they do not offer comprehensive perception into the unique nature and meaning of the exhibits, which can be applied to a wide variety of animal-based attractions.

This chapter will propose an alternative typology of exhibits in captive-based animal attractions, based on the seminal work of Kellert (1985), who described nine basic wildlife values. Although these values represent general attitudes towards animals and nature, it is argued that they also best explain the various ways in which animals are displayed and exhibited in most, if not all, animal-based attractions. While some attractions might be characterised by a single wildlife value, most attractions include exhibits that represent diverse wildlife values. The chapter will describe these values and their expressions in various animal displays and provide illustrations from contemporary animal-based attractions.

Attitudes Towards Animals

In recent years, many efforts have been directed towards establishing the relatively new field of anthrozoology, i.e. the study of relations between people and animals. As part of the development of this field of study, the International Society for Anthrozoology (ISAZ) was established in 1991; this was followed by the launching of the *Anthrozoös* and *Society and Animals* academic journals, which are dedicated to investigating human–animal relations. Anthrozoology encompasses many fields of research and draws from a broad range of disciplines, such as psychology, psychiatry, political science, cardiology, behavioural science and others (Schneider, 2005). In any case, the main focus of anthrozoologist studies is the examination of human attitudes towards animals.

There are several reasons for researchers' growing interest in the public's attitudes towards animals. First, animals today are tightly incorporated into people's lives, particularly as companion animals. This has led to efforts to investigate the influence of companion animals on the individual, on families and on society as a whole (e.g. Albert & Bulcroft, 1988; Cohen, 2002). Secondly, some studies support the idea of a close link between caring for animals and caring for people (e.g. Henry, 2004; Taylor & Signal, 2005). Therefore, examining attitudes towards animals may have important implications for the fields of psychology and education. Third, there are growing concerns for the way animals are treated in society, not only in scientific laboratories and industrial farms, but also in areas such as entertainment and transportation. Finally, contemporary efforts towards conservation and preservation of wildlife and the natural environment have also led to the need to investigate the attitudes of the public at large towards animals. As noted by Peyton and Langenau (1985), wildlife professionals find it difficult to make policy and management decisions without knowing what is acceptable to the public.

As a result of these and similar concerns, the need to develop theories and tools to capture and examine the public's attitudes has been widely recognised. One of the notable first attempts to describe and measure attitudes towards animals was undertaken by Kellert (1985, 1991). In his typology, Kellert portrayed the following nine basic wildlife values:

(1) Humanistic
(2) Moralistic
(3) Utilitarian
(4) Negativistic
(5) Dominionistic
(6) Naturalistic
(7) Ecologistic
(8) Scientific
(9) Aesthetic

Table 3.1 Basic animal values

Term	Meaning
Humanistic	Interest and strong affection for individual animals, particularly companion animals
Moralistic	Concern for the right and wrong treatment of animals, with strong opposition to exploitation and cruelty towards animals
Utilitarian	Concern for the practical and material value of animals or their habitats
Negativistic	Avoidance of animals due to indifference, dislike or fear
Dominionistic	Interest in the mastery and control of animals, typically in sporting situations
Naturalistic	Interest and affection for wildlife and the outdoors
Ecologistic	Concern for the environment as a system, for interrelationships between wildlife and natural habitats
Scientific	Interest in the physical attributes and biological functioning of animals
Aesthetic	Interest in the artistic and symbolic characteristics of animals

Source: Kellert (1985, 1991)

Each value is applicable to a person in varying degrees. Table 3.1 provides a short summary of each of the wildlife values, which will be further clarified later in the chapter. For example, one can score high on the humanistic value, in the sense of loving and caring for pets, and at the same time, score high on the utilitarian value, in the sense of favouring animal experimentation and the rearing of animals for food. Another person might score high on the ecologistic value, advocating conservation efforts, but score low on the moralistic value, in accepting the use of hunting and fishing as tools for managing wildlife.

Following the development of the typology of basic wildlife values and their respective scales, several extensive investigations tracked animal-related attitudes among socio-demographic groups and major animal activity groups (Kellert, 1978, 1980, 1996). A thorough discussion of these studies is beyond the scope of the current chapter. However, it is worthwhile mentioning the findings regarding two relevant groups related to the context of captive-based animal attractions, namely, zoo enthusiasts (defined as those who frequently visit zoos at some point in their life) and rodeo enthusiasts (those who indicate frequent rodeo attendance). An examination of the characteristics of these groups illustrates the inherently different wildlife values each attraction type emphasises.

The repeat zoo visitors were found to have stronger naturalistic attitudes than the general population – but lower attitudes than those found in groups like nature hunters and bird-watchers. They were also characterised by exceptionally high humanistic attitudes. Therefore, Kellert (1978, 1980) concluded that the zoo enthusiasts were more motivated by a general affection for animals, than by a special interest in wildlife. They expressed high moralistic and naturalistic attitudes, indicating concern for the welfare of the animals and their natural habitats. On the other hand, rodeo enthusiasts were characterised as having very strong dominionistic and utilitarian attitudes. This seems to reflect the nature of the activity, which is realised in conveying physical dominance and control over the participating animals. These findings provide initial evidence that diverse animal-based attractions attract people with varied wildlife values. Consequently, the latter can serve as an effective means of differentiating the attractions (or individual exhibits) in a way that contributes to the understanding of their appeal among different groups.

Wildlife Values in Animal Exhibits

Although animal displays/attractions might not necessarily genuinely adopt and/or practice the wildlife value with which they are associated, they are geared towards appealing to the variety of wildlife-related values that people hold. In addition, particular displays might feature more than one value, although, typically, there is one dominant wildlife value portrayed by a display.

The aesthetic value is the only wildlife value described by Kellert that is not applied in the suggested typology of animal exhibits. The aesthetic value refers to an interest in artistic display and the visual appeal of wildlife (Kellert, 1978). As noted by Kellert (1996: 15) 'the aesthetic outlook tends to place primary focus on the larger, more colorful, mobile, and diurnal species'. Indeed, it was found that, generally, people have clear aesthetic preferences with regard to animal species, as charismatic vertebrates (e.g. lions, bears, swans and primates) and companion animals (Bjerke *et al.*, 1998; Kellert, 1993; Phillips & McCulloch, 2005). Despite the significance of this value in understanding people's attitudes towards animals, as well as their behaviour in animal-based attractions, it appears to be too inclusive to distinguish specific attractions and/or exhibits. For this reason, although the aesthetic viewpoint is highly relevant to the understanding of the attributes of animal exhibits, the current typology focuses on the other eight values, which characterise more clearly distinguishable types of animal exhibits.

Naturalistic exhibits

Kellert (1996: 11) suggested that the naturalistic wildlife value 'emphasizes the many satisfactions people obtain from the direct experience of nature and wildlife'. Encounters with the natural world have been shown to provide both mental and physiological benefits for humans (Sundstrom *et al.*, 1996). This can take expression in a variety of recreational settings, such as hunting, fishing, wildlife feeding and birding. The notable appeal of the naturalistic value is well expressed in modern animal-based attractions, which feature a prominent and evident shift towards a naturalistic presentation of captive animals (Tomas *et al.*, 2002).

In this regard, the development of captive animal displays is often described with reference to first-, second- and third-generation exhibits (Tribe, 2004). The first generation of animal exhibits was characterised by barred cages in which the animals lived nearly their entire lives and 'were presented as if they were felons', with very little regard to issues such as animal welfare and hygiene (Coe & Lee, 1996: 1). In the second generation of animal exhibits, the cages were replaced with larger cement enclosures, which were usually surrounded by moats (Tribe, 2004). The animals' health and hygiene conditions in these facilities were significantly improved in comparison to the first-generation exhibits (Coe & Lee, 1996). The third generation of animal exhibits, however, in which animals are located in natural design surroundings, marks the most significant change in the nature of animal displays in attractions. The reasons for this transformation were the growing concerns and awareness of animal welfare issues, as well as changes in visitors' tastes, who expect the experience at the attractions to simulate media representation of wildlife (Hughes *et al.*, 2005; Moscardo, 2008).

As noted by Catibog-Sinha (2008a), many animal-based attractions have taken certain actions to improve the naturalism of their exhibits, such as creating miniaturised ecosystems that imitate the natural habitats of the exhibited wildlife and providing more dynamic and spacious roaming areas for the animals. Animal welfare concerns and evidence of visitors' expectation to observe the 'natural' behaviour of the animals have led modern animal-based attractions to integrate environmental enrichment into the design of wildlife displays (Markowitz, 1982; Mellen & MacPhee, 2001). Davey (2007: 367) defines environmental (or behavioural) enrichment as 'an animal husbandry principle that aims to improve welfare provision for captive animals by increasing the behavioral choices available in order to encourage natural behavior and breeding'. He further states that it includes the incorporation of both natural elements – or 'exhibit naturalism' (e.g. rocks, vegetation and water features) – and artificial objects that stimulate species-specific behaviour (e.g. toys, scents and sounds). Other techniques that can be used to enhance the naturalism of exhibits and/or encourage the animals to express natural behaviour are the integration of ecologically relevant sounds in the exhibits (Woods, 1998) and mixed species rotation exhibits that increase the available space and provide more behavioural opportunities for the animals (Coe, 2004).

More recently, attempts to improve the representation of nature in animal-based attractions have led to the development of what is currently termed the fourth generation of animal exhibits, or 'immersive exhibits'. Moss *et al.* (2008) explain that immersive exhibits differ from merely naturalistic exhibits in their design of visitor areas. More specifically,

> in the immersive exhibit both the visitor and the animals share the same landscape, themed to represent the animal's natural environment... Animals may still be separated from the public in enclosures; but to the visitor, the barriers are discreet and unobstructive. (Moss *et al.*, 2008: 27)

Examples of exhibits that create an immersive experience include: walk-through, underwater tunnels in aquariums; walk-through exhibits of free-range wildlife without observable barriers between the visitors and the animals; and natural exhibits that incorporate multiple small viewpoints in a way that replicates animal observation in the wild (Moss *et al.*, 2008).

Ecologistic-scientific exhibits

Although there are important differences between the ecologistic and scientific values, in most cases these seem to converge in animal-based attractions and, therefore, will be regarded here as a single type. While the ecologistic wildlife value stresses the interdependence among species and natural habitats, the scientific value refers to a deeper understanding of the physiological, biological, and behavioural attributes of the animals. However, the common denominator between these approaches is the 'assumption that through systematic exploration of the biophysical elements of nature, living diversity can be comprehended and sometimes controlled' (Kellert, 1996: 13). In addition to naturalistic value, these values are well expressed in modern animal-based attractions, especially in related environmental education and conservation efforts, and in many cases, serve as the main justifications for their existence (Jamieson, 2006; Mason, 2000).

To achieve environmental education and conservation goals, many animal-based attractions present biological characteristics and facts about the animals and encourage visitors to support environmental initiatives. Fraser *et al.* argue that,

> the social experience of zoo-going offers one of the few venues for families... to explore and establish a relationship to the natural world; in the face of the biodiversity crisis, zoos may offer these families a place to renegotiate their relationship to an unseen but desirable wild nature. (Fraser *et al.*, 2008: 282)

Thus, the exhibited animals in attractions can be seen as 'animal ambassadors', representing their wild counterparts, thereby enabling visitors to connect with the natural world and better understand it.

The ecologistic-scientific value is mainly expressed in the highlighting of certain displays that include endangered species, in addition to information provided on the efforts and activities of the organisation to preserve that species – both *ex situ* activities (outside the wildlife's natural habitat; i.e. through genetic management and captive breeding) and *in situ* activities (within the wildlife's natural habitat; i.e. habitat protection programmes and reintroduction of endangered species back into the wild) (Tribe, 2004). Even though this value is evident to some extent in many animal exhibits and in attractions in general, some exhibits are characterised by an exceptionally dominant ecologistic affinity. One such a site is The Trail of the Elephants exhibit at Melbourne Zoo in Australia. As noted by Smith and Broad (2008), one of the main goals of the exhibit is to offer visitors various learning opportunities regarding conservation issues. More specifically, the attempt is to stress that Asian elephants are under threat and that even individual visitors can take action to save them from extinction. In this case study, it was suggested that the immersive-naturalistic design of the exhibit contributed to the length of the visitors' stay and attention and, hence, to their exposure to conservation messages. Therefore, certain integrations of diverse wildlife values in animal exhibits, such as the naturalistic and ecologistic-scientific approaches, can be highly effective in achieving the attractions' goals.

Humanistic exhibits

The humanistic value refers to the emotional identification people experience in the presence of animals, which can include expressions of companionship, bonding, attachment and intimacy (Kellert, 1978). This strong affection towards animals often leads to 'humanising' the animals; i.e. giving it a name and associating the animal with human characteristics (i.e. anthropomorphism) (Kellert, 1996). Although humanistic attitudes are usually directed towards companion animals in the home setting, evidence of this approach can be observed in some modern animal exhibits and shows, which are highly popular in modern animal-based attractions.

One prominent example of the humanistic value in animal exhibits is the petting zoo that many attractions include in their activities. Petting zoos allow visitors – mainly, but not exclusively, children – to pet, feed and/or ride on a variety of exhibited animals, such as rabbits, goats, llamas and donkeys. In most cases, the visitors can buy special food at the site and feed the animals, thus deriving pleasure from nurturing and caring for them. Petting zoos are also highly popular in settings such as fairs, malls and agritourism attractions (Barbieri, 2002; McGehee & Kim, 2004). It should be noted, however, that the use of petting zoos (especially in small attractions) is heavily criticised by animal rights groups on the grounds of cruelty to the exhibited animals, which may result from visitors' careless behaviour that can cause injury or death to the animals, lack of staff supervision, overcrowding, inadequate bedding and facilities, and lack of veterinary care (Animal Rights Coalition, 2009). In addition, these attractions, when not managed responsibly, can lead to serious health threats to visitors (Zoltak, 2005).

Another example of a dominant humanistic value in animal-based attractions is the highly popular animal show, which includes choreographed performances of trained animals, such as marine mammals, pets and birds. Many of these shows anthropomorphise the animal performance, and visitors derive pleasure from watching the animals behave in a human-like manner (e.g. walking on two legs, kissing, hugging, clapping hands and communicating with their trainers). Indeed, shows featuring marine mammals were found to be one of the main attractions of marine zoos and theme parks. The Anheuser Busch Sea World parks (Lück & Jiang, 2008) are the most prominent example. Another humanistic-orientated show at Sea World is 'Pets Ahoy!' in which dogs, cats, birds and other domesticated animals give a human-like performance.

Dominionistic exhibits

The dominionistic wildlife value is principally orientated towards opportunities to demonstrate prowess, mastery and dominance over animals, usually in sport or competition contexts (Kellert, 1978). As argued by Kellert (1996: 20), 'by successfully challenging nature and wildlife, people derive feelings of self-reliance that are hard to achieve in an untested relationship or by simply experiencing nature as a spectator'. This is presumably the most ancient wildlife value, as most of the world's main religions have supported or at least enabled the domination of man over the non-human world (Waladau, 2006). Moreover, the earliest captive collections of wildlife were mainly influenced and characterised by the dominionistic value, as primeval rulers kept large menageries of animals as a sign of their strength and prowess, occasionally demonstrated by slaughtering entire collections (Jamieson, 1985).

The dominionistic value is apparent in some types of animal attractions nowadays, even though, for the most part, these exist outside the mainstream of the tourism industry. Rodeo and bullfighting, in which the main goals are to gain control and demonstrate the competitor's mastery over the animal (which, in the case of the latter, ends with its death), are still prevalent in certain parts of the world, despite heavy criticism (Bailey, 2007; Cobb, 2003). Dominionistic displays of animals can also be found in more ordinary forms of animal-based attractions. An example of one such attraction is Gatorland, an animal theme park in Orlando, Florida. The main attraction is the gator wrestling show, in which a wrestler drags an alligator to the stage, gains control over it and performs various stunts with the animal. The dominance of the wrestler is manifested in a variety of activities, such as forcing the gator to open its mouth while the wrestler places his/her head inside. In addition, children are permitted to sit on the alligator's back at the end of the show. Another dominionistic show in Gatorland is the 'Gator Jumparoo', in which alligators are manipulated by performers to jump four to five feet out of the water to retrieve food.

Utilitarian exhibits

Kellert (1978: 11) explained that activities influenced by the utilitarian wildlife value are compelled 'by practical considerations of the animal's utility and thus its potential to return some kind of tangible material reward'. Although in certain eras, animals were sometimes worshipped as gods, they have, for the most part, been used for various human needs and purposes (Orams, 2002). Indeed, the utilitarian approach towards the non-human world has prevailed since early history, when animals were perceived as a means to an end, rather than an end in themselves, and were widely used in areas such as food production, agriculture and transportation, scientific research, and entertainment and amusement (Bowd, 1984).

Somewhat surprisingly, attractions and displays that stress the utilitarian value towards animals are relatively uncommon. Nevertheless, the rising popularity of tourism in the countryside and rural areas has led to the emergence of some utilitarian-based animal attractions. Decreases in revenues from agriculture, as well as increases in the demand for vacations in rural areas (Fleischer & Pizam, 1997), have led many animal farms to open their gates to visitors, and in many cases, to offer Bed and Breakfast accommodation. Besides informational tours of the farms, many of these open farms provide an opportunity for a 'hands-on' experience, in terms of cuddling, feeding and handling animals, as well as practical demonstrations of milking cows, sheep shearing and butter making (Wilson, 2007). The emphasis of these and similar attractions and displays is clearly on the utilitarian value of animals and the ways in which they contribute to human life.

Moralistic exhibits

As noted by Kellert (1996: 23), 'the moralistic value has been especially associated with concern for ethical treatment of animals and nature' and its 'central focus is right and wrong conduct toward the nonhuman world'. More specifically, people with a very strong moralistic attitude tend to reject what they perceive as non-justifiable forms of exploitation of animals, e.g. sport hunting (Kellert, 1978). In light of this view, on the surface, moralistic expressions in animal-based attractions seem like a paradox, as animal rights advocates tend to reject the justifications for the existence of any such sites – in many cases, even if the latter features exceptionally humane treatment of animals or contributes to goals such as education and conservation (e.g. Jamieson, 1985; Regan, 1995). In fact, the rise of the animal rights (or moralistic) position has led to a reduction in the use of animals in the tourism industry, such as the shift in the UK from observing dolphins in captivity in dolphinariums to watching them in the wild (Hughes, 2001) and the growing popularity of animal-free circuses (Shani & Pizam, 2008). Indeed, it is relatively rare for displays in animal-based attractions to present a dominant moralistic message, as this position is often subversive against the existence of the sites themselves.

Surprisingly, however, the moralistic wildlife value can be noticed in some attractions that involve the display of animals. Big Cat Rescue in Tampa Bay, Florida, is a non-profit, educational sanctuary that provides permanent shelter for big cats rescued from circuses, amusement shows or private homes. The main educational message of the site (which also serves as an attraction, for all intents and purposes, with regular tours, close encounters with the cats, special events, kids' activities and merchandising) is the need to abolish the use of big cats for entertainment or private use, since holding wildlife in captivity is unnatural and morally wrong. In addition to participating in educational activities and events on big cats, the visitors are also encouraged to put pressure on legislators to promote laws that will prevent the exploitation of big cats.

The New York and California shelters of Farm Sanctuary are perhaps an even clearer example of an animal-based attraction with moralistic exhibits. Farm Sanctuary is a non-profit organisation providing refuge, lifelong care and rehabilitation for rescued factory farm animals, as well as promoting awareness of issues related to animal rights in factory farms. In addition to their utility as animal sanctuaries, both locations also serve as visitor centres, where visitors can directly interact with the animals. The main activities are geared towards educating visitors about the living and slaughtering conditions of animals in industrial farms and the need to abolish them, as well as towards promoting a vegan lifestyle. The farms also offer gift shops, accommodation, retreats, special events and conferences. These examples demonstrate that animal-based attractions and the moralistic wildlife value might not necessarily be mutually exclusive.

Negativistic exhibits

The negativistic value is manifested by hostile and negative feelings towards the natural world, or certain parts of it, such as dislike, fear and aversion (Kellert, 1980). Previous studies have found that certain species are more likely to arouse such feelings, especially snakes and various types of invertebrates, such as bugs, cockroaches, stinging insects, spiders, mosquitoes and grasshoppers (Kellert, 1993; Philips & McCulloch, 2005). Interestingly, many current animal-based attractions utilise the negativistic wildlife value in their exhibits, although their function in these cases is obviously to attract visitors to confront their feelings of fear or revulsion. A variety of attractions has established insect zoos, wherein visitors can watch the aforementioned species, which typically generate mixed reactions of disgust, recoiling and magnetising. In addition, the negativistic value can be realised in various entertainment and competition shows. A contemporary example is the 'Fear Factor Live' show at Universal Studios in Orlando, Florida, in which people from the audience participate in interactive assignments and contests involving encounters with spiders, snakes, roaches and scorpions.

Furthermore, the negativistic value and its paradoxical appeal are also used for promotional purposes. In September 2006, as part of its 'Fright Fest' to be held the following month, Six Flags Parks announced a special contest in which people who ate a live Madagascar hissing cockroach could skip to the front of the line. In response, the People for the Ethical Treatment of Animals (PETA) issued a formal protest of Six Flags, demanding – unsuccessfully – that they cancel the promotional contest. In an official message to the media, PETA asserted:

> Presumably, the cockroach was chosen for this "gag" because of the species' extremely negative image. However, this much-maligned invertebrate possesses keen senses, is quite docile and has an amazing evolutionary history. (Moran, 2006)

Table 3.2 Types of exhibits in animal-based attractions

Types of exhibits	Description
Naturalistic	Exhibits in which the animals are presented in natural and semi-natural surroundings, with the incorporation of elements and techniques to enhance the impression and experience of a natural setting
Ecologistic-scientific	Exhibits in which the emphasis is on delivering environmental and conservational messages and encouraging activism on behalf of visitors, as well as fulfilling visitors' intellectual curiosity with regard to the physical, biological and behavioural characteristics of the animals
Humanistic	Exhibits in which animals are displayed in a way that allows visitors to express affection for them, and/or displays which present animals performing human-like behaviours
Moralistic	Exhibits that stress and promote various animal rights messages – principally, an opposition to cruelty towards and exploitation of animals
Utilitarian	Exhibits wherein the practical and material value of the animals to humans is emphasised through demonstrations and/or hands-on activities
Dominionistic	Exhibits that, in most cases, involve shows aimed at displaying mastery and power over animals
Negativistic	Exhibits that include shows and displays that focus on presenting animals with a negative, scary or repulsive image

Overview

The purpose of this chapter is to introduce a typology of animal exhibits in animal-based attractions that is founded on the exhibit/attraction's dominant wildlife value. The basic wildlife and nature values suggested by Kellert (1985) serve as the conceptual framework in constructing the typology and illustrating the attitudes towards animals, emphasised by each type of exhibit. Specifically, seven exhibit types were depicted (Table 3.2); yet, it was stressed that various wildlife values can coexist in a single exhibit, in addition to the possibility that exhibits in a single attraction will be characterised by a similar value.

The typology was mainly based on the existing body of knowledge on animal-based attractions, which is still relatively limited (Frost & Roehl, 2007), as well as participant observations that were conducted at various attractions. Thus, although the typology illustrates the diversity and complexity of animal exhibits in modern tourist attractions, more empirical evidence on visitors' attitudes and reactions to diverse animal exhibits is required to validate the suggested typology and its scope. Future studies should also focus on uncovering the socio-demographic profile of visitors to different types of animal exhibits and uncovering the managerial and ethical challenges involved in each of the exhibit types. It is hoped that the suggested detailed typology of animal exhibits will contribute to the understanding of animal-based attractions and may instigate discussions on tourist–wildlife relations, while providing theoretical underpinnings for future research in this under-studied field.

Chapter 4

Ecotourism and the Commodification of Wildlife: Animal Welfare and the Ethics of Zoos

STEPHEN WEARING AND CHANTELLE JOBBERNS

Introduction

Current directions in ecotourism reflect an increasing tendency towards the commodification of nature. The quest for profit from nature-based activities, particularly tourism, has spawned an industry lacking an ethic of care for nature and, specifically, the animals used in this new ecotourism regime. Economic rationalist approaches often place economic incentive before the intrinsic and intangible values of nature. This often results in the inappropriate development or use of natural resources and changes the capacity of the resource to meet the expectations of users. Trends in the provision of ecotourism experiences, such as larger numbers of people using nature and more commercially orientated groups, coupled with competition for higher economic returns, see a need for the consideration of the rights of animals and the practices that have evolved as a result of this new ecotourism regime.

The practice of displaying animals in captivity is often defended as a necessary form of education for the general public, and one avenue towards increasing public awareness of the need for conservation. This argument has been supported by the global ecotourism industry to justify zoos and aquariums as an educational and conservation tool, as well as the increasing visitation of tourists to protected areas to view animals in their natural habitats. However, the validity of this role is questionable given the loss of freedom for these animals and the excessive exploitation of protected areas for tourism. This chapter provides an examination of the ethical issues surrounding the capture and use of animals for tourism, entertainment and education with a focus on the subsequent treatment of these animals.

Ecotourism: Sustainability, Ethics and the Role of Animals

In order to critique the claim that captive animal viewing in zoos and aquariums serves educational and conservation purposes, a brief overview of sustainability and ecotourism must first be reviewed in order to understand the context in which zoos and aquariums are defended. Sustainability (and ecotourism as a form of sustainable tourism) is a vague, contested concept, easily manipulated to support and enhance the power of industry interests and those who stand to gain (Mowforth & Munt, 2008). Neoliberal economic policy has served to influence ecotourism and related protected area policies in ways that afford little room for intangible values, either natural or cultural (Staiff *et al.*, 2002). Moreover, with ecotourism promoting protected areas to the marketplace, there is now an expectation that they should be required to yield financial return. Central to this regime are the animals that these areas are often established to protect (Figgis, 2000).

The inevitable outcome of ecotourism in most protected areas is the need to provide animals for observation and interpretation (Wearing & Neil, 1999). A new type of tourist has emerged that requires a higher degree of interaction with nature: 'people who require environmentally compatible recreational opportunities... where nature rather than human-ity predominates' (Kerr, 1991: 248). These ecotourists are interested in visiting wilderness, national parks and tropical forests, and in viewing birds, mammals, trees and wildflowers. One of the most notable differences that has emerged is in expenditure, where veteran ecotourists are estimated to be willing to spend more than general tourists for the experience. These ecotourists 'on average, would spend 8.5% more for services and products provided by environmentally responsible suppli-ers' (Wight, 1994: 41). Wearing and Neil (1999) suggest that the ecotourist is more concerned with development and fulfilment, which includes self-education. This circumstance has created the opportunity for an increase in the provision of education and interpretation in nature and wildlife-based activities for a customer that is likely to pay a rate higher than that for traditional tourism experiences.

Through the commodification of wildlife, considerations of the impact of tourists on the environment, including the welfare of wildlife, have been displaced in lieu of potential profits. Genuine concern exists regarding the health and survival of wildlife in high volume tourist areas (Anathaswamy, 2004). The short-term impacts of ecotourism report negative behaviour changes in wildlife, including the disruption of breeding patterns, dependency on humans for food, high infant mortality rates and death (Anathaswamy, 2004; Cunningham-Smith *et al.*, 2006; Hughes & Carlsen, 2008b; Mau, 2008). The positive impacts of ecotourism are disputed among academics. They include 'awareness of, and empathy for wildlife and the natural areas in which they live' (Hughes & Carlsen, 2008b: 148), economic benefits for developing nations, the protection of natural environments and feeding wildlife in urban environments, which may aid the survival of local animal populations forced from their habitat due to encroaching development (Anathaswamy, 2004; Hughes & Carlsen, 2008b). Lemelin (2006) conversely maintains that there is no evidence supporting claims of respect and empathy for wildlife, nor educational benefits.

A motivating factor of the ecotourist is to seek natural habitats and explore unchartered territory. Their pursuit to see increasingly rare and exotic wildlife may be more damaging to the natural environment than mass tourism, due to increased travel distances and urban impacts on remote areas (Lemelin, 2006; Wall, 1997). It has been suggested that offering alternatives and satisfying the wants of the ecotourist could be achieved through forms of captive animal viewing (Tremblay, 2008).

Captive animals raise questions of ethics and rights. The rights of individual animals have been contested and debated for centuries. Commonly viewed as 'things' to be used for food, clothing, transport, entertainment, experiments and sport (DeGrazia, 2002; Mullin, 1999; Newkirk, 1999; Singer, 1977), dominated and exploited by humans and considered less than the human race, their needs and wants are reduced to minimal significance (Singer, 1977). Humans discriminate against animals in the same way they would discriminate against a person because of their gender, cultural heritage or sexual orientation (DeGrazia, 2002; Mullin, 1999; Newkirk, 1999; Singer, 1977). Singer (1977: 12) referred to this is as 'speciesist', and argued that there is no reason to 'refuse to extend the basic principle of equality of consideration to members of other species'.

Different views towards human beings relationship with nature and animals can be encapsulated in different environmental ethics perspectives, including conservation ethics, the ethics of the environment and anthropocentric ethics. Conservation ethics maintains that the environment and its resources should be conserved and maintained for future generations. Conserving the environment is a by-product of ensuring that humankind will thrive and have the same access to natural resources in the future. The ethics of the environment is a view whereby the environment is given the same respect and moral considerations afforded to humans. Finally, anthropocentric ethics is the view that acknowledges humans as the only beings worthy of moral considerations (Holden, 2003). The latter view dominates the tourism industry, where the individual rights and needs of animals are rarely considered through the consumption and production process of ecotourism.

Animals as Commodities: What has Ecotourism done to Influence the Zoo and Marine Park?

The practice of collecting and exhibiting wild animals has its origins in Ancient Egypt. Private collections, or menageries, were reserved for the rich and powerful. They were symbols of wealth and power, and entertainment for their owners (Bulbeck, 2005; DeGrazia, 2002; Newkirk, 1999). Exotic animals, in particular from the plains of Africa, were symbols of the power, wealth and expansion of the British Empire. They were souvenirs of travels abroad in a time when only the wealthy had the means to travel, and reaffirmed status and prestige (Mullin, 1999).

The zoo of the 20th century was argued to have emerged as a medium through which the population could be educated in morals and ideals. Zoos claimed that their existence was to protect species through conservation efforts, education and research, however, zoos have been the subjects of much criticism and many believe that the modern zoo stood for economic benefits and the 'endorsement of modern colonial power' (Bulbeck, 2005: 17). Zoos today closely align their organisations with conservation and education, and reinforce and justify their existence through their contributions. Conservation and education places great emphasis on species preservation in both wild and captive populations, and in the process disregards individual animal welfare and the rights of individual animals (Millar & Houston, 2008a, 2008b).

In this era of technology, education as a primary argument for justifying captive animals is becoming obsolete. Museums could provide equal, if not greater educational opportunities, while providing visitors with close animal encounters (Moss, 1961). Holograms, documentaries and films dedicated to wildlife have critics arguing that the zoo as a primary educational platform is unfounded and conveys the wrong message about the relationship between humans and animals, where animals are considered inferior and under the control of humans (Jamieson, 1985; Moss, 1961; Mullin, 1999).

The quality of life in captivity differs across the estimated 10,000 zoos worldwide (DeGrazia, 2002; Newkirk, 1999), from featureless cages in Romania (Born Free Foundation, 2008) to exhibits that closely resemble the natural habitat in the USA (Unknown, 2008c). Animals in zoos are the feature attraction, and therefore valuable assets. It is common for organisations to view their animals as commodities; stock to be traded, loaned, sold, or even killed and disposed of, depending on changing market trends and consumer tastes (Newkirk, 1999).

Animals are 'managed' and live in enclosures designed for easy cleaning, explaining the presence of concrete in 'natural' environments. Animals, typically wary of humans, are lured to areas for public viewing by techniques such as heated sand (Bulbeck, 2005; Cain & Meritt, 1998). A change to animal enclosures gives the perception of improvement – replacing iron bars with glass forgoes animals free-flowing air. Animals such as monkeys lose the mental stimulation and activity that swinging on bars could have provided to alleviate boredom (Bulbeck, 2005; Cain & Meritt, 1998). Other cosmetic changes include improvements to an animal's enclosure that they are unable to use or enjoy. The greenery surrounding the gorillas exhibit at Taronga Zoo in Sydney, Australia, is separated from the gorillas by an electric fence in order to protect it. 'Backstage' images differ greatly from the enclosures portrayed to the public, and many animals retreat to empty cages devoid of stimuli (Bulbeck, 2005).

The level of stimuli and activity that the foremost enclosure could offer is not enough for many of the animals, and does not compare to a life in the wild. Crowcroft (1978) noted the limits of the zoo enclosure, and acknowledged that gorillas, in particular, experience constant boredom, bound by the limits any enclosure could offer. He justified keeping an animal that could never be truly happy by stating that it was better to have a bored gorilla, than to have no gorillas (Crowcroft, 1978).

The size, intelligence and activity level of particular animals presents a valid rationale that certain animals are not suited to captivity. The tiger lives a solitary life and roams over his/her large territory searching for food and may cover anywhere from 16 to 32 km every day. No zoo enclosure could replicate this (Moss, 1961). Similarly, the polar bear is also an animal that walks large distances every day in search of food and water, distinctly different to their life in captivity. Polar bears have developed behavioural problems and die younger than their wild counterparts (Engelbrecht & Smith, 2004; Smith, 2003). Gus, the polar bear from Central Park Zoo in New York, made headlines when his depression forced staff to administer Prozac – the first zoo animal in history to receive antidepressants (Newkirk, 1999). In 2003, zoologists at Oxford University concluded that large, roaming, nomadic predators, such as tigers and polar bears, exhibit high stress and neurotic symptoms when kept in captivity, and it is estimated that 'captive polar bears spend 25% of their day pacing' (Clubb & Mason, 2003). Elephants are considered to be extremely intelligent beings, and researchers have recently discovered that they can recognise them-selves in mirrors, a level of self-awareness previously thought to be possessed only by humans, apes and dolphins (Szabo, 2006). Elephants have been observed helping sick family members, are keen problem solvers – building tools to reach higher branches – and researchers have witnessed elephants in Africa displaying signs of post-traumatic stress disorder (PTSD). Researchers believe the PSTD stems from a long and violent history of family breakdowns through culling, poaching and a loss of habitat. PTSD-related behaviours include abnormal startle response, depression, unpredictable asocial behaviour and hyper aggression (Bradshaw et al., 2005). These findings highlight the importance of family and herd stability, and reflect negatively on the capture of elephants for zoos, where parents and older relatives may have been killed in order to capture young animals (Newkirk, 1999), and on current zoo conditions where some elephants live alone, or in small groups of two or three animals.

Wild elephants are constantly moving, active and may walk tens of miles each day (Help Elephants, 2008). Without constant movement and exercise, elephants face health problems ranging from foot and joint disease, to 'arthritis, digestive disorders and neurotic behaviors resulting from severe confinement' (Help Elephants, 2008). The Association of Zoos and Aquariums (AZA) minimum outdoor space requirement for a single adult is 1800 sq. ft, and an extra 900 sq. ft must be added for each additional animal; 1800 sq. ft is the equivalent of six parking spaces (AZA, 2003).

Distressed zoo visitors have witnessed animals exhibiting behaviours such as head bobbing and restless pacing (Bulbeck, 2005). These behaviours, along with walking in circles, rocking back and forth, self-mutilation and sucking the bars of their cages are referred to as 'psychosis' or 'zoochosis' (Newkirk, 1999). This last behaviour has also been witnessed in pigs on factory farms confined to cages so small that they are unable to turn around (Newkirk, 1999). The Born Free Foundation is an advocate for wildlife, and has investigated over 100 zoos across North America, Europe and the UK. Their findings concluded that zoo animals exhibit these signs of abnormal behaviours due to a lack of stimulation and boredom. These behaviours, according to Phil Murphy, Head of Clinical Psychology for Mental Handicap in Norfolk England, 'can still be found in institutions caring for our most severely mentally disturbed patients' (Newkirk, 1999: 66). Investigations conducted by PETA across the USA found several species of bears exhibiting stereotypical behaviour. Frustrated animals were observed pacing, walking in tight circles and swaying or rolling their heads (PETA, 2009).

Neglect, cruelty and death that occur behind the scenes are rarely reported. Recent reports of abuse have plagued Melbourne Zoo, where accusations of animal abuse and neglect were led by the RSPCA, zoo experts and zoo staff. One allegation involves Dokkoon, a 13-year-old elephant allegedly stabbed 'more than a dozen times with a sharp metal spike.... The elephants seemed obviously distressed, standing back to back, vocalising and defecating' (Millar & Houston, 2008a). The incident was witnessed and reported by a staff member, who described the actions of the trainer in question as 'inappropriate and excessive'. The response from the Acting Zoo Chief Executive, Matt Vincent, was that actions taken by the trainer were warranted given the 'potential risk to staff'. The elephants are also kept under control by electric cattle prods (Millar & Houston, 2008a).

An Alternative to Zoos? Wildlife Release Programmes

The Species Survival Plan (SSP) Programme is a cooperative plan between North American zoos and aquaria to 'help ensure the survival of selected wildlife species' (SSP, 2008). The SSP for each particular species includes breeding management 'in order to maintain a healthy and self-sustaining population that is both genetically diverse and demographically stable' (SSP, 2008). SSPs also facilitate and 'participate in a variety of other cooperative conservation activities, such as research, public education, reintroduction and field projects' (SSP, 2008). AZA (2008) do not believe that the reintroduction of species to natural ecosystems is the solution to ensuring the survival of endangered species. AZA is a group that represents the largest and wealthiest zoos and aquaria, including marine parks, in North America. The reluctance on their part to commit to release programmes questions their motivations and priorities.

Captive African lions are being successfully rehabilitated in Antelope Park, Zimbabwe. The aim of the African Lion Environmental Research Trust (ALERT, 2009) is to successfully release captive-born lions into the wild through a four-stage process. There are currently 71 lions in the programme, and 24 waiting for release into Stage 2 where:

> the lions are given the opportunity to develop a natural pride social system in a minimum 500 acre enclosure. They have plenty of game to hunt, and their progress is monitored closely, however all human contact is removed. Lions remain in stage two until such time that the pride is stable and self-sustaining. (ALERT, 2009)

ALERT may also introduce rehabilitation programmes for other African predators, including the cheetah, leopard, African wild dog, jackal, hyena, serval and caracal (ALERT, 2009). This programme, which has experienced significant success, could be developed for species outside Africa. Volunteer programmes, where participants volunteer their time and pay a fee (US$3590 for 1 month), help to fund the rehabilitation programme and buy food for the lions (African Impact, 2008). This rehabilitation programme is not a government, zoo, SSP or conservation initiative. It was founded in 2005 by Andrew Conolly, who purchased Antelope Park in 1987. Included with the purchase of the park were six captive lions and cubs. The idea and plan to rehabilitate lions developed from observing the cubs' natural instincts and behaviours while exercising them on walks. Conolly believed that if the cubs natural instincts could be harnessed, release would be possible (ALERT, 2009).

Under the 'Guidelines for Consideration' on the AZA webpage concerning the reintroduction of captive animals, the first mentioned is 'sufficient funding' (AZA, 2008). The business model established by ALERT could be the foundation from which other rehabilitation programmes could be established, where volunteer participation – both locals and tourists – is subject to a fee, which is invested directly into the programme. This method of funding could prove to be extremely successful given the unique experience offered, and the rise in popularity of volunteer tourism.

Marine Parks and Aquaria: Justification for Captive Viewing

Marine parks and aquaria are criticised for keeping captive animals, particularly cetaceans such as dolphins and orcas. Researchers question the capabilities to cater to the needs of such large and complex animals (Engelbrecht & Smith, 2004; Hoyt, 1992; Williams, 2001). Academics in favour of captive animal viewing, stress the positive impacts, such as the alleviation of stress and natural degradation to the environment and wildlife (Ryan & Saward, 2004; Tremblay, 2008).

Ryan and Saward (2004) classify captive animal viewing as ecotourism. However, classifying captive animal viewing as ecotourism negates the contribution of ecotourism to genuine sustainable tourism through the mistreatment of these captive animals. Living conditions vary among marine parks, and while regulations and standards exist, the stringency of regulation depends on the country or state (Carwardine, 2001; Hoyt, 1992; Smith, 2003; Williams, 2001). Countries have prescribed minimum pool sizes and critics argue that standards were set to coincide with the size of existing pools in marine parks (Carwardine, 2001; Hoyt, 1992; Smith, 2003; Williams, 2001).

Captivity affects every aspect of an orca's life. Tight family units are separated; tank sizes are inadequate and filled with chlorinated water; animals are required to perform shows daily; and animals experience loss of freedom, high infant mortality rates and the premature death of adults. Autopsies performed have found a multitude of diseases, and stress has been labelled a possible contributing factor in 38 of 74 deaths (Carwardine, 2001; Engelbrecht & Smith, 2004; Hoyt, 1992; Williams, 2001).

Regulations now govern the capture of orcas in most waters, and increasing public disapproval of wild captures has forced marine parks and aquaria to focus on captive breeding programmes to preserve their captive numbers (Carwardine, 2001; Hoyt, 1992; Smith, 2003; Williams, 2001). Captive breeding programmes are criticised as they perpetuate and sustain captive populations. Organisations exhibiting orcas maintain that captive viewing contributes to education and conservation (Carwardine, 2001; Hoyt, 1992; Smith, 2003; Williams, 2001), however, their motives are considered economically driven, as Sea World parks receive around US$400–500 million per year from visitor revenue with as much as 70% of their income derived directly from visitors interested in orcas (Williams, 2001).

Research conducted in aquaria in the UK questioned the strategy of education through signage, and found that 83% of visitors did not read the signs at live exhibits apart from the animal's name, and 95% of visitors failed to read the entire sign. The report concluded that visitor motivations influenced the level of interest at exhibits. Less than 45% of the aquaria offered educational talks or special events, less than 45% offered educational packs and 23% did not have a website. The study found evidence of incorrect signage at exhibits, and staff citing incorrect information. The study concluded with recommendations that the public could be better educated through documentaries (Casamitjana, 2004). Marine parks are considered to contribute the least to education. Critics question the educational value of watching whales and dolphins in choreographed acrobatic performances (Engelbrecht & Smith, 2004).

The threat of extinction through hunting, poaching and loss of habitat has pushed conservation to the forefront of environmental issues (DeGrazia, 2002). Conservation is a legal requirement of all aquaria in the UK; however, aquaria play a role in promoting the keeping of exotic fish as pets, and indirectly contribute to the destruction of coral reefs and over fishing. Aquaria in Europe send mixed signals regarding conservation and the importance of protecting wildlife, as visitors can purchase souvenirs of corals, shells, dried starfish and seahorses in gift shops. Conservation claims by aquaria are misleading, as only 1.8% of individuals displayed in UK aquaria are threatened (Casamitjana, 2004). The Humbolt penguin is the only animal part of the European Endangered Species Programme, and none have been released (Carrell, 2004).

Species survival is impeded by live captures. Sandbar sharks mature slowly – a 17-year-old immature female has been recorded – and the wild population is rapidly declining (Casamitjana, 2004). Whale sharks are listed as an endangered species, however, aquariums in Japan and the USA continue to exhibit and replace stock with live captures (Cohen, 2008; Goodman, 2007). Okinawa Churanmi Aquarium in Japan displayed a total of 16 whale sharks over a period of 18 years. Survival in captivity ranged from 3 days to 6 years, compared with life projections of up to 100 years for whale sharks in the wild. Of the 16 whale sharks, 13 died in captivity and 7 were injured during transit and survived less than 2 months (Casamitjana, 2004; Goodman, 2007). Georgia Aquarium in the USA lost two male whale sharks within months. Marine biologists suggest that the number of captive deaths indicate that the species is not suited to captive life (Goodman, 2007).

Little evidence supports the contribution of marine parks to the survival of whales, dolphins and seals. The contribution to *in situ* projects is miniscule, with Sea World funding US$4 million on conservation and stranding efforts (Kestin, 2004). The industry has heavily lobbied the International Whaling Commission to preclude whales and dolphins from their 'jurisdiction'. The inclusion of whales and dolphins would give them international protection under the International Whaling Commission, preventing future live captures (PETA, 2006).

Whale Watching

The overnight growth of the whale watching industry has 'industrialised the ocean' (Corkeron, 2004: 848). Short-term impacts, such as increased boat noise and traffic, are affecting whales, while the long-term consequences remain unknown (Corkeron, 2004; Jelinski *et al.*, 2002; Milius, 2004). Whale watching has been classified as a form of non-consumptive ecotourism, however, whales have been witnessed changing their behaviours in the presence of tourist boats (Corkeron, 2004; Jelinski *et al.*, 2002).

The international whale watching industry is valued at over US$1 billion (Hoyt, 2001), and attracts oven nine million people annually. Orca populations, especially off British Columbia and Washington State, are targets of tourist boats (Jelinski *et al.*, 2002), and as potential economic profit entices the involvement of pro-whaling countries, such as Japan, Norway, Iceland and Russia (Gillespie, 2003), whale watching is now being viewed by some as 'an acceptable form of benign exploitation' (Gillespie, 2003: 408).

Short-term impacts involve continuous increasing levels of boat noise and boat traffic (Corkeron, 2004; Jelinski *et al.*, 2002; Milius, 2004; Morton & Symonds, 2002). Milius (2004) claims that increased boat noise has resulted in killer whales calling up to 15% longer to communicate with fellow pod members, and scientists are unable to determine the long-term consequences. One possible theory is that the longer calls are equivalent to humans adjusting their voices to be heard (Milius, 2004). Morton and Symonds (2002) report that the whales may experience loss of their 'directional hearing capabilities' (Morton & Symonds, 2002: 73), and Corkeron (2004) indicates research demonstrating that noise is the contributing factor of behavioural changes evident in killer whales. Ebersole (2003) reports on a pod of killer whales in Prince William Sound, whose population has declined rapidly over the past 10 years, attributed to noise pollution from increased boat traffic, which is thought to have disturbed their hunting patterns.

The long-term consequences may be as serious as lower activity and reproduction levels, affecting pod survival (Jelinski *et al.*, 2002). Commercial vessels follow and track the whales, which in some cases lead to whales altering their movements (Jelinski *et al.*, 2002). Off Washington State, the number of vessels trailing only three pods of whales has risen from none to 70, in just over 20 years, and research indicates that each pod may be trailed by an average of 22 vessels on any given day. Pods in Canada still recovering from live captures, have now been listed by the government as 'threatened' and of 'special concern' (Morton & Symonds, 2002: 71).

Conclusion

Ecotourism necessarily requires the commodification of wildlife and its habitat – it creates a market value from the observation of animals. It sits between the absolutes of conservation and commercial sale, where the direct human 'gaze' of wildlife is central to the experience with all the possibilities for disruption that such viewing brings (Ryan & Saward, 2004). But, given its alignment to alternative tourism (Wearing & Neil, 1998), it should also provide a mechanism to improve the plight of animals that are central to its function. This chapter would suggest that alternative tourism has a long way to go before it is able to claim any form of value adding to the existence of animals. Also, any claim to have included an ethic that could be aligned to Singer's (1977) appears to be a long way off. Of particular importance is the notion of improving the welfare of animals through their recognition via the education of the tourist through interaction with them – with the ecotourist and animals as active participants in the construction and meaning making of the experiences there is the possibility of the movement of the animal to a more central role in the overall agenda of ecotourism, including some form of ethics based around animals. This may allow movement away from their marginalisation and sole linkage to economic imperatives. We would suggest that with ecotourism, the global commodification of animals is almost complete. As the economic benefits of ecotourism have increased and the recognition of animals as central to this, given anthropocentric Judeo-Christian traditions, nature is inescapably commodified, especially since 'every state of nature must be socially reproduced' (Eder, 1996: 24). Further, with the advent of consumerism 'commodifying almost all aspects of social life' (Macnaghten & Urry, 1998: 26), the commodification of nature is in itself highly contested and so are the rights of animals within this contest.

It is contended here that for ecotourism to philosophically align itself to environmental ethics and to present itself as an alternative form of tourism (Wearing & Neil, 1998), it must incorporate some intention to include in its agenda the rights of animals (included in this is the welfare of animals). Research suggests that the welfare of animals has become an issue due to the need to sustain them for commercial exploitation within the ecotourism experience, but the notion of rights for animals in ecotourism appears to be a distant hope. We would contend that for a movement towards the rights of animals within the ecotourism experience, decommodification principles and practices must be introduced into the global ecotourism industry. If ecotourism cannot offer an alternative path (Wearing & Neil, 1998) towards the rights of animals, it loses the right to distinguish itself from the mainstream ideas of tourism and becomes just another market niche in that industry. We are concerned with outlining the complexity of the role of animals in ecotourism, suggesting that in neoliberal regimes, such as Australia, the USA, Canada and England, there is a need to ensure a conscious agenda of decommodifying the role of animals in the ecotourism experience.

It is clear that we live in a world of limited natural and environmental resources and that human kind must restrain the exploitation of the resources that have become so characteristic of the collective needs of developed countries. There is a conflict between the individual needs of people to protect the environment and the market's needs for production of profit. As such, organisations operating under the banner of ecotourism may need to accept and ensure a closer focus on the rights of animals in order to validly differentiate themselves from a tourism industry otherwise dominated by the exploitative attitudes of free market principles.

Chapter 5

The Rhetoric versus the Reality: A Critical Examination of the Zoo Proposition

LIAM SMITH, BETTY WEILER AND SAM HAM

Introduction

Many nature-based and wildlife-based tourism attractions make statements outlining their purpose as being, in part, to engender positive attitudes and behaviours towards nature and wildlife (AZA, 2006; WAZA, 2005; Mayes *et al.*, 2004; Orams, 1997; Manfredo & Driver, 2002; Ballantyne & Packer, 2005; Ballantyne *et al.*, 2008, 2009; Zeppel & Muloin, 2008). Perhaps because of a need to demonstrate moral and ethical validity, zoos are particularly strong in their emphasis on behavioural and attitudinal impacts. Although there is evidence to support zoos delivering on these goals on-site, there is comparatively little evidence for a sustained shift in attitudes or behaviour once visitors have left the site (Fraser & Wharton, 2007; Adelman *et al.*, 2000; Smith *et al.*, 2008).

The reasons for the lack of demonstrable evidence to support zoo rhetoric are many. They include insufficient research, inadequate or poor research design, and visitors who may not be interested in being changed (Smith *et al.*, 2008). There are also questions about whether zoos are constructing their experiences in ways that lead to changes in visitors' attitudes and behaviours. Experiential elements of a zoo experience that may be important in fostering attitudinal and behavioural change include the communication content, the communication delivery, as well as the emotion evoked as part of the interaction between animals and visitors. Despite its emphasis in some rhetorical statements, emotion is a relatively under-explored variable in contributing to the depth of nature-based tourism experiences and the subsequent impact on cognition and behaviour (Knopf, 1987; Farber & Hall, 2007).

The purpose of this chapter is to critically examine the proposition that zoos can use emotion to influence attitudes and behaviour in the long term. More precisely, the chapter examines the rhetoric and the reality of using zoo experiences to foster pro-wildlife behaviour, as organisational statements about their ability to influence attitudes and behaviour is widespread. We will first present, critique and then deconstruct the proposition that zoo experiences induce emotion in visitors, which can then be used for a positive effect on visitors' attitudes and behaviour. Theories and empirical evidence supporting the proposition are contrasted with those that do not. Through this process, an agenda for future research into the impact of emotions on visitors' pro-wildlife behaviour becomes apparent.

The Zoo Proposition

At all levels of zoo administration, there is a stated desire to encourage zoo visitors to become better environmental citizens (see, e.g. ARAZPA, 2003; AZA, 2006; Patrick *et al.*, 2007; WAZA, 2005). Zoos often seek to encourage better environmental citizenship by requesting or suggesting pro-wildlife behaviours that visitors can undertake to decrease threats to wildlife and habitats. Behaviours of interest range from those that visitors do on-site, such as recycling and making donations to conservation programmes, to those that visitors do once they have left the zoo, such as putting up nest boxes in their backyard, planting native trees or volunteering for conservation projects (Smith, 2009).

The strategy that many zoos employ in an attempt to influence behaviour is through providing a combination of experiences and interpretation. A premise of this approach is that zoo experiences can lead to emotional connections with animals, which can promote a desire in visitors to engage in behaviours perceived to be helpful to the animals they encounter. If, as part of visitors' experiences, behaviours are suggested to them, there is an increased likelihood they will engage in them. This proposed theoretical sequence, termed 'the zoo proposition' for the purpose of this chapter, is found in many zoos' organisational statements, as well as in the strategies of regional and world zoo associations (see, e.g. ARAZPA, 2003; AZA, 2006; WAZA, 2005). As one example, the Education and Training section of the World Association of Zoos and Aquariums (WAZA) Conservation Strategy identifies four outcomes that zoo education should strive to achieve (WAZA, 2005: 37):

- To excite, enthuse and interest people about the natural world.
- To encourage understanding of conservation issues and visitors' individual roles in them.
- To develop public support and action to address conservation concerns.
- To provide a range of experiences, materials and resources for the diversity of visitors, to enable them to make informed choices in their daily lives that benefit the environment and wildlife.

Put more succinctly,

The educational focus should induce a feeling of wonder and respect for the web of life and our role in it; it should engage the emotions and build on this experience to create a conservation ethic that can be carried into action. (WAZA, 2005: 38)

Despite such assertions, the process through which zoos claim to influence their visitors is largely untested by research in a zoo context. Zoos do have some advantages over other organisations interested in influencing behaviour, in that they are, ostensibly, more easily able to induce emotion through the facilitation of interactions between wildlife and people. They also have the opportunity to capitalise on these emotions to request behaviours face-to-face with a relatively attentive audience (Smith & Broad, 2008). However, evidence demonstrating that these advantages are actually leading to impacts on zoo visitors' behaviour is lacking (see e.g. Adelman *et al.*, 2000; Balmford *et al.*, 2007; Smith *et al.*, 2008; Manubay *et al.*, 2002; Dierking *et al.*, 2004).

Empirical Research Relevant to the Zoo Proposition

Despite the assertion that emotion may be an important precursor to shifts in attitudes and behaviour, limited research has examined the proposition. Studies on all three of the primary constructs (emotion, attitude and behaviour) *have* been researched in zoos. For the most part, research has tended to concentrate on the amount of knowledge visitors gain during a zoo visit and some visitors' attitudes, although studies on attitudes and behaviour as outcomes are becoming more common (see e.g. Adelman *et al.*, 2000; Balmford *et al.*, 2007; Smith *et al.*, 2008; Manubay *et al.*, 2002; Dierking *et al.*, 2004; Kruse & Card, 2004; Nakamichi, 2007). Emotion, despite its status as an important antecedent in the zoo proposition, remains the least explored of the three constructs.

One notable exception is the Myers *et al.* (2004) study assessing the emotion and emotional arousal of zoo visitors while viewing three different zoo exhibits (snake, okapi and gorilla), using an experience sampling method. Although their comparative findings were interesting (people had more 'good' emotions at the gorilla exhibit), the study was not designed to examine the impact of visitors' emotions on other outcomes of interest, such as attitudes and behaviour. A conclusion of the Myers *et al.* (2004) study was that the emotion–behaviour relationship represents an important focus for future research.

Although not directly measuring individual components of an experience, such as emotion or emotional arousal, some studies have attempted to demonstrate the impact of a whole zoo experience on short-term behaviour. In a study directly related to the zoo proposition, Swanagan (2000) investigated the relationship between levels of visitors' interaction with elephants and two subsequent behaviours – signing a petition to keep the ban on the importation of ivory and taking solicitation cards to send to politicians about the issue. Based on finding that visitors who had a more intense experience with elephants were more likely to fill out solicitation cards, Swanagan concluded that a link between the experience and subsequent behaviour might exist. However, another study (Stoinski *et al.*, 2002) looked at the relationship between viewing confronting images of the wildlife trade likely to evoke emotion and the related behaviours of signing a petition and taking solicitation cards. Unlike Swanagan, Stoinski and colleagues did not find a relationship between the experience and the behavioural outcome. Those viewing more confrontational images were no more likely to take a solicitation card or sign a petition than those who viewed benign images. Although there are notable differences between the studies, in that respondents in Swanagan's study probably experienced positively valenced emotions through the viewing of live animals and respondents experienced negatively valenced emotions from viewing confronting images, it is clear that more research examining the experiential elements of an experience, including emotion, is necessary.

Other studies focus on behavioural outcomes but do not isolate particular experiential elements to explain why change would occur. For example, Manubay *et al.* (2002) measured brochure pick-up as a measure of visitor interest in seeking additional information following a zoo experience. Similarly, Dierking *et al.* (2004) used a list of pro-environmental behaviours from a national survey to determine the impact of a zoo experience on visitor behaviour. In both these cases, and others (e.g. Balmford *et al.*, 2007; Smith & Broad, 2008), a direct relationship between the [emotional elements of the] experience, the messages communicated and the behavioural outcomes was not apparent.

Deconstructing the Process

Theory and research in other contexts provide some insight into the links suggested in the zoo proposition, most notably between emotion and attitude and between attitude and behaviour. In varying contexts, these connections have ranged from tenuous to strong. In reference to the link between emotion and attitude, emotion can play a pivotal role in the formation and movement of attitudes (Petty *et al.*, 2003). Support for this idea can be found in studies indicating that mood state can influence the efficacy of persuasive messages (as determined by a shift in attitude), particularly where the valence of the message matches the valence of the mood (DeSteno *et al.*, 2004; Agrawal *et al.*, 2007).

In reference to the link between attitudes and behaviour, when attitudes are strong and accessible (Kraus, 1995), or when attitudes are formed through substantial cognitive effort or direct experience with an attitude object (Fazio & Zanna, 1981; Petty & Cacioppo, 1986), they can be predictive of certain behaviours with respect to that object. Consistent with these findings are studies showing that when the attitude object is itself a behaviour, a person's attitude towards the behaviour itself will be predictive of whether the particular behaviour is carried out (Ajzen, 2005; Ajzen & Fishbein, 2005). As an example, a generally positive attitude towards wildlife will not be predictive of whether an individual will donate to the World Wide Fund for Nature (WWF). A positive attitude towards the *behaviour* of donating to WWF however, would be more consistently predictive of the behaviour. Recent studies in national parks and protected areas have indeed shown that impacting visitors' attitudes towards pro-environmental behaviours can increase compliance with requests to carry out those behaviours in the short term (Ham *et al.*, 2007).

Thus, a key issue with the zoo proposition is that a conservation ethic, in so far as such a thing exists, can be seen as a generally positive attitude towards the concept of conservation, which is made up of many components. Therefore, the prospect that such an ethic might result from short, infrequent zoo visits is highly unlikely without support from other experiences that influence other components of the attitude. Furthermore, even if such a general attitude could be induced or influenced during a zoo visit, it would not be very predictive of specific conservation or pro-environmental behaviours (Ajzen & Fishbein, 2005). Based on this pattern of research findings, a modified version of the zoo proposition, removing reference to general attitudes, might state that:

> Zoo experiences induce emotion in visitors and this emotional state can, in combination with persuasive requests to perform a specific behaviour in behalf of an animal or species, influence attitudes toward, and the undertaking of the specific requested behaviour.

Despite a lack of evidence demonstrating the impact on long-term behaviour, this modified zoo proposition may have some foundation. By identifying emotion as a component in the psychological journey that zoos wish their visitors to take, zoos have identified an ingredient that can influence behaviour. In other contexts, researchers have shown support for this idea; for example, DeBergerac (1998), Waldron (1998) and Smith (2007) all used case studies to illustrate the impact of strong emotional experiences on the lives and behaviours of those who have them. That zoos are capable of providing strongly emotional experiences between visitors and featured wildlife, distinguishes them from other organisations attempting to influence pro-environmental behaviour. In other words, animal encounters could create an emotional state in zoo visitors, which makes them more receptive to persuasive messages aimed at influencing their behaviour.

While theory has helped redefine the zoo proposition and provides some support for it, particularly for the emotion–behaviour link, further subdivision would aid in outlining an agenda for future research.

Consider that there are at least five steps for the transition outlined in the modified zoo proposition to occur. First, emotion must be evoked. Second, attention must be directed towards the behavioural request made in the zoo communication. Although attention to an emotion-eliciting message ought to occur automatically in most cases (Lang, 2000), attention to behaviour requests in a zoo environment may be more difficult to achieve because of the possible presence of other emotionally arousing stimuli. Third, information processed as a result of attention-paying needs to be encoded into either short-term or long-term memory. While the relationship between memory and emotional arousal is well-established (Cahill & McGaugh, 1995), the degree to which zoo requests for behaviour are encoded and remembered needs to be measured. Fourth, if the request is attended to and encoded, the zoo visitor has to appraise the behaviour in several ways, such as assessing the magnitude of the problem, the efficacy of the requested behaviour at addressing the problem, and the individual's assessment of her/his ability to perform it among other competing priorities. The fourth step ultimately should result in a positive appraisal of the encoded message and the formulation of a positive attitude towards the requested behaviour. The final step necessary in realising the zoo proposition is the translation of the intention into action.

Studies by both Myers *et al.* (2004) and Smith (2009) confirm that zoo experiences can indeed evoke emotional responses, providing some support for the first step. Some studies examining visitors' recall of behaviour requests show that they are remembered at the end of zoo visits (Smith *et al.*, 2008; Smith, 2009), suggesting that requests are often encoded into short-term memory (steps two and three). However, studies on emotional cues contradict this, demonstrating that emotion can serve to consume attention and prevent attention being paid to non-emotional cues (Christianson & Loftus, 1987; Heuer & Reisberg, 1990; Mather *et al.*, 2006). Studies examining visitors' stated behavioural intentions as visitors leave zoos suggest that many say they intend to perform the requested behaviours (step four). However, those with a follow-up assessment of actual or reported behaviour have shown little change in behaviour (see, e.g. Adelman *et al.*, 2000; Dierking *et al.*, 2004; Manubay *et al.*, 2002; Smith *et al.*, 2008). Thus, there appears to be limited long-term influence on behaviour, suggesting that visitors do not follow through on stated intentions (step five). Conversely, studies that have used on-site behaviours as the behaviour of interest have often found visitors willing to participate (see, e.g. Hayward & Rothenberg, 2004; Manubay *et al.*, 2002; Swanagan, 2000).

Although there is little, and conflicting, evidence for the original zoo proposition, it appears that there is some support for the modified proposition presented. However, two areas present as suitable for closer scrutiny, and represent areas where future research into the zoo proposition should focus. These areas are the relationship between emotion and attention, and the transitioning of positive attitudes towards behaviour into behaviour.

Future Research: Using Emotion for Attention

From the evolutionary perspective of emotions, emotional arousal promotes attention to a central cue or the dominant stimulus, which, in turn, facilitates approach or avoidance behaviours (Lang, 2000; Talmi et al., 2007). While it is not always shown to be true that attention and emotional arousal coincide, within most theoretical frameworks the two are intimately related. Indeed, the function of emotional arousal is thought to be that of directing attention to emotional cues (Ohman et al., 2001) and emotional cues consume attentional resources, and an individual's capacity for processing information unrelated to the source of emotion is limited (see limited capacity processing – Lang, 2000). Tangential information surrounding memory of the emotional cue can be less reliable, leading to a so-called 'weapon-focus' found in eye-witness accounts of violent crime, where attention becomes so focused on the emotional cues that other information is lost (Heuer & Reisberg, 1990; Christianson & Loftus, 1987; Mather et al., 2006).

Thus, one possibility that appears to contradict the zoo proposition and directly challenges the second step (attending to the request), is that the emotions visitors feel as part of an interaction with wildlife may distract visitors away from requests to perform behaviours. In other words, visitors become too focused on the source of their emotion (the animal) such that they are not able to pay attention to information about and requests to perform behaviours that can assist the animal at hand. Two studies lend some support to this assertion. Although not significant, Stoinski et al. (2002) found lower action recall after emotionally evocative images were viewed. More convincingly, Smith (2009) found a small but significant negative correlation between recall and emotional arousal during a birds-of-prey show for first-time visitors to the show. Repeat visitors reported lower levels of emotional arousal which, as Smith argues, may afford visitors the opportunity to attend to messages rather than be distracted by the birds.

The possibility of distraction is of paramount importance to zoos as they attempt to focus the attention of visitors on their requests for pro-wildlife behaviours. It is likely that the animal itself is acting as an emotional cue, meaning that processing of related information, particularly behavioural requests, may not occur. Thus, the colour of a tiger's eyes and the sharpness of its teeth may receive substantial attention, while information about the endangerment of tigers and ways they can be helped may not. Two solutions to this problem are apparent. One alternative would be to separate, both spatially and temporally, communication activities from interactions with the animals so that the emotional content of the interaction doesn't distract the visitor's attention from the message. This, of course, raises other questions, such as how far they should be separated and whether zoo visitors will even be interested in information about wildlife without the wildlife present. Studies on zoo signs suggest not (Churchman, 1985; MacDonald & Ham, 2007), largely leaving the challenge to zoo staff to communicate requests.

A second and more theoretically justified solution would be to put emotion into a persuasive appeal such that the attention-drawing power of the appeal simultaneously focuses visitors' attention on the message being communicated. Studies involving viewer attention to emotive television messages have supported the idea that emotional content draws attention to the message and leads to encoding (Lang, 2000). Thus, emotional appeals may be able to compete on a more even basis with animal-induced emotion. Studies examining processing where two emotional cues are present suggest that simultaneous processing can occur, although sometimes not consciously (Anderson & Phelps, 2001). In a zoo, of course, this alternative raises questions about which emotion(s) should be evoked to compete with the animal as well as which emotions are effective at influencing behaviours of interest. Research is needed to test the distraction hypothesis. The two proposed solutions (separation and competition) also require research to determine their efficacy at addressing the issue of distraction.

Future Research: Translating Attitudes and Intentions into Behaviour

A second area identified for future research is how to aid the translation of a positive attitude towards behaviour and intention to perform the behaviour into actual behaviour. A number of studies have shown that zoo experiences can have an impact on on-site behaviours and intentions to perform future behaviour (Adelman *et al.*, 2000; Manubay *et al.*, 2002; Swanagan, 2000; Stoinski *et al.*, 2002; Smith *et al.*, 2008; Balmford *et al.*, 2007), but the subset of studies that included a follow-up investigation into long-term impacts showed minimal impact once visitors had returned home. For example, Adelman *et al.* (2000) showed that while commitment to conservation action increased immediately after visiting the National Aquarium in Baltimore, 6–8 weeks later it had returned to pre-experience levels. Manubay *et al.* (2002) demonstrated an initial increased interest in environmentally responsible behaviour, but found that it did not persist over time.

Similarly, Dierking *et al.* (2004) found that levels of intended conservation action rose initially after visiting a conservation station at Disney's Animal Kingdom, but 2–3 months after visiting the exhibit, they reverted to their original level. Smith *et al.* (2008) found changes in visitors' intentions at the zoo exit and reported behaviour in follow-up interviews 6 months after they visited the zoo. However, all reported changes (for recycling) were associated with the distribution of recycling bins by the local municipality. Conversely, visitors who stated an intention to perform another behaviour (moving road kill off the road so that carrion-feeding birds are not hit by passing cars) were not facilitated or reinforced in any other way and no changes in reported behaviour were found.

The observation that on-site behaviours and intentions for future behaviour seem to be more easily influenced than off-site behaviours is worth exploring. In other contexts, consistency between intention and behaviour has also been low (Ajzen, 2005; Orbell & Sheeran, 1998; Sheeran, 2002; Sutton, 1998), with one meta-analysis of meta-analyses suggesting that behavioural intention accounts for 28% of variance in behaviour (Sheeran, 2002). Sheeran (2002) suggests a number of possible explanations for low intention–behaviour consistency, including measurement, behaviour type, intention type, properties of behavioural intentions and personality variables. Other explanations can be added, including bias in the research conducted, too much time passing between the formulation of an intention and the opportunity to act, and also that zoo experiences are effective in motivating behaviour in the short term only. Components of a zoo experience that may be responsible for motivating action include an individual's personality, normative influences and the emotion felt during it (as per the zoo proposition).

A number of theoretical perspectives, such as protection motivation theory (Rogers, 1975), theories of planned behaviour and reasoned action (Ajzen, 1991), personal norms (Harland *et al.*, 1999), stages of change (Prochaska & Velicer, 1997), the elaboration likelihood model (Petty & Cacioppo, 1986), implementation intentions (Gollwitzer & Sheeran, 2006) and emotional appeals (see previous discussion) inform how behaviour can be influenced and practical tools are readily available to influence behaviour, such as community-based social marketing (McKenzie-Mohr & Smith, 1999) and Cialdini's weapons of influence (Cialdini, 2001). Research is needed into the applicability and, more importantly, the efficacy of these frameworks and tools in a zoo context, with a particular focus on addressing the intention–behaviour gap.

On-site behaviours may be important because they represent an outlet for visitors to manifest the emotions they feel, but represent only a small subset of behaviours that can assist wildlife (Smith, 2009). Thus, research is needed to determine how best to use the on-site emotions and resultant positive attitudes towards pro-wildlife behaviours to facilitate off-site behaviour. Some studies have shown that memories of events can re-induce the emotion felt at the time (Tarrant *et al.*, 1994). If, as Smith (2009) suggests, off-site pro-wildlife behaviours are of greater interest to zoos, then post-visit communication between the zoo and their visitors should perhaps aim to re-evoke these emotions. Doing so requires an extension of the relationship between zoos and their visitors beyond the time they are on-site and the conditions under which post-visit communication most effectively operates requires research.

Conclusion

This chapter investigated whether there is theoretical and empirical support for zoo rhetoric surrounding their ability to use emotion to influence visitors' pro-wildlife behaviour. Deconstructing the process revealed some theoretical support for a refined zoo proposition and also revealed two key areas for future research. The first area for future research is to investigate the possibility that zoo animals may distract visitors' attention away from behaviour requests. It is possible that interacting with wildlife in zoos may consume visitors' attentional resources, making it difficult for zoos to communicate any other information, including information on actions that visitors can take to help the species concerned. Determining the answer to this question involves testing the efficacies of temporal and spatial separation of emotional arousal from request as well as testing the efficacy of competing emotional cues. Research is also needed to investigate how the desirable attitudes and intentions visitors frequently express on-site can be translated into future action. In particular, comparisons between different methods of communication and behaviour-change strategies (including on-site action) will lead to a better understanding of how to use the zoo context to best achieve zoos' stated desire to influence pro-wildlife behaviour.

Chapter 6

Conservation, Education or Entertainment: What Really Matters to Zoo Visitors?

SHARON LINKE AND CAROLINE WINTER

Introduction

For centuries, humans have valued other species not only as a key source of food and clothing, but also as a means of entertainment, education and spirituality. Humans also have a long history of capturing a selection of species that are perceived to hold greater values, demonstrated by a range of characteristics, such as aesthetic appeal, size, rarity and novelty. The diverse nature of captive wildlife exists on a continuum, ranging from complete confinement to complete freedom, and from a conservation/education viewpoint to one of providing entertainment (Shackley, 1996). According to the World Zoo Conservation Strategy (IUDZG/CBSG (IUCN/SSC, 1993), the term 'zoo' is now used for institutions that exhibit two characteristics: they house a collection of wild (non-domesticated) animals; and they display at least part of this collection to the public. Using these characteristics, Tribe (2004) concluded that despite their variation in composition and naming, it is appropriate to term all captive wildlife institutions as 'zoos', including those that use other titles, such as aquariums and fauna parks.

Given that most people in western societies live in urban environments, Morgan and Hodgkinson (1999: 228) argue that 'zoological parks are considered to be the most important source of contact between people and animals in modern society'. The Australian Bureau of Statistics' (ABS) household census for 2005–2006, found that 35.6% of the Australian population aged 15 years and over, or 5.7 million people visited a zoological park or aquarium in the 12 months prior to the survey (ABS, 2008). According to the Zoos Victoria Annual Report 2007/ 2008, which incorporates the three major zoos in Victoria: Melbourne Zoo (MZ), Werribee Open Range Zoo (WORZ) and the Healesville Sanctuary, in that period, Zoos Victoria attracted 1,556,000 visitors (Zoos Victoria, 2008c).

Zoos also contribute significantly to the national economy. Operating as a tourist attraction, they create employment, purchase goods and services, receive overseas tourists which instigates foreign exchange, reinvest any surpluses in zoo development, and also directly and indirectly attract visitors to the local area (Tribe, 2001). A census of the Australian zoo industry in 1996–1997, found that it had almost 8 million paid admissions, an annual turnover of $142.4 million, generated an operating surplus of $16.3 million and employed almost 2000 people in 65 organisations (ABS, 1998).

This chapter concerns two of the Zoos Victoria properties that exhibit substantially different animal enclosures – MZ and WORZ. MZ is located approximately 4 km north of Melbourne's Central Business District (CBD) and it attracted 970,000 visitors in the 2007/2008 financial period (Zoos Victoria, 2008c). WORZ is located approximately 35 km west of Melbourne's CBD, and in 2007/2008 attracted 285,000 visitors (Zoos Victoria, 2008c). The research reported here, sampled visitors from each zoo and compared their reasons for visiting and their attitudes towards the main role of zoos.

The Roles of Zoos

There has been an understanding within zoo-based research that the three key roles of zoos relate to conservation, education and entertainment (Turley, 1999). Equally, it has been argued that these multiple roles are often conflicting and can be difficult to adequately manage (Mason, 2000; Pickersgill, 1996; Shackley, 1996). Reade and Waran (1996) found that a general public sample regarded entertainment as the least important role of zoos, but for a sample of actual zoo visitors, the main motivations were, in fact, entertainment based. Using a qualitative method, Turley (1999) explored UK zoo managers' perceptions of the objectives of zoos, but found that the direct influence of conservation on encouraging zoo visits was relatively unexplained. Turley suggests that conservation may provide a moral justification for visiting the zoo, and therefore it has an indirect influence on visitor numbers.

As Tribe (2004) argues, a major issue for zoos is in fulfilling their entertainment purpose in attracting visitors without having to compromise their other roles. An investigation conducted by Tribe (2006) on the attitudes of visitors towards the role of conservation at four Australian zoos and four UK zoos found that many visitors believed both conservation and education to be key roles of the zoo. The study concluded, however, that a situation has emerged for zoos whereby 'people visit them mainly for recreation, but they believe that their main role is actually in conservation' (Tribe, 2006: 9). Tribe and Booth (2003) argue that there is a lack of knowledge about the influence that the role of conservation has on visitor experience and satisfaction, as well as the effect that zoos' participation in conservation has on visitation levels. This, in turn, means that zoo management may, in fact, be missing out on potential financial benefits by not embracing the selling tool of conservation (Tribe & Booth, 2003). Smith and Broad (2008), however, conclude that the findings from their study on visitors to the Trail of the Elephants at MZ support the claim that, to some extent, zoos play a role in educating the public about conservation.

The shift towards the importance of the conservation role in zoos has resulted in the 'modern' zoo, which in order to deserve that title, feels obligated to educate the public about nature and participate in conservation activities (van Linge, 1992: 115). They also focus on species preservation and scientific research rather than on entertainment (Jamieson, 1995). This is due to the realisation that the future of a modern zoo is dependent, to a significant extent, on public support (Higginbottom *et al.*, 2001). As a managed visitor attraction, ultimately it is the satisfaction of visitor requirements and expectations that will determine their future. This means that zoos must be clearly, positively and appropriately positioned in the mind of the prospective visitor (Turley, 1999). The visitor today is better informed, more travelled and much more environmentally conscious than that of previous decades. This, however, has not led to the downfall of zoos, but rather a shift towards the conservation objectives in order to match popular tastes (Shackley, 1996).

According to the World Zoo and Aquarium Conservation Strategy, published by the World Association of Zoos and Aquariums (WAZA, 2005), in order for zoos to play an active role in conservation they must:

> Face opposition head-on, by understanding criticisms, adapting where necessary and explaining their actions in a way that gains public support. They must also make clear to the general public that their mission is one of conservation, which is conducted in tandem with the highest welfare standards. (WAZA, 2005)

The Structure and Design of Zoos

The trend towards conservation is evident in the design and operation of zoos, with a continual movement towards more naturalistic physical environments. Zoos have changed from traditional exhibits of bars and concrete, to enclosures that feature natural environments (Hughes *et al.*, 2005; Jamieson, 1995; Ryan & Saward, 2004; Shackley, 1996; van Linge, 1992). The modern naturalistic habitats offer a contrast to the cages, bars and concrete of the traditional urban zoo (Pickersgill, 1996).

These changes to more naturalistic exhibits are also said to reflect changes in visitor attitudes (Hughes *et al.*, 2005; Ryan & Saward, 2004), resulting in an increase in public awareness of, and interest in, animal species (Reade & Waran, 1996). Empirical evidence of this is demonstrated in Shackley (1996), who discovered in her zoo visitor survey that visitors – particularly those in the younger category (15–24 years) – would rather see animals in a safari park situation than in cages.

The move towards naturalistic exhibits may also be beneficial in helping all zoos to escape the 'menagerie' or 'gaol' labels (Nimon, 1990). Therefore, the improvement in enclosure design can lead to zoos becoming more attractive as tourist destinations, and therefore be of financial benefit (Tribe, 2004), as well as improving animal welfare and conservation (Ryan & Saward, 2004). Shackley (1996) predicted that in the future, zoos will be divided into two distinct categories. They will either be small zoos with limited numbers of species in natural environments, providing large amounts of information, or they will be larger zoos with a wider range of species living in reconstructed habitats, employing the latest technology in visitor interpretation. However, both types of zoos will need to concentrate on research and breeding programmes rather than existing primarily for human recreation.

Although many of the smaller urban sites no longer contain the primitive enclosures of the past, the issue of space restraints on captive animals still remains. Progress has been made in the design of zoos through the development of large open range sites. According to the above definition, MZ is classified as a traditional zoo due to its urban spatial restrictions. As its name suggests, WORZ differs in that it is a large open range site covering over 225 ha. It is mainly open savannah, which is viewed by taking a 45-min bus tour, with some smaller exhibits accessed via walking trails (Zoos Victoria, 2008a).

Theoretical Framework

Until very recently, there has been a lack of research on zoos, in particular on zoo visitors, with even less on comparisons between different sites (Mason, 2000; Shackley, 1996; Tribe, 2004; Turley, 1999). One way in which zoo visitors can be understood is through examining their attitudes and behaviours. It is known that attitudes influence behaviour through intentions, which are conscious motivations to carry out a behaviour or act in a particular way (Eagly & Chaiken, 1993). Other factors intervene in this relationship, such that behaviour can be seen as a product of attitudes, social expectations, beliefs about and evaluation of the consequences of the behaviour, and the ability to perform the action (Pearce, 1988). Therefore, these factors can influence the actual behaviour of which zoo the visitor chooses to attend.

The Theory of Planned Behaviour was developed to extend the Theory of Reasoned Action and to account for those behaviours that are not voluntary (Eagly & Chaiken, 1993). This model details several fundamental assumptions – that intention immediately precedes actual behaviour; intention is determined by attitude towards the behaviour, the subjective norm (being what they think the reactions of others will be) and the perceived behavioural control of the individual; these determinants are influenced by the behavioural, normative and control beliefs; and that these beliefs vary due to a number of background factors (Ajzen & Fishbein, 2005). Attitudes that are based on direct experience with the attitude object are better predictors of behaviour than attitudes formed without the experience or based on second-hand information (Ajzen & Fishbein, 2005; Cialdini *et al.*, 1981).

The study reported in this chapter adopted part of these models and examined the relationship between the attitude towards the behaviour, and the behaviour. This was analysed through the visitors' attitudes towards the roles of the zoo, and their actual behaviour exhibited through attendance at a particular zoo site – MZ or WORZ. Attitudes are generally stable and deeply held, but in analysing the behaviour of a visit to the zoo, it is realistic to acknowledge that other more variable reasons can influence behaviour and that they may change from one visit to the next.

Method

In 2007, two focus groups were conducted to explore visitation experiences of zoos and help assess the questions from other research for use in this project. The eight participants included six females and two males, aged from 20 to 50 years. The information gained from these groups was used to inform the development of the main data collection method, a quantitative questionnaire.

The data were collected using a researcher-assisted questionnaire, which contained the following sections

- The reasons for the visit were measured using nine five-point Likert scale items, the majority of which were from Tribe (2006). Three items were slightly altered to ensure that they corresponded with only one role of a zoo. Prior research (Reade & Waran, 1996; Ryan & Saward, 2004; Shackley, 1996; Tribe, 2004; Turley, 1999) was consulted in making these changes.
- Attitudes towards the three main roles of zoos (conservation, education and entertainment) were measured using a set of 13 five-point Likert scale items. These items were based on discussions from the focus groups, and were from prior research (Ryan & Saward, 2004; Shackley, 1996; Tribe, 2004, 2006). Four items were reversed to prevent 'Yay saying'.
- Visitation habits, method of transport used, socio-demographic information, including detail on other members of the visiting party and *Friends of the Zoo* membership was also sought (Zoos Victoria,

2008b). The format of these questions closely matched that of Sweeney Research, who has conducted an annual survey of visitors at each of the Zoos Victoria properties since 2004 on behalf of Zoos Victoria.

A pilot study on a sample of 30 people was conducted at MZ and some minor changes to the questionnaire were made as a result. The final questionnaire was administered to zoo visitors aged over 18 years at MZ and WORZ during August and September 2007, in a non-holiday period and both weekdays and weekends. The survey times were selected by a simple random sampling technique and the visitor sample was chosen by approaching people who were seated in the food outlet areas. The total number of completed questionnaires was 190, with 108 from MZ and 82 from WORZ, with an overall response rate of 84.4% (225 people had been approached). Three records were removed from the MZ sample because of incomplete responses to some questions, leaving a final data set of 187.

Results

Visitation habits

Just over half of the total sample ($n = 109$, 58%) had visited a zoo in the past year, and of these, MZ was the most popular ($n = 75$, 69%). For the remainder of the sample, 28% had visited between 1 and 5 years ago, and 14% had last visited a zoo more than 5 years ago. No significant differences were found between the samples for *Friends of the Zoo* membership.

Overall, the sample was predominantly female ($n = 137$, 73%), with similar proportions at MZ (74%) and WORZ (70%). The WORZ sample was significantly older than the MZ sample. The largest percentage of participants was in the 30 to 39-year-old range (32.1%), comprising 34.3% of the MZ sample and 29.3% of the WORZ sample. A higher proportion of younger people, aged 18–24 years (14.8%) were in the MZ sample, compared with 9.8% for WORZ. A higher proportion of the older (40–49 and 50–59 year groups) participants were represented in the WORZ sample (Table 6.1).

Table 6.1 Age groups (%) by sample

Age groups (years)	18–24	25–29	30–39	40–49	50–69	>70	Total (%)
MZ	14.8	9.3	34.3	24.0	15.7	1.9	100
WORZ	9.8	7.3	29.3	28.0	24.4	1.2	100
Total	12.6	8.4	32.1	25.8	19.5	1.6	100

The sample from MZ was more likely to have a pre-school age child accompanying them (45.4%) than at WORZ (37.8%). For the total sample, the majority of groups (48.9%) consisted of parents and children, which was slightly higher at MZ (53.7%). Grandparents accompanied 16% of groups. More groups of friends visited WORZ (19.5%) than MZ (7.4%).

Reasons for visiting

The results for the descriptive analysis of items designed to measure visitors' reasons for visiting the zoo are shown in Table 6.2. For the total, MZ and WORZ, the three strongest items related to Entertainment. For the total sample, the most important reason was item R1 to *Have a fun day out* (mean = 4.58), followed by item R2, to *See lots of different animals* (mean = 4.48). Mann–Whitney U tests indicated that for all but two items (R2 and R8) the WORZ sample scored significantly higher means than MZ.

Attitudes

Table 6.3 details the items that measure visitors' attitudes towards the roles of zoos. All of the means are greater than '4', indicating that the sample 'agreed' or 'strongly agreed' with the items. No differences were detected between the means for MZ and WORZ. According to the Theory of Planned Behaviour, the higher reasons for visiting the zoo indicated by the WORZ sample would be reflected in higher scores for their attitudes, and there would be significant differences to the MZ sample. In order to resolve this apparent incongruity, further analysis was undertaken by clustering the sample (Table 6.4).

Reasons for visiting

The clusters showed a similar pattern of reasons for visiting, as shown in Table 6.2. Cluster 2 held significantly stronger reasons for visiting than Cluster 1 for the two Conservation items (R6, R7), one Education item (R9) and one Entertainment item (R4) (Table 6.5). For four of the five Entertainment items, no difference was detected between the clusters. In both clusters, the Entertainment reasons were stronger than those for Conservation and Education. The lowest reason for Cluster 1 (and second lowest for Cluster 2) was to *Contribute to wildlife conservation.*

Attitudes towards zoos

T-tests indicated that Cluster 2 held significantly stronger attitudes towards the role of zoos than Cluster 1 for all the items except A4

Table 6.2 Reasons for visiting the zoo today – descriptive analysis

Item No.	Reason for visiting	Melbourne zoo		Werribee open range zoo		Total		Sig. (p)
		Mean	SD	Mean	SD	Mean	SD	
Entertainment								
R1	Have a fun day out	4.48	0.61	4.71	0.56	4.58	0.59	0.00
R2	See lots of different animals	4.50	0.67	4.46	0.63	4.48	0.65	0.55
R3	Spend time with family/friends	4.19	0.93	4.52	0.84	4.33	0.90	0.00
R4	Be in a pleasant outdoor space	4.02	0.89	4.38	0.68	4.18	0.82	0.01
R5	Escape pressures of daily life	3.29	1.35	4.01	1.12	3.61	1.30	0.00
Conservation								
R6	Help support rare or endangered animals	3.55	1.11	3.91	1.02	3.71	1.08	0.03
R7	Contribute to wildlife conservation	3.34	1.09	3.85	0.98	3.57	1.07	0.00
Education								
R8	Educate my children about animals	3.88	1.46	3.96	1.31	3.92	1.39	1.00
R9	Learn about wildlife	3.66	1.04	4.14	0.86	3.87	0.99	0.00

Note: Scale: 1 = not at all important; 2 = not so important; 3 = neutral; 4 = important; 5 = very important. SD = standard deviation.

Table 6.3 Attitudes towards zoos: Descriptive analysis

Item No.	Attitude item	Melbourne zoo		Werribee open range zoo		Total	
		Mean	SD	Mean	SD	Mean	SD
Entertainment							
A1	Zoos provide a variety of animals for us to look at	4.66	0.50	4.57	0.59	4.62	0.54
A2	I do not consider zoos to be entertaining[a]	4.56	0.75	4.52	0.82	4.54	0.78
A3	Zoos provide a pleasant day out	4.50	0.62	4.54	0.57	4.52	0.60
A4	Zoos provide a place to take the children as a treat	4.41	0.75	4.30	0.78	4.36	0.76
Conservation							
A5	Breeding endangered species is an important role of zoos	4.59	0.61	4.68	0.61	4.63	0.61
A6	Zoos support wildlife conservation	4.49	0.73	4.63	0.60	4.55	0.68
A7	Zoos play an important role in conservation	4.39	0.77	4.54	0.72	4.45	0.75
A8	It is not a role of zoos to conserve species[a]	4.40	1.02	4.48	1.05	4.43	1.03
Education							
A9	Information about the animals does not need to be provided to visitors[a]	4.71	0.57	4.77	0.57	4.74	0.57
A10	The education of school children is an important role for the zoo	4.56	0.70	4.67	0.50	4.61	0.62
A11	Educational displays in zoos are important	4.47	0.66	4.50	0.61	4.48	0.64

Table 6.3 (*Continued*)

Item No.	Attitude item	Melbourne zoo		Werribee open range zoo		Total	
		Mean	SD	Mean	SD	Mean	SD
A12	It is important that the zoo educates all visitors	4.31	0.68	4.39	0.66	4.34	0.67
Other							
A13	Zoos do not have any worthwhile role[a]	4.72	0.73	4.87	0.54	4.79	0.65

Note: Scale: 1 = strongly disagree; 2 = disagree; 3 = neither agree nor disagree; 4 = agree; 5 = strongly agree. SD = standard deviation.
[a]Data have been reverse coded.

Table 6.4 Distribution of samples across the clusters

	Cluster 1	*Cluster 2*	*Total*
MZ	41 (40%)	62 (60%)	103 (100%)
WORZ	31 (38%)	50 (62%)	81 (100%)
Total	72 (39%)	112 (61%)	184 (100%)

Table 6.5 Reasons for visiting the zoo – significant differences between clusters

Item No.	*Reason*	*Cluster 1*	*Cluster 2*	*Sig. (p)*
Entertainment				
R4	Be in a pleasant outdoor place	3.89	4.35	0.00
Conservation				
R6	Help support rare or endangered animals	3.25	3.98	0.00
R7	Contribute to wildlife conservation	3.06	3.87	0.00
Education				
R9	Learn about wildlife	3.48	4.11	0.00

(*Zoos provide a place to take the children as a treat*). A composite mean was then calculated for the three attitude types (Entertainment, Conservation and Education). Items A9 and A13 were excluded. Cronbach's alpha reliability tests are shown in Table 6.6. The result for Conservation was respectable (0.72), Education was minimally acceptable (0.68) and the low result of 0.59 for Entertainment was unacceptable (DeVellis, 1991: 85).

The mean for each cluster (Table 6.6) was calculated for Entertainment, Conservation and Education. *T*-tests indicated that the magnitudes of the means for Cluster 2 were significantly higher than Cluster 1. Within each cluster, paired sample *t*-tests showed that Cluster 1 did not distinguish between Conservation and Education. The highest mean for Cluster 2 was Conservation and for Cluster 1 it was Entertainment. Cluster 1 was significantly younger than Cluster 2, having twice the proportion of members in the 25–29 age bracket and half the number in the 40–49 age bracket.

Table 6.6 Attitude means by cluster

Attitude	Items	Cronbach's alpha	Cluster 1 mean	Cluster 2 mean
Entertainment	A1, A2, A3, A4	0.59	4.36	4.63
Conservation	A5, A6, A7, A8	0.72	3.99[a]	4.86
Education	A10, A11, A12	0.68	4.11[a]	4.72

Note: *t*-tests showed significant differences between the clusters for the three means.
[a]Indicates there were no significant differences between means *within* clusters.

Discussion

The study was based on the notion that behaviour, at least in part, is influenced by a person's values and attitudes. Given the differences in the layout of the two zoos, along with increasing public demand for greater space for the animals, it could be expected that each zoo would attract a different clientele. It could also be expected that the visitors from each zoo would be distinguished by differences in the magnitude of their attitudes towards the role of zoos and, subsequently, their reasons for visiting. In the first stage of the analysis, the WORZ sample showed stronger reasons for visiting than those at MZ. This can partly be explained by the greater effort required to access WORZ due to its distance from the city and relative lack of public transport. Both groups indicated that their strongest reason for visiting was for entertainment followed by education and then conservation.

No differences, however, were detected in the attitudes of the two samples. A clustering of the sample helped to distinguish two different groups with significantly different reasons and attitudes for visiting. Significant differences for all but one attitude item and approximately half the reasons for visiting distinguished one cluster from the other. The original two site-based samples were distributed across the two clusters with remarkable similarity: 40% of each sample in Cluster 1 and 60% in Cluster 2. Cluster 1 stated their strongest attitude towards the role of zoos was Entertainment and their reason for visiting scores for Entertainment were also higher than for Education or Conservation. Cluster 2 indicated higher attitude scores towards the role of zoos as being Conservation and Education, with the lowest score for Entertainment. This was at odds with their reasons for visiting, which recorded higher scores for Entertainment.

The results from this study suggest that people visit a zoo primarily for entertainment, regardless of their attitudes towards their role. It should also be considered that modern zoos make a substantial effort to provide education that is also entertaining. Clearly, information that is presented in an enjoyable format is more likely to generate greater attention and interest from an audience that that which is dull. There is not necessarily any reason why motivations for education and entertainment are mutually exclusive. Further studies in this field could extend the way in which these two aspects of visitation are measured.

For the two zoos studied here, visitation appears to be independent of the nature of the zoo. Today's zoos undertake a considerate effort to create 'zooscapes' that appear natural and attractive for their human visitors. While WORZ has the attraction of larger enclosures, MZ has made a substantial effort to create an aesthetic zooscape, which tends to overshadow the fact of the much smaller enclosures for the animals. It could perhaps be worthwhile determining the impact of these design features on visitor perceptions in relation to conservation, entertainment and education. It is also probable that people who hold stronger negative attitudes towards zoos do not attend them or they visit other natural places, such as parks and protected areas, and thus are not captured at on-site studies. Given the significance of zoo design on the animals themselves, it is important that future work be undertaken to fully recognise the real uses to which animal viewing holds for human audiences.

Part 2
New Developments

Zoos are dynamic institutions. As was discussed in the first section of this book, over the last 30 years or so, they have changed dramatically in response to changing social attitudes to animals. In addition, zoos have been forced to change by the same competitive forces that affect all tourist attractions. Faced with competition from other attractions and entertainment options, zoos need to continually develop new ways of exhibiting animals and providing for tourists. Like all attractions, they need to constantly adjust to what Butler (2006) described as the 'Life Cycle' of success, decline and renewal.

Furthermore, whatever innovations zoos bring in, they are likely to be copied by other zoos and possibly even other attractions. Thus, for example, the successful development of walk-through tropical rainforest exhibits in the 1980s gave the pioneers a competitive advantage. However, they could only retain that advantage for a short period because they could not copyright or otherwise monopolise the idea. Other zoos successfully developed their own rainforest exhibits, indeed they were also introduced in aquaria, museums and even shopping malls. In the 2000s, the success of penguin exhibits (complete with Antarctic micro-climates) is leading to their spread. The opposite also works. When Seal Rocks opened on Philip Island (Australia), its private owners advertised it as the 'Zoo of the Future'. At a time when IMAX and the internet were breaking new ground, much was made of its live projection of wild seals broadcast from offshore rocks. However, it quickly failed, and so, seemingly, did any notion that zoo visitors would prefer live video footage over live animals (Frost, 2003).

These competitive forces are also seen in the development of specialisations. Many zoos have realised that it is uneconomic to try for a wide range of animals and so there has been a trend to less exhibits, ideally better done (Shackley, 1996). A number of zoos have chosen to market themselves as 'bio-regional', focusing on the fauna of the local region. Examples include the Arizona-Sonora Desert Museum (USA), Alice Springs Desert Park (Outback Australia) and Healesville Sanctuary (south eastern Australia). The attraction for tourists to a region is the chance to see the distinctive wildlife (and flora) of the region and these zoos have tended to be more viable than generic wildlife parks.

A variation on this idea occurs at Zoo Montana, located in Billings, USA. This is a bio-regional zoo, but it aims to include wildlife from both Montana and regions of the world at the same latitude (45°–49°).

Accordingly, there are wolverines, Grizzly bears and bald eagles, but also Siberian tigers and deer. Billings is between Yellowstone National Park (190 km west) and the Little Bighorn Battlefield National Monument (100 km east). Zoo Montana has been successful in developing a small tourism niche, with its endemic and exotic wildlife providing a reason for tourists visiting either Yellowstone or Little Bighorn to also stop at Billings.

The first two chapters in this theme provide examples of the successful development of innovation tourism products. Dobson explores the recent growth of aquaria, particularly focusing on how they present and interpret sharks. In the past, sharks tended to provoke feelings of fear and disgust, but contemporary interest is more complex, combining fear with fascination for the powerful predator and a growing realisation of their endangered status. Henderson examines the development of the Singapore Night Safari. In this case, this new product was specifically developed to complement other tourist experiences within Singapore. It is also important to note that there is nothing that limits a night zoo in Singapore and other attractions are beginning to experiment with the concept.

The following two chapters perhaps take a more subversive attitude towards new developments. Hannam considers the case of Mumbai Zoo. Initially developed to satisfy local tastes, it held little to attract international tourists. Accordingly, plans have been developed to re-invent this attraction as a modern zoo with an emphasis on conservation, greater attention to animal welfare and immersive exhibits. However, in a familiar tale, these plans have been postponed. The final chapter by Frost takes an historical approach in comparing the evolution of zoos, theme parks, protected areas and museums. The message is that these attractions are closely related and their operators have often looked to others for new ideas.

Chapter 7

Fun, Fascination and Fear: Exploring the Construction and Consumption of Aquarium Shark Exhibits

JOHN DOBSON

Introduction

Zoos and public aquaria often justify keeping animals in captivity on the grounds that they actively contribute towards the conservation of animals through mechanisms such as scientific research and visitor education (Hutchins *et al.*, 2003). Alternatively, critics argue that, in reality, zoos and aquaria make minimal contributions towards the conservation of the natural environment and are more focused on using animals to entertain paying visitors (Jamieson, 1985). Beardsworth and Bryman (2001) see a blurring of the boundaries between the role of zoos as sites of conservation and entertainment as they transform both structurally and ideologically. They identify the impact of Disneyisation as zoos adopt the principles of Disney to appeal to the post-tourist, who seek instant pleasure and are less concerned with authentic experiences. Speigel and Schubel (2001: 5) see this as potentially problematic and consider the mix between education and entertainment as a battle-ground, noting the pressures of ensuring 'numbers through the gate' and the need to satisfy and impress.

This chapter explores the paradox in the representation of sharks that can exist in aquaria when attempting to mix conservation-based objectives with the commercial need to provide an enjoyable and memorable visitor experience. A qualitative methodology was used to collect data. This entailed the observations of shark exhibits at ten aquaria from around the world and semi-structured interviews with four senior aquaria staff. The observations focused on how shark exhibits are constructed, the nature of the interpretive messages provided, how sharks are represented in exhibits, in promotional material and in merchandising, and also how visitors reacted to seeing sharks in exhibits. The semi-structured interviews focused on developing an understanding of how aquaria perceive they present sharks to visitors and the contributions that they make to shark conservation.

Sharks, Conservation and the Monster Image

For many people, the marine environment is an unfamiliar, alien, yet intriguing world. Exposure can be limited to information provided by the media (e.g. television documentaries) and direct experiences are often confined to immediate coastal environments, such as beaches and the inter-tidal zone (Evans, 1997). In western culture, this lack of contact between the general public and marine environments is a 'major causal factor in the relatively low status of marine conservation' (Evans, 1997: 239). However, the survival of the human species is closely tied to the health of ocean ecosystems. Oceans act as a climate regulator, absorbing significant amounts of carbon dioxide and emitting approximately 70% of the planet's oxygen into the atmosphere (Polidoro *et al.*, 2008). Despite this, many oceanic ecosystems and species are threatened by anthropocentric activities, such as coastal development, over-fishing and pollution.

The threat to oceanic ecosystems is exemplified by the problems facing elasmobranchs (sharks and rays). Sharks and rays are particularly vulnerable to human activities due to their nature as predators located at or near the top of the food chain. They tend to have K-selected lifestyles characterised by late sexual maturity and give birth to relatively few young, making populations vulnerable should sexually mature animals be taken out of the system (Camhi *et al.*, 1998). Both sharks and rays are targeted to supply the growing demand for fins (used in shark fin soup) and cartilage (used in traditional oriental and alternative medicine) (Watts, 2001, 2003). The IUCN Red List of threatened species lists 50 shark and 76 ray species as globally threatened (those species classified as being critically endangered, endangered or vulnerable) (IUCN SSG, 2008). Perhaps of more concern is that 47% of sharks and rays are listed as data deficient (Polidoro *et al.*, 2008), reflecting the lack of knowledge and research that has been undertaken to assess the impact of human activities on global populations (Camhi *et al.*, 1998). Many shark and ray populations are therefore in need of urgent conservation. Unfortunately, developing conservation strategies for sharks and rays is hampered by sharks, and to a lesser extent rays, having a poor public image (Crawford, 2008; Dobson, 2008). A number of authors have recognised and discussed the tendency of humans to associate negative human character traits with some animals (see, e.g. Baker, 2001; Bishop, 2004; Midgley, 1995). Bishop (2004: 108) notes that throughout history some animals have been constructed as 'an essence of deviance and pathology'. This is certainly true of sharks, as Midgley (1995: 31) noted when observing a television documentary about sharks:

> [it began] emphatically, with the words, "These are the world's most vicious killers." Vicious? No evidence appeared in the film, incidentally, to suggest that sharks ever kill except in hunger or self-defence.

Dobson (2006, 2008) discusses that the negative construction of the shark has a long tradition in western society and identifies that contemporary media constructions of sharks continue to perpetuate the image of sharks as mindless killers in the mould of Peter Benchley's fictional monster shark, *Jaws*. In recent years, rays have also suffered some negative public perception through the unfortunate death of Australian naturalist and zookeeper, Steve Irwin, who was killed by a stingray while snorkelling on the Great Barrier Reef in 2006. This widespread negative perception of sharks has led Martin (1993) to consider that changing the public's perception of sharks is central to ensuring their conservation. Several authors have discussed if exposing humans to the natural environment has the potential to affect attitude change (Beaumont, 2001; Cassidy, 1997; Zajonic, 1968) and Dobson (2007) notes the potential for tours to observe sharks in the wild has the potential to positively influence participants' perception of sharks. However, as stated above, accessing the oceanic environment, and sharks in particular, can be problematic. There are a number of limiting factors that can restrict tourists' ability to see sharks in the wild. These limiting factors can include the need to have achieved a scuba qualification, the geographical location of many tours and the cost (Figure 7.1).

Figure 7.1 Aquaria can be an effective mechanism for bringing sharks and humans together. (Photo: John Dobson)

One mechanism that allows people to bridge the gap between themselves, the oceanic environment and sharks is the public aquarium. Both Gendron (2004) and Martin (1993) argue that displaying sharks and rays in public aquaria is an effective tool in helping to overcome the constraining factors listed above and making direct and effective contributions to the conservation of sharks and rays. Gendron (2004) sees animals displayed in public aquaria acting as ambassadors for species in the wild. She argues that such ambassadorship can then help visitors gain an understanding of the sharks and rays, the threats they face and instil visitors with a conservation ethic. Gendron (2004: 525) considers that a key aim of any aquarium displaying sharks should be to 'engender respect for elasmobranchs and build positive emotional connections by de-bunking the many myths that surround sharks'. Such myths include the belief that sharks deliberately seek out and attack people, medicines from shark cartilage can cure or prevent cancer and that sharks are able to re-grow their fins once they have been removed (Gendron, 2004). The next section provides a brief history of the development of aquaria and the display of sharks.

Aquaria

As with zoos, the keeping of fish has a long history. Roman, Egyptian and Chinese societies reportedly kept fish for both food and ornamental reasons (Jarvis, 2000; Luck, 2008a). In Victorian Britain, the keeping of fish in bowls was particularly popular in certain social circles (Jarvis, 2000), leading to the opening of the first public aquaria, the fish house, at London Zoo in 1854 (Nightingale *et al.*, 2001). Soon after, a number of other aquaria opened in major cities, such as Dublin, Berlin and Brussels (Jarvis, 2000). Although interest in aquaria declined in the late 19th century (Jarvis, 2000), there has been a particular resurgence in the popularity of aquaria in the last 30 years. Nightingale *et al.* (2001) identifying now as the 'Age of Aquaria'. Part of this resurgence in interest can be explained by the role that aquaria have had in urban redevelopment schemes. This has helped expand the reach of aquaria with a number of cities situated away from coastal areas incorporating an aquarium in their urban regeneration schemes. Many of the world's major cities have an aquarium as part of their tourist offerings, including London, Sydney, Auckland, Singapore, New York and Cape Town. Aquaria range in size from small-scale institutions displaying marine species from local waters, such as those found in some small British seaside resorts (e.g. Ilfracombe and Tenby), to large flagship aquaria found in major cities, such as the Two Oceans Aquarium in Cape Town and the Georgia Aquarium in Atlanta. Marine parks, such as Sea World and Ocean Park in Hong Kong, are the largest marine-based attractions, combining aspects of aquaria with those of theme parks. As with their terrestrial counterparts, zoos, aquaria are immensely popular. Markwell (2008) considers that 'the lasting popularity of aquaria reflects our fascination with marine life' and that a public aquarium 'fascinates and intrigues because it provides windows into a sublime world that is mostly remote and inaccessible to the majority of visitors'.

Since public aquaria were first developed in the late 1800s, various elasmobranch species have been exhibited (Koob, 2004). Hamburg Aquarium in Germany was one of the first aquaria to put sharks on public display in 1864, followed by several other major European aquaria displaying a variety of small sharks (such as dogfish and catsharks) (Koob, 2004). The New York Aquarium was one of the first institutions to exhibit larger shark species, displaying smooth hammerhead, blue, nurse and sand tiger sharks with mixed success around 1896 (Koob, 2004). In the USA, expositions and fairs were popular attractions in the 1800s and frequently contained an aquarium as part of the display, which often exhibited sharks and rays. In the 1860s, P.T. Barnum is known to have displayed sharks along with Beluga whales (Luck, 2008a) and the 1893 World Columbian Exposition in Chicago displayed 24 dogfish, 2 stingrays and 4 sand tiger sharks (Koob, 2004).

Sharks and rays have remained popular attractions in modern aquaria. The 2008 AES International Captive Elasmobranch Census identified that 9578 individual sharks and rays were displayed in 129 aquaria around the world (AES, 2008). Small species, such as catsharks and bamboo sharks, are the most frequently displayed sharks alongside larger coastal species, such as the sand tiger and nurse sharks (Dobson, 2008). However, significant improvements in shark husbandry techniques have also allowed larger pelagic species, such as the whale shark, tiger shark and, for short periods, the great white shark, to be kept in captivity (Dobson, 2008). These larger species often act as celebrity animals; the Monterey Bay Aquarium has experienced a significant rise in visitor numbers each time it has put a great white shark on temporary display (Grayson, 2006), and over 3 million visitors have seen the whale sharks on display at the Georgia Aquarium in Atlanta, USA (Gross, 2006).

Sharks as Aquaria Icons

The representation and interpretation of animals by human beings has changed over time in tune with changing cultural values (Bishop, 2004). Humans utilise animal representations as 'icons of otherness' (Bishop, 2004: 107) and they can be used to both attract and repulse humans. Animals (such as pandas and tigers and various cetaceans) have frequently been used by conservation organisations as flagship species in order to raise awareness about the need to conserve the natural environment or to help raise money for conservation efforts (Walpole & Leader-Williams, 2002). Animals are also used by the tourism industry as icons to help both promote and allow prospective tourists to connect with destinations (Tremblay, 2002; Smith *et al.*, 2006a, 2006b).

Certain key attributes go towards the making of an animal icon. Of central importance is that the animal possesses positive charismatic traits, such as being approachable or being perceived as cute (Tremblay, 2002). Tremblay (2002) also considers that the ability to anthropomorphise the animal's actions is an important factor in creating an icon, as people are more likely to find an animal appealing if it demonstrates human-like characteristics (such as positive social habits, playfulness and curiosity). Conversely, animals considered to have 'negative charisma' are those that display unappealing characteristics, such as scavenging behaviour, or those that can be perceived as dangerous and are therefore not appealing to tourists. Smith *et al.* (2006a) identify species such as the red back spider and box jellyfish are characteristic of Australia, but owing to the negative characteristics associated with them, they cannot be considered as wildlife icons that can be used to help promote the country. However, there are several animals, perceived as dangerous, that can inspire interest in tourists and act as wildlife icons. In relation to the saltwater crocodile, Tremblay comments:

> the saltwater crocodile is interesting at many levels as it is primarily associated with traditional and contemporary perception of mythical fears and other sensationalist aspects that make the species sometimes attractive and other times repulsive to humans. (Tremblay, 2002: 179)

As with the saltwater crocodile, the shark is another species that people can find repulsive, yet intriguing. As with Tremblay's description of the saltwater crocodile, for many this constructed image of the shark now embodies all that is dangerous about the ocean, while, paradoxically, it can also be seen as attractive due to its perceived wild, dangerous and untamed nature (Dobson, 2008).

Many of the observed aquaria utilised shark imagery to help promote the attraction, some of which can be read as utilising the 'shark as monster' construction described above. The National Aquaria of New Zealand utilises a ferocious-looking shark as its emblem (Figure 7.2), while in September 2007 the queuing area at Kelly Tarlton's Aquarium in Auckland, New Zealand, displayed nine large posters featuring sharks, which ranged from pictures of graceful Hammerhead shoals and one of a large basking shark, to more stereotypical pictures of a great white shark leaping out of the water, jaws wide open, and a close-up picture of a shark's teeth. Shark feeds and shark dives are often heavily promoted by

Figure 7.2 A rather ferocious-looking shark has been adopted as the emblem of the National Marine Aquarium in Napier, New Zealand. (Photo: John Dobson)

some aquaria and can utilise the 'shark as monster' construction. The Sydney Aquarium advertises its Glass Bottom Boat and Shark Feed trip with the line 'it's an adrenaline-pumping moment when you see that iconic fin break the water's surface, but you can relax in perfect safety'. Similarly, Sea World in Australia describes its Shark Encounter, which allows people to feed sharks, as 'the ultimate Shark Encounter and an exhilarating shark feeding session with the world's most feared predators. You'll come face to face with large sharks including potentially dangerous species such as the magnificent Dusky Whaler shark'. A sign outside Sea World's Shark Encounter in Florida in 2005 described the exhibit as the 'World's largest collection of dangerous sea creatures'.

These images utilise the negative stereotype that western societies have constructed around sharks and can be one of the first challenges that aquaria face when using sharks as attractions. Aquaria have followed zoos in arguing that they have made the transition from centres of entertainment to acting as centres of conservation that attract visitors. However, aquaria are commercial organisations that need to generate interest in their product, thus negative shark imagery is used as a 'hook' to get people interested in visiting the aquaria. One aquarium representative stated in reference to using sharks as promotional tools:

> There is a delicate balance with sharks. We have to accept bringing people in through the door by saying "Wow these things are deadly killers" otherwise it is difficult to get people interested. Once they are here we try to break down those negative connotations.

This need to 'hook' people and get them interested in visiting an aquarium links to Pine and Gilmore's (1999) concept of the experience economy. They argue that consumers are becoming much more discernable in their spending and are looking for experiences that engage them in a personal way and for experiences that linger in the memory. This need to attract visitors and engage and provide them with memorable experiences that will possibly make them want to return can then place further pressure on generating a memorable experience that also educates people about shark conservation. The next part of the chapter will explore how sharks and rays are utilised in aquaria as central aspects of the visitors' experience.

Bringing the Visitor and Shark Together

In many aquaria, larger sharks and rays form part of the central exhibit where a range of species are displayed in large tanks. These large tanks are often the focal point of the visit and have the greatest visitor dwell time (personal communication, Two Oceans Aquarium). Many aquaria have followed the lead of Kelly Tarlton's Aquarium in Auckland, New Zealand, which was the first aquarium in the world to offer its visitors the opportunity to walk through an underwater acrylic tunnel. Tunnels are now fairly commonplace in many aquaria and provide visitors with a multi-dimensional view of the various species on show. Shark exhibits are often themed by geographical location (e.g. the Mediterranean tank at the National Marine Aquarium in Plymouth, UK), where sharks are presented with a range of other species from a similar region. Specific shark/predator themes are also used, for example Sea World, Florida, themed its exhibit as the Shark Encounter; the I and J Predator Exhibit is the focal point for displaying sharks at the Two Ocean's Aquarium in Cape Town; and Kelly Tarlton's Aquarium in New Zealand has a dedicated shark tank. Rays and small sharks (such as dogfish and bamboo sharks) are often displayed in pools that are frequently given a rock pool theme, with some aquaria actively encouraging visitors to touch the rays. At some aquaria, encounter opportunities have moved beyond the acrylic tunnel or viewing window into exhibit tanks, with visitors being allowed to dive with sharks.

These focal points, which bring visitors and shark and rays together, provide significant opportunities to educate visitors about the species they are viewing. In response to the growth in concern of keeping animals in captivity, zoos and aquaria have repositioned themselves over the past 20 years as centres of conservation. The education of visitors has been a central activity in this repositioning, and the World Association of Zoos and Aquariums identifies environmental education as one of their key visions:

> Zoos and aquariums with their unique resource of live animals, their expertise, and their links to field conservation will be recognised as leaders and mentors in formal and informal education for conservation. The educational role of zoos and aquariums will be socially, environmentally and culturally relevant, and by influencing people's behaviour and values, education will be seen as an important conservation activity. (WAZA, 2005: 35)

Gendron (2004) believes that there has been a shift in the messages relating to sharks that aquaria have promoted over the last 30 years. During the 1970s, at the height of the *Jaws* phenomena, Gendron (2004: 522) suggests that aquaria promoted a 'fascination through fear', as exemplified in 1977 by Sea World San Diego's display of a frozen great white shark accompanied by interpretive material highlighting that the shark was caught in waters frequented by tourists. The following year, the same park opened its Shark Aquarium and, according to Gendron (2004: 522), the interpretation was limited to basic information about the species on display and 'displayed little else except a prehistoric shark (Carcharodon megladon) jaw. Background music was ominous and suggestive of dangers lurking beneath the waves'.

Gendron goes on to identify that in the 1980s, this message of fear began to change towards one of sharks as being *misunderstood*. During this period, aquaria began to illustrate how unlikely it is to be killed by sharks and that they were the threatened species in need of protection. This message then moved towards what Gendron (2004: 524) describes as the *new message*, which promotes the shark as an important part of the marine ecosystem and its role as an indicator of a healthy oceanic environment.

Observations at the aquaria established that a range of interpretive methods, including interpretive panels, models, talks (often tied in with shark and ray feeds), guide books and audiovisual displays were used to project a range of messages to visitors about sharks and rays. By far the most common information provided to visitors was the name of the species (often accompanied by its scientific name), its geographic distribution and conservation status, as listed by the IUCN Red List. Interpretation relating facts about shark biology was also common; much of this related to basic facts such as how long sharks have existed in the world's oceans, how to distinguish between sharks and other fish species and the nature of the shark skeleton. The nature of the shark's senses was also a focal message with information being related concerning the ability of a shark to detect a drop of blood in water and that sharks have a sixth sense (they are able to detect weak electrical signals through their lateral line and ampullae of Lorenzini).

Some interpretation focused on projecting the 'sharks as misunder-stood' and 'the new message' categories. This was exemplified by a display at The National Marine Aquarium in Plymouth, UK, which was organised in conjunction with The Shark Trust. Six interpretive panels were used to project messages relating to sharks as being a misunder-stood species and the need to conserve them owing to their importance in the oceanic ecosystem. Each panel had an evocative title (iconic, threatened, majestic, endangered, dramatic and disappearing) with an associated image accompanied by some text. These panels projected some of the most powerful statements relating to the essential role that sharks have in regulating the oceanic ecosystem, the threats that they face from humans (the 'threatened' panel suggested that 75 million sharks are killed each year and the 'endangered' panel identified that three sharks are killed every second to supply the soup fin trade) and the limited threat that sharks pose to human beings.

One major problem facing the interpretation of sharks was the draw of the sharks themselves. At all the aquaria observed during this research, many people tended to focus on the sharks in the exhibits rather than engaging with the interpretation provided. On seeing the shark, visitors' own constructions of sharks were brought to the surface. Some visitors espoused positive comments concerning the sharks, adorning them with positive adjectives, such as 'awesome', 'graceful', 'beautiful', 'powerful' and 'fantastic'.

However, the viewing of sharks also allowed negative constructions to surface. This was particularly evident when adults were visiting with small children, some of whom emphasised the imagined 'shark as monster', which has only one desire – to eat children. One adult was observed saying to a young girl 'Shall we feed you to the sharks? They like little babies, little baby shark biscuits. Are you a little baby shark biscuit?' Other comments made between adults and children included 'Look at that big shark, it will gobble you up, they like tasty little boys' and 'Look Jack! Shaaaark! Look at his teeth, look at his teeth. Oh my gosh! Do you think it wants to eat you?' One display of a number of large sharks led one young male to comment to his friends 'Look shark infested waters, fancy a swim with Jaws and his mates?' He then proceeded to hum the Jaws theme tune. The killer myth was not only restricted to sharks. The unfortunate death of Steve Irwin helped generate interest in rays (personal communication, Kelly Tarlton's Aquarium) and resulted in them being identified as 'killers'. Two teenage boys made the following comments while viewing rays:

BOY 1: Wow! Look! Manta rays, they can kill you with an electric shock.
BOY 2: Yeah, that's what killed Steve Irwin.
BOY 1: They are really dangerous more so than a shark.

In the above example, the boys were mistaken about the species they were viewing, the species of ray that killed Steve Irwin and how dangerous rays are to human beings. After a couple of minutes looking at the ray, the boys moved on; neither explored the interpretive panel on the side of the tank. Other misunderstandings about the nature of sharks were also observed, included the myth of the size of a great white 'that shark is 3 metres a great white is 10 metres'. In reality, male great whites rarely grow above 4 m and females 5 m (Compagno *et al.*, 2005).

Interpretive talks on sharks and rays are common in aquaria and prove to be very popular and can take advantage of this popularity through the promotion of positive messages. Observed talks provided information similar to other interpretive methods described above (biological facts, sharks as misunderstood and sharks as oceanic regulators). Knudson *et al.* (2003) caution that most people who attend interpretive talks have weak listening skills and only retain approximately 10% of the relayed information. However, the strength of such talks appears to lie in their ability to enable staff to personally challenge any negative constructions or misunderstandings that visitors may have relating to sharks and rays.

Visitor (referring to a tank full of rays)**:** Are these the things that killed Steve Irwin?
Aquarium Staff Member: No mate, these are not the same species as the ray that was involved in his death. But look, the thing that you have got to remember is that Steve was very unlucky. These things are not really dangerous they are very placid otherwise I wouldn't be stood in the water with them. Steve was just unlucky and out of his area of natural expertise, the ray was probably scared and just defending itself.
Visitor: Oh really, I thought they were dangerous.
Aquarium Staff Member: Not really. Like anything you have to be wary of them and respect them, but essentially they are not looking to hurt you.

For one female visitor, a shark talk also helped in debunking the myth that all sharks must continue to swim in order to stay alive. Referring to a group of nurse sharks lying still at the bottom of a tank, she asked 'those shark look dead... I thought sharks can't stop swimming'. To which the staff member responded:

> No they are quite alright. They are nurse sharks and they are able to do that. People think all sharks need to keep swimming, but that is not true. Great whites yes, nurse sharks no; they are quite all right they are just resting. In the wild they feed at night and rest in the day.

Many aquaria now utilise shark and ray feeds as ways of attracting visitors. These feeds can be very popular, with many aquaria advertising feeding times on websites so that visitors can appropriately time their visits if they so wish. This growth in the popularity of feeds, especially shark feeds, needs to be carefully managed as they can be a mechanism that has the possibility of reinforcing negative constructions. As stated previously, people are fascinated by the perceived danger that lies in sharks and this can be embodied in watching sharks feed, as arguably it is what people most associate with sharks. Feeds can be done either at the surface or by divers underwater. It appears to be imperative that shark feeds are accompanied by talks that actively tackle misconceptions and reinforce positive constructions of sharks. On seeing divers enter a tank to feed sharks, a visitor raised concerns that the sharks would attack the divers, 'won't the sharks get them?' to which a staff member replied, 'no it will be alright, it is safe otherwise we wouldn't allow it. The sharks on display are not really dangerous and our divers are well trained'.

Although Gendron (2004) identified that the messages that aquaria were promoting moved from 'fascination with fear' to more positive messages being relayed about sharks, there were aspects of some aquaria that continued to exploit the 'fascination through fear' aspect of sharks evidenced through quasification (the use of model animals; Beardsworth & Bryman, 2001) and merchandising.

A number of aquaria utilised model sharks within their displays, which were often mounted with open jaws, teeth showing. Great white sharks were popular models on display, possibly reflecting the most recognisable shark and acting as a substitute for the real shark, which is extremely difficult to keep in captivity. Some of these representations can be read as projecting a negative stereotypical image of the great white shark. Underwater World in Singapore utilised a holographic great white shark (Figure 7.3), which appeared to jump out at passing tourists, mouth open. An animatronic great white shark was suspended from a ceiling at the National Maritime Aquarium in Plymouth and was strategically positioned so that visitors would not see it until they rounded a corner, at which point the body would move and its jaws

Figure 7.3 Holographic representation of a great white shark on display at Underwater World, Singapore. (Photo: John Dobson)

would open and close. This resulted in one woman picking up a little girl saying 'oh my word look at that, quick before he eats us' and then running down the corridor.

The paradoxical nature of using sharks to attract visitors while also educating them is demonstrated in London Sea Life Centre's Shark Walk, which opened in 2009. This display provides visitors with the opportunity to walk above the main display tank and look down on the sharks. Positive interpretive messages relay biological facts and information on threats to sharks, such as '300 million sharks are killed every year with some populations down by 90%'. This positive aspect of the display is contrasted against the creation of a tense atmosphere. The entrance to the display is advertised as 'take the shark walk if you're brave enough!' and the dim lighting and background music matched Gendron's (2004: 522) description of the atmosphere at Sea World San Diego's shark exhibit in 1977 as 'ominous and suggestive of dangers lurking beneath the waves'.

The final part of the visitor experience at many aquaria is the souvenir shop. Beardsworth and Bryman (2001) identify that merchandising has become a vital revenue stream for zoos and aquaria through the Disneyisation process. Merchandising also allows institutions to project their message beyond the immediate experience through branded merchandise. Shark-based merchandise again helps illustrate the paradoxical situation of both promoting sharks in a positive light while also trading on the 'fascination with fear' and 'shark as monster' messages. Books with titles such as *I Love Sharks* and *Discover Sharks* are frequently

Figure 7.4 Shark Attack photo booth at Sea World, Florida. (Photo: John Dobson)

set alongside titles such as *Shark Attacks* and *Scary Creatures: Sharks*. Iconic animals can also be found recreated as toys in aquaria gift shops, with charismatic animals, such as cetaceans and clown fish, particularly prevalent. Shark toys were also common, however, these tended to represent the stereotypical negative image of the shark, mouth open, teeth showing, ready to bite (these toys were often positioned next to representations of the friendly, smiling dolphin). A particularly memorable souvenir came in the form of a stress ball in the shape of a shark that, when squeezed, disgorged a balloon of red liquid from its mouth with severed human limbs floating inside. In 2005, Sea World in Florida offered their visitors the chance to purchase a shark attack photograph from a stall directly outside the exit of their shark encounter exhibit. For a few dollars, you could pose inside the mouth or on top of a model of a great white shark and pretend to be eaten alive (Figure 7.4). In relation to some of the negative representations of sharks within merchandise, one respondent commented 'unfortunately it sells'.

Conclusion

Aquaria provide the public with the opportunity to connect with the oceanic environment and a guaranteed viewing of selected marine animals. Sharks have been displayed in public aquaria for over 100 years and remain important exhibits today. The attractiveness of sharks can be partly explained by the negative characteristics that have been attributed to them by western society, with sharks frequently being constructed as monsters and man-eaters by the media. The importance of sharks as attractions can be seen by the use of shark imagery in promotional material by many aquaria. Some of this promotional material for some aquaria can be read as selling the stereotypical western construct of the shark and is contradictory to the stated aims of many aquaria in helping conserve sharks and breaking down the many misconceptions associated with them. This paradox is further developed in the construction of the shark exhibit, where positive conservation messages about sharks can be mixed with models, shark jaws, merchandise and experiences (such as the Shark Walk in London) that again help re-enforce negative views of sharks. The rise of the experience economy and post-tourist can place pressure on aquaria to ensure that visitors have an enjoyable and memorable experience in order to ensure commercial viability. Those tasked with exhibiting sharks therefore walk a difficult path between providing thrills through perpetuating the negative western construct and selling sharks as the threatened species most in danger from human activities.

Chapter 8
Singapore Zoo and Night Safari

JOAN C. HENDERSON

Introduction

Singapore Zoo and Night Safari are interesting examples of zoological gardens, and their study affords insights into the ways in which such centres have evolved in recent decades, the manner in which they function as visitor attractions, other roles performed and operational and management challenges. The cases also reveal certain characteristics of Singapore in general and as a tourist destination, including its development and marketing strategies. These represent the key themes of the chapter, which is organised into sections considering the past, present and future, with a separate discussion about animal welfare issues. The focus is on Singapore Zoo and Night Safari, but reference is made to Jurong Bird Park, which has been under the same management since a restructuring exercise in 2000.

Historical Background

Singapore is a former British colony and attained self-government in 1959. It later joined the Federation of Malaysia, but was expelled in 1965 after political differences, and became an independent republic. There were initial fears about Singapore's future and doubts about its survival due to its small size (approximately 683 km^2) and the absence of natural resources. However, the government of the People's Action Party (PAP) under Lee Kwan Yew adopted a policy of radical economic restructuring and comprehensive physical planning. This drive towards development was to transform the island into a modern, industrialised, urbanised and prosperous city state. The PAP administration has retained power and is defined by its pursuit of order and control, which extends to economic, physical and social arenas (Henderson, 2005). Such an agenda has directed decisions about land use with priority given to maximising the commercial potential of scarce land. Space was allocated for a zoo and separate bird park to provide leisure opportunities for residents, and also to enlarge the attractions inventory and boost the country's fledgling tourism industry.

Singapore Zoo dates from the 1960s when the Public Utilities Board (PUB), responsible for the reservoirs and surrounding rainforest in the centre of the island, proposed that some of this Central Catchment Area be used for recreation. A committee was set up under the PUB chairman to explore the possibilities of a zoo and a report was submitted to the government in 1969. The positive recommendation was supported and approximately 88 ha were dedicated to the project, although the zoo was only to occupy 28 ha and the remainder was reserved for subsequent developments. An initial sum of S$9 million was invested from public funds and consultants and personnel were recruited in 1970. Construction work began in 1971 and the Singapore Zoological Gardens opened in 1973 with 270 animals from over 72 species and a staff of 130 (Hooi & Wan, 1999; Sharp, 1994).

The zoo is modelled on the open zoo concept (Harrison, 1992), pioneered by Hagenbeck in Germany in the early 20th century, who rejected the conventional reliance on cages and indoor displays (Rothfels, 2002). The emphasis is on creating environments akin to natural habitats with appropriately landscaped spaces for the animals to roam relatively freely. Obtrusive barriers are kept to a minimum with the installation of wet and dry moats to divide visitors and exhibits. Moats are sunken or obscured by greenery so that they are not obviously apparent, resulting in a sense of nearness to the animals among observers. Dangerous beasts capable of surmounting these obstacles are put in enclosures with glass screens.

In the 1980s, the zoo started to organise night tours, which proved very popular, giving rise to the idea of a night zoo that would be the first of its kind in the world. The feasibility of the venture was favoured by Singapore's balmy tropical nights and the fact that being close to the equator, the sun sets regularly at around 7.30 pm throughout the year. The Night Safari opened in 1994 after four years of planning and three years of construction on 40 ha of secondary forest adjacent to the zoo. The initial cost was S$63 million and the intention was to give 'guests the unique experience of exploring wildlife in a tropical jungle at night' (Night Safari, 2009). Designers employed sophisticated lighting techniques to illuminate, but seemingly not disturb, the animals.

Developments since Opening

The two sites have developed since their inception in terms of what they offer visitors and how they are managed. With regard to the zoo, by the 1990s, there seemed to be an awareness that its approach to presenting animals was no longer that unusual and could be found in other zoological gardens around the world. This realisation prompted efforts at 'modernising the zoo, reinventing it as a unique tourist attraction and maintaining its place at the cutting edge of zoo design'. One example was a 'master re-development plan' with the tag line 'Journeys to Wild Places', in which the in-house creative design team worked with local and foreign consultants on several projects (Design for Life, 2009).

Product development is illustrated by the Fragile Forest, opened in 1998 at a cost of S$4.5 million and seeking to replicate a walk in a tropical rainforest, which was 're-themed' seven years later (WRS, 2006). A second themed attraction, the Hamadryas Baboons: The Great Rift Valley of Ethiopia, was launched in 2001 and simulates the arid semi-desert savannah woodlands that are home to these primates (*The Straits Times*, 2001). Recently, there has been fairly aggressive expansion with new animal arrivals and fresh and rejuvenated exhibits (WRS, 2006, 2007, 2008). The S$10 million Rainforest KidzWorld was finished in 2008 and purports to 'redefine experiential fun learning amidst a natural setting' (WRS, 2008: 3). Aspects of the physical infrastructure, such as park entrances, have also undergone improvements, as have food and beverage facilities, the latter in a bid to create 'more opportunities for revenue and profit growth' (WRS, 2006: 28).

Dedicated nocturnal zoos remain rare, although some zoos do occasionally have special night or evening events and the concept has been adopted elsewhere in Asia. Chiang Mai Night Safari in the north of Thailand commenced operations in 2006, professing to be twice the size of that in Singapore (Chiang Mai Night Safari, 2009), and there is a night zoo in the Chinese state of Guangzhou. Cairns in Australia advertises Cairns Night Zoo, but the exhibits appear limited and the other forms of entertainment at the venue are highlighted (Cairns Night Zoo, 2009). Nevertheless, over the years, the Night Safari too has added new features and enhanced those in existence in order to retain a competitive edge (WRS, 2006, 2007, 2008).

Wildlife Reserves Singapore (WRS) was set up in 2000 to overhaul and oversee the operation of the zoo, Night Safari and Jurong Bird Park collectively. Jurong Bird Park has its origins in the late 1960s and is located on 20.2 ha in an industrial zone, representing a more natural space for the benefit of locals and tourists. It has an open design, featuring free flying aviaries and now has over 9000 birds from 600 species (Jurong Bird Park, 2009).

Temasek Holdings, a government-linked investment body, owns 88% of WRS and 12% is held by the Singapore Tourism Board (STB), the National Tourism Organisation (*The Straits Times*, 2008). Its stated objective is to be a 'world class leisure attraction, providing excellent exhibits of animals and birds presented in their natural environment, for the purposes of conservation, education and recreation' (Singapore Zoo, 2009a). The Chief Executive of the zoo had been associated with it for 30 years and initially headed WRS, but left in 2002. His replacement resigned after one year and the former Executive Director of the zoo and Night Safari with a background in marketing took charge. There was also a new Executive Chairman of the Board of Directors, who initiated a plan to 'strengthen the national iconic status of the three parks' (WRS, 2008: 15). Reorganisation and what was described in Singapore's leading newspaper as a 'management revolution' then occurred. Change was reflected in new offices and redesigned uniforms (*The Straits Times*, 2008), as well as selective revamping, instances of which have already been cited.

WRS currently has about 100 office employees and 450 field workers and endeavours to cultivate a 'culture of learning among the staff and to equip them with the skills to excel in their job' (WRS, 2008: 48). Training and development schemes are undertaken and there has been cooperation with official training agencies to introduce accredited workforce skills qualifications (WRS, 2007).

Current Facilities

The two sites support a range of attractions, amenities and activities. The zoo has over 2500 specimens from 315 species, 16% of which are threatened. Visitors can walk through the grounds or take the tram service and there are elephant rides as well as pony and horse and carriage rides in the children's play area. At the Night Safari, there are about 1000 animals from over 100 species, almost one third of which are under threat. Many of these are nocturnal and on view in 'naturalistic habitats' organised into eight zones (Himalayan Foothills, Nepalese River Valley, Indian Subcontinent, Equatorial Africa, Indo-Malayan Region, Asian Riverine Forest, South American Pampas and Burmese Hillside), which can be explored on three walking trails and by open tram (Night Safari, 2009).

Assorted specialised tours are available for an extra fee; namely, Fragile Forest Behind the Scenes, Reptile Garden Behind the Scenes, Great Rift Valley of Ethiopia Feeding and Wild Discover at the Zoo and Safari Adventure at the Night Safari. There are three 'showtimes' at the zoo (Rainforest Fights Back, Splash Safari and Elephants at Work and Play) and the Night Safari's 'Creatures of the Night' is staged three times every evening.

The Night Safari has a 600-seater Ulu Ulu Safari restaurant, where 'Borneo Tribal Performances' take place twice a night, and the more informal Bongo Burgers, accessible to those without park tickets. The zoo has self-service and fast food restaurants, an al fresco dining area and a pizzeria. The Jungle Breakfast promises the chance to share breakfast with orangutans and selected other animals, while Lunch with Lions allows participants to dine 'alongside the king of beasts'. There are four speciality shops at the Night Safari, trading in wildlife-themed stationery items, handicrafts, glow in the dark objects and animal-themed jewellery.

The zoo has a retail space selling miscellaneous souvenirs and a convenience store. Both have ice cream outlets and mobile sales carts are utilised during weekends and peak days.

Individuals and companies can hire out venues at the zoo and Night Safari, but the choice is wider in the former where there are 25 options. These are variously labelled and include 'cocktail' (Elephants of Asia, Tiger Trek, Australian Outback and Treetops Trail), 'outdoor' (Pavilion-by-the-Lake, Garden Pavilion, Reservoir Picnic Site and Palm Park) and 'indoor' venues (Forest Lodge). Help is available for arranging birthday and wedding parties and other functions. Dinner Safari packages, for example, for business customers, combine an 'elephant greeting with fruit feeding' at the zoo with a 'safari-themed dinner' and tram ride at the Night Safari.

The zoo closes at 6 pm and the Night Safari is open from 7.30 pm until midnight and tourists are encouraged to move from one to the other, passing the interim period in the latter's restaurants, which start serving at 6 pm. Admission charges are S$18 for the zoo and S$22 for the Night Safari, with a 50% reduction for children, and advance online booking is possible. Combined tickets grant entry into all three WRS parks (S$45) or any two (S$32). In addition, there are four types of membership schemes for families or individuals (Friends of the Zoo, Feather Friends, Wildlife Unlimited and Wildlife Unlimited Plus) covering 1–2 years. There is also a Corporate Friends programme whereby companies contribute S$5000 (gold) or S$3200 (silver) annually and animals can be sponsored or adopted by organisations or members of the public.

The Zoo and Night Safari as Visitor Attractions

As discussed earlier, Singapore is a small country that has undergone rapid industrialisation and urbanisation. It is densely populated and land is in short supply. Physical characteristics impose constraints on tourism, but a policy of investment in new attractions and aggressive marketing by the STB has assisted in the achievement of some success as an international destination (Tan *et al.*, 2000; Teo & Chang, 2000). Visitors declined slightly in 2008 to just over 10 million after a record high in 2007, attributed to the economic climate, but further expansion is predicted in the long term (Singapore Zoo, 2009b).

Development and promotion within the context of leisure markets has shifted over the years and now focuses on large scale and modern purpose-built attractions and events. The city state is also sold as a centre for shopping and several new malls purporting to be 'iconic' have been constructed. Two integrated resorts incorporating casinos are due to be completed by 2010, typifying the new style of product and positioning; as does the Singapore Formula One Grand Prix, which was inaugurated in

2008. Nevertheless, natural and cultural heritage have retained a place in formal strategies and the zoo and Night Safari are prominent in official advertising, which stresses the numerous awards, national and international, they have received.

Considerable attention is also given to marketing by WRS, which produces a variety of materials, logos having recently been refreshed, and strategic campaigns are aimed at locals and tourists. Overseas marketing is concentrated in North Asia and Malaysia and sales missions are regularly conducted to South Korea, China and Japan. Meetings, incentives, conferences and exhibitions business contribute significantly to revenue and these buyers are also targeted.

There are programmes of special events, some linked to the season, and Halloween was celebrated in 2007 at the Night Safari by 'Halloween Horrors'. Visitors reportedly enjoyed

> horrifying fun along the Haunted Rainforest Trail and on board the Halloween tram and Halloween Cocktail Express. To enhance the experience, a Doom Buggy zipped along the tram route while ghosts and ghoulies were planted at every corner of Night Safari to scare visitors on foot. (WRS, 2008: 42)

As well as devising their own events, the parks participate in wider tourism initiatives, such as the annual Singapore Food Festival, when Night Safari trams are converted into dining cars for the Gourmet Safari Express, and traditional Ethiopian coffee ceremonies are held next to the zoo's Hamadryas exhibit (*The Straits Times*, 2002). The parks are also often chosen by World Gourmet Summit organisers looking for novel locations.

The Night Safari is on the itinerary of many tourists from overseas who constitute over 80% of visitors, whereas they represent about 25% of the zoo's ticket sales (WRS, 2007). The zoo is thus a popular leisure attraction for locals and especially families, although domestic tourism is constrained in Singapore because of its size and ease of access to neighbouring countries with a wider array of tourism resources. Some residents have, however, complained about the entrance charges to both the zoo and Night Safari and, according to one analyst, the STB is 'pushing' to make admission prices 'lower for regional travellers and local families' (Euromonitor, 2009).

Nevertheless, there have been increases in attendance over the past few years and 3.6 million visited the three WRS parks in 2007–2008 (WRS, 2009a). The zoo is the most frequented and had 1,632,800 visitors in 2008, up from 1,062,000 in 2003; respective statistics for the Night Safari are 1,423,100 in 2008, up from 552,000 in 2003. Volumes are forecast to grow further in the five years up until 2013 (Euromonitor, 2009).

Table 8.1 WRS revenue and expenses 2007–2008

Sources of revenue	Contribution (%)
Admission	41
Food and beverage	26
Trams/panorail	12
Retail	9
FOB/FOZ/WU membership schemes	4
Sales from photography and animal rides	2
Adoption and donations	2
Others	4
Expenses	39
Staff costs	
Net depreciation and property and plant and equipment write-off	16
Cost of sales	13
Maintenance expenses	10
Marketing A&P	7
General and administration	5
Utilities	5
Animals and bird fees and vet expenses	3
Professional and consultancy	2

Profits started to be earned by WRS in 2004 and rose steadily thereafter alongside revenues. A total of S$87.8 million was generated in 2007–2008, the last year for which figures are published, and details can be found in Table 8.1 together with information about expenses, which totalled S$79 million (WRS, 2009a). Government grants, corporate sponsorship and public donations are still, however, accepted (*The Straits Times*, 2008).

Future Prospects

Writing in the WRS 2007–2008 Yearbook, the Chief Executive Officer said:

great things lie ahead. With our total integration between Jurong Bird Park, Singapore Zoo and Night Safari, Wildlife Reserves Singapore has truly grown into an all-rounded leisure attraction with a mission to break new ground in animal conservation and education. The shared expertise of our long-serving staff and economies of scale will no doubt result in stronger branding for the organisation, creative heights in marketing and our continued leadership among Singapore's top attractions. (WRS, 2008a: 3)

The latest announcement heralded an S$140 million 'river safari theme park' to be ready by 2011 and situated on part of the Central Catchment Area originally designated for recreation. Some of the zoo and Night Safari aquatic animals will be transferred there and key selling points will be new species, boat rides and exhibits of freshwater habitats. It is expected to draw at least 750,000 extra visitors (*The Straits Times*, 2009) and sailing on the stretch of reservoir abutting the zoo has already been introduced.

Other Functions: Education and Conservation

In addition to acting as visitor attractions that afford amusement and entertainment, zoos commonly profess to assume and exercise other responsibilities pertaining to conserving wildlife and promoting learning. The zoo and Night Safari have been active in education and conservation, encompassing research, and this has continued under the WRS umbrella, as suggested by the Chief Executive Officer's statement previously quoted. An education outreach programme is directed at school children and students, educators and the general public. An Education Department arranges interactive outdoor sessions, teachers' workshops, talks, conducted tours and student volunteer programmes. These may have a commercial dimension and a 'Personal Effectiveness through Animal Wisdom' youth camp was held recently, which it was hoped would 'serve as an effective platform to engage youths, a market segment that has always been a challenge to penetrate' (WRS, 2007: 18). School visits are also hosted and 171,500 were organised in 2007–2008, a year that also saw a conference where Asian zoo educators met.

In terms of research, WRS engages in animal exchange and cooperative work with local universities and overseas zoos. A new S$3.6 million Wildlife Healthcare Research Centre, enabling visitors to view animals being operated on through a video link, enhances the zoo's capabilities in the field and adds to what the visitor can experience. It is also used to train veterinarians and veterinary nurses attached to non-governmental organisations (WRS, 2006). Investment is ongoing in selected regional conservation programmes and regular campaigns communicate conservation messages, striving to heighten awareness of the threat of extinction facing some species and issues related to climate change. There have also been collaborative efforts with bodies such as the World Wildlife Fund for Nature in global initiatives.

Questions of Animal Welfare

There is a long-standing debate about the ethics of putting animals on display and the consequences for their physical and psychological well being. A topic of particular contention is the animals being required to perform in a demeaning manner, contradictory to natural behaviour and potentially dangerous. Many zoos have stopped performances deemed to be unacceptable and place great stress on their education, conservation and research roles. These are depicted as contributing positively to animal welfare and the environment in general, a stance aligned with mounting popular interest in and understanding of environmental matters. Good practice in animal husbandry and display techniques by zoological gardens is now perhaps expected by visitors and thus makes sense in terms of satisfied customers, as well as being ethically sound. However, the actual level of commitment among zoos to conservation has been questioned by critics (Fravel, 2003; Rothfels, 2002) and meeting these obligations and balancing them with any commercial imperatives may engender dilemmas that are not easily resolved.

WRS has a policy and guidelines on animal welfare and ethics founded on those of the World Association of Zoos and Aquariums, of which it and the three subsidiaries are all members. The six underlying principles are summarised below (WRS, 2009a).

(1) Conservation and survival of species.
(2) Improvement in standards of animal welfare based on latest best practice and available information and guidelines from other organisations.
(3) Promotion of the interests of wildlife conservation, biodiversity and animal welfare.
(4) Encouragement of research and dissemination of results.
(5) Promotion of public education and awareness.
(6) Cooperation with the wider conservation community to assist in maintaining global diversity.

The areas that the guidelines apply to are animal welfare, the use of animals in presentations, exhibit standards, acquisition of animals, transfer of animals, contraception, euthanasia, mutilation, research using zoo-based animals, release-to-the-wild programmes, escapes to the wild, deaths of animals while in care and external wild animal welfare issues. Separate statements outline policies on animal acquisition and animal relocation in greater detail and a third deals with 'animal shows, contact and training'. WRS asserts that 'animal shows/contact will mainly focus on fostering, educating and conveying conservation awareness of endangered species of flora and fauna', while having an 'entertainment component', which is necessary to catch the public's notice. An Animal Welfare and Ethics Committee exists and is called on to review situations and ensure that animal welfare and dignity are not damaged (Singapore Zoo, 2009a).

Nevertheless, the zoo has confronted criticism from a local charity named ACRES (Animal Concerns Research and Education Society). The presence of the organisation is worthy of note as civil society in Singapore is agreed to be undeveloped, partly due to regulation of groupings suspected of having a political agenda (Koh & Ooi, 2000). ACRES mounted a campaign in 2005 to 'end the use of animals in animal shows at the Singapore Zoo and Night Safari', maintaining that 'circus-style tricks' had been observed there. An account on its website describes some success, referring to discussions with WRS, which led to modifications to the shows whereby any 'tricks' were removed and 'natural, species appropriate behaviours' were encouraged (ACRES, 2009).

The condition of the zoo's polar bears was another complaint of ACRES, which contended that a tropical climate was unsuitable for such creatures, despite the air-conditioned den and misting fans, and that their open-air enclosure was too small. The bears had already been the subject of media reporting beyond Singapore with stories of how they had 'started turning green'. The phenomenon was explained by algae, produced by the hot and humid climate, attaching itself to the bears' hair, and was treated with a hydrogen peroxide solution (BBC, 2004).

ACRES prepared a report, presented to the zoo in 2006, which argued that the two bears (a female and her male offspring) were demonstrating physical and behavioural signs of stress (ACRES, 2009). The zoo announced that it would make the male bear (Inuka) available for transfer to a zoo in a temperate climate on the death of the mother who was too old to be moved, a step in conformity with its aspirations to be a rainforest zoo and not a response to external pressures (Reuters, 2006). However, the WRS Animal Welfare and Ethics Committee recommended in early 2007 that Inuka remain in Singapore because he had been born there and was acclimatised. The age of the bears, 16 and 30, indicated that they were doing well and the proposed transfer of the younger, in combination with the loss of his mother, would be very distressing. Inuka would therefore 'continue to be the Singapore Zoo's ambassador for the conservation and educational thrusts regarding climate change through-out his whole life' (WRS, 2009b).

Conclusion

Singapore Zoo was a creation of the new republic and has evolved alongside the city state to establish itself as a well-known visitor attraction that is popular with tourists and residents. There has been substantial investment in innovation and upgrading of exhibits with a view to retaining its appeal in an age of increasing competition for leisure consumers' time and money. The Night Safari is indicative of a willingness to experiment with novel concepts and skill in their execution. Improvements have also been regularly made to the infra-structure and amenities, complementing the core animal displays in appreciation of the demands of customers and their increasing sophis-tication. Marketing is not neglected and campaigns, too, have demon-strated originality and creativity. In addition to organisation endeavours, the National Tourism Organisation advertises the sites as nature-related diversions of interest to visitors. Therefore, they have value in augment-ing and diversifying the destination's offerings, which are heavily dependent on urban features.

Product development and associated marketing by the zoo and Night Safari seem to have intensified in recent years, perhaps linked to management restructuring, and there is evidence of a greater focus on revenue and profit. A strong commercial orientation does not preclude zoological gardens from the satisfactory exercise of other functions arising from their role as centres of animal protection, conservation and learning. The two domains can be compatible, with scope for productive synergies, but there are also possibilities for tensions. The zoo and Night Safari have not been immune from accusations about animal exploitation and the need to strike a balance between education and entertainment applies as much to the interpretation and presentation of natural heritage as it does to the cultural arena.

Singapore is a place of constant change driven by the perceived imperative of sustaining economic development and retaining its financial rewards. Tourism is an essential tool to be utilised in pursuit of this goal and is given a high priority, marked by efforts to ensure a world-class attractions inventory. At the same time, there has been mounting recognition of the significance of quality of life issues beyond material possessions and this embraces the environment and opportu-nities for residents to come into contact with nature. In combination, these forces suggest that the zoo and Night Safari will continue to be formally regarded as important resources that serve economic and social purposes.

Nevertheless, operators confront the challenge of maintaining and enlarging the appeal of the parks, maximising revenues and profits, without compromising the stated commitment to animal welfare and the furthering of conservation causes. These tasks are made more formidable in an era when many residents and tourists may be somewhat tired of conventional attractions and in search of novelty and excitement, attributes not always associated with zoos. It will therefore be interesting to monitor the cases of the Singapore Zoo and Night Safari in the 21st century and their responses to dynamic market conditions that, together with the environmental movement, would seem to raise questions about whether zoological gardens of whatever sort and standard have a future.

Chapter 9

Heterogeneous Spaces of Tourism and Recreation at Mumbai Zoo, India

KEVIN HANNAM

Introduction

India is widely known to have a unique fauna, including mega-vertebrates such as tigers, elephants and rhinoceros. Many of these animals can be seen in the wild in numerous national parks around the country. Indeed, for many international tourists, this is the primary means by which they engage with India's natural world. However, for much of the Indian population, living in the expanding Indian metropolises, the primary means by which they engage with the Indian natural world is through the zoos that were set up by the British colonial administration in the 19th century. Thus, there are many zoos in the urban centres of India that serve as a key recreational experience for local inhabitants, but most are in a very poor state of repair and are frequently criticised by international visitors. Mumbai (Bombay) zoo is located inside the Veermata Jijabai Bhosale Udyan Botanical Gardens (formerly the Victoria Gardens) of Mumbai. Today, this is one of India's most problematic zoos because of its high domestic visitation rates (many of whom are prone to teasing the animals), high levels of urban pollution and uncoordinated administration and management (Walker, 2001). This chapter seeks to investigate this zoo as a heterogeneous space for both visitors and animals.

Tourism, Zoos and Heterogeneous Spaces

In his seminal paper on tourism and zoos, Mason (2000) argues that zoos are a form of living museums. He goes on to discuss that zoos are important from a tourism perspective in terms of amusement and education. The most important function of zoos is arguably their educational aspect in making animals available for the tourist gaze. In addition, they generate excitement in visitors who would otherwise never see such animals, particularly charismatic and rare mega-vertebrates, in real life except in films (Bostock, 1993; Shackley, 1996; Ryan & Saward, 2004). Although zoo visitors motivations may be varied and complex, it is generally recognised that zoos may provide important cognitive and affective educational experiences for visitors (Churchman, 1985; Hunter-Jones & Hayward, 1998). Turley (2001: 8), meanwhile, has emphasised the importance of zoos as social recreational experiences, particularly for children who 'both facilitate and, in their absence, inhibit zoo visiting'. Furthermore, she notes that previous research has argued that many zoo visitors are only mildly interested in the animals per se, with the actual visit having more importance as a family social event: 'the zoos' largely outdoor, park-like setting and consequently less rigid visitor flow, facilitate the social behaviour which is the predominant zoo activity' (Turley, 2001: 6).

Beardsworth and Bryman (2001) discuss the birth of the modern zoo in the late 18th and early 19th centuries in terms of a disciplined space for the animals themselves. They note that

> Within the artificial confines of the menagerie or zoo, almost total control is exercised by humans over the animal's movements and activities, with minimal opportunity for the animal to exercise its own preferences and priorities. (Beardsworth & Bryman, 2001: 5)

They argue that just like a prison or hospital, the zoo has inmates, however, these are animals rather than humans and they are subject to the processes of surveillance:

> In other words, the *powerless* are at all times subject to the gaze of the *powerful*, subject (irrespective of their own preferences) to constant scrutiny, monitoring and examination. For example, confined animals may be subjected to a "scientific gaze" or more specifically, a "zoological gaze". That is, they become objects of analysis in the discourses of such disciplines as ethology, parasitology, reproductive biology, animal nutrition and so on. More generally, they become the objects of a kind of "recreational gaze" on the part of the general public who form the principal audience for the zoo's presentations. (Beardsworth & Bryman, 2001: 5–6)

Bostock (1993: 109) notes that contemporary 'zoo architecture often seems to have been a rather misguided pursuit, aimed at pleasing human taste instead of serving the animals' own interests'. He goes on to further argue that the 'best' enclosures are 'naturalistic' ones that provide the 'illusion' that the animals seen are 'in the wild', but such 'furnishings' may be for the benefit of the human visitors as much as they are actually for the animals themselves (Bostock, 1993: 113). Furthermore, he concludes that there are 'obviously' grades of keeping animals in 'prison-like' captivity with the unintentional and intentional unpleasantness of such captivity being morally wrong (Bostock, 1993: 122).

Indeed, most contemporary 'traditional' zoos in the West remain in urban locations that restrict the mobility of animals and tend to portray animals out of context (Shackley, 1996). Due to this sense of the animals being out of context and because of competition from other urban tourist attractions, many zoos, particularly in the West, have found recent times difficult (Stevens, 1988; Linge, 1992). As Mason (2000) notes,

> If zoos are viewed as unacceptable visitor attractions by some people, then they may fail to provide appropriate educational messages, particularly in terms of conservation. The conditions in which animals are kept may even deter visitors and there is currently some evidence to support this. (Mason, 2000: 336)

However, Ryan and Saward (2004) point out that

> there is an argument that market forces may lead to the betterment of zoo design to the advantage of animal welfare and conservation programmes, and to the financial advantage of zoos by being more attractive to visitors. (Ryan & Saward, 2004: 249)

Catibog-Sinha (2008) argues that zoos in developing countries still operate under substandard conditions and many are managed mainly for amusement and entertainment. Mason (2000) cites the objections to zoos by the British zoologist, Gerald Durrell, as follows:

> I discovered to my dismay that a very high percentage of zoos were bad. ...they had no real motivation and were simply run as showcases... The animals were badly fed and badly caged for the most part, and the breeding results (if any) were poor. Very little scientific study was done... and the attempts to educate the zoo-going public were poor at best. (Quoted in Mason, 2000: 334)

Although Durrell was reflecting on his experiences with UK zoos, it remains to be seen whether such objections apply to zoos in the developing world. The aesthetics and purpose of zoo design in developing countries, of course, is fraught with difficulties because of funding.

From a more theoretical perspective, Whatmore (2002) draws on the work of Foucault, in order to unsettle the taken for granted status of animals as material objects in heterogeneous spaces. Furthermore, she develops the concept of hybridity in relation to human–animals relations:

> In place of the geometric habits that reiterate the world as a single grid-like surface open to the inscription of theoretical claims or universal designs, hybrid mappings are necessarily topological, emphasizing the multiplicity of space-times generated in/by the movements and rhythms of heterogeneous association. The spatial vernacular of such geographies is fluid, not flat, unsettling the

coordinates of distance and proximity; local and global; inside and outside. (Whatmore, 2002: 6)

Whatmore argues that

> efforts to refigure wilderness as a heterotopic space, on the "inside", are an important first step to challenging the binary geographies of "nature" and "society" and the associated purifications of human and animal lives. …the notion of wildlife … is a relational achievement spun between people and animals, plants and soils, documents and devices in heterogenous social networks which are performed in and through multiple places and fluid ecologies. (Whatmore, 2002: 14)

Furthermore, Edensor (1999) notes that heterogeneous tourism spaces can be conceptualised as rich and varied transitory spaces where various actors (human and non-human) produce a changing symphony or different rhythms. Following Edensor (1999) and Whatmore (2002), in this chapter I thus seek to analyse Mumbai's zoo as a heterogeneous space. Firstly, however, I note some of the contextual aspects of tourism, recreation and zoos in India.

Tourism, Recreation and Zoos in India

As a large and significant developing country, India has a wealth of cultural and natural resources for the development of tourism. Unlike many other developing countries, only recently has India's government made tourism development a priority. Nevertheless, India has always appealed to middle-class foreign tourists, particularly, it has been argued because of various enduring Orientalist representations (Bhattacharya, 1997). Just over half of India's foreign tourists come from Western Europe and North America and the vast majority are non-package 'backpacker' tourists who stay for at least a month (Hottola, 2005). India's tourism also has a marked seasonality, focused on October to March, and has largely failed to develop any European-style 'package' tourism industry except in places such as Goa and more recently in the state of Kerala (Saldanha, 2002; Sreekumar & Parayil, 2002). It has been acknowledged that contemporary tourism in India faces an image problem due, in part, to poor accommodation, transport and sanitary conditions, as well as tiresome bureaucracy and political uncertainty (Chaudhary, 1996).

In the early 1990s, India's tourism witnessed growth rates well above average world figures. Tourist growth rates then slowed and international arrivals have not kept pace with global rates of increase, despite the economic liberalisation that has taken place. This is because of the relatively low priority and lack of urgency afforded to tourism development by the Government of India (Raguraman, 1998). Domestic tourism is still on the rise, however, as the new Indian middle classes look to spend their disposable income on tourism and leisure (Bhardwaj, 1998; Rao & Suresh, 2001). It should be remembered, though, that over one third of the domestic tourists in India are, in fact, on religious pilgrimages of one kind or another (Bandyopadhyay *et al.*, 2008). The Indian government is, however, beginning to recognise the importance of diversifying its tourism products, and, in terms of this diversification, religious, heritage and nature-based tourism has been particularly highlighted (Joseph & Kavoori, 2001; Hannam, 2005). Zoos, however, have been rather under recognised as a potential tourism resource in India.

In her recent historical review of zoos in India, Walker (2001) has distinguished three phases of zoos in India. The first phase began with the Maharajas or Princes and continued into the colonial state. The second phase, post-Independence, was supported by the central and state governments of India, and Walker then argues that a third stage is just beginning in the 21st century with a review of zoos in India. Walker discusses how princely menageries kept for intellectual curiosity, scientific enquiry and hunting predate public zoos, but these were nevertheless often open to guests. Indeed, she cites Edwards, who argues that: 'zoologists of the early nineteenth century drew much inspiration from collections in India and elsewhere in Asia, rather than the other way round' (Walker, 2001: 252). Mullan and Marvin (1987) argue that although the formal, traditional zoo was later imposed on India during the British colonial period, they clearly drew on these earlier collections. Similarly, Grove (1996) also notes that many of the early colonial experiments with conservation also drew on indigenous practices in India and elsewhere in the colonial world. Walker (2001: 254) goes on to discuss how a certain Colonel Flower inspected India's zoos in 1913 and commented how 'an enormous number of animals are herded together in no particular order' and that it was a 'very, very sad sight to see the large number of crippled or aged animals which were kept there alive instead of being put out of their misery' in a case of 'misdirected kindness'. She further notes that many of the zoos in the major Indian cities of Calcutta (Kolkata), Madras (Chennai), Bombay (Mumbai), Trivandrum and elsewhere under colonialism were open to both Indian and European visitors and were particularly enjoyed by children, but the management of India's zoos during this period remained solely under the control of the British administration who were mainly interested in the loss of game for sport than in any real conservation effort. Initially, after independence in 1947, the Indian Board for Wildlife instituted a special 'Zoo wing' to review the welfare and scientific utility of India's zoos. In 1972, the

Indian Wildlife Protection Act made provisions for the management and development of new zoos in India. As Walker (2001) notes in this regard:

> many [of these zoos] were founded, no doubt, simply to keep up with the next city of state; zoos had become a token of prestige. . . . it is safe to say many of the zoos were set up for the wrong reasons. Time [has] proved this to be the case when they deteriorated, lacking the continued personal interest of the individual who set them up, and without a mechanism to ensure their proper upkeep. (Walker, 2001: 286)

By 1975, there was great concern about the quality of zoos in India. After reviewing the zoos, an expert committee recommended the setting up of a central coordinating body to monitor and administer the zoos of India. But it wasn't until the late 1980s that the Central Zoo Authority (CZA) was finally established and enshrined in the 1991 Zoo Act of the Indian parliament. The main functions of the CZA were to specify minimum standards for zoos in India, to periodically evaluate them and to coordinate training, research and educational programmes. However, it was also given the power to 'de-recognise' zoos after inspection. This is fraught with some difficulties though, not only because of the bureaucracy that this entails, but also because of the country's diverse religious and social customs, which largely prevent the taking of life even if it is to end suffering.

Thus, in the contemporary period, Walker (2001) notes that

> in India, a country with a history of extreme kindness to animals on the one hand and inordinate cruelty on the other, there were until recently well in excess of 300 collections of wild animals in captivity registered with the Central Zoo Authority. (Walker, 2001: 251)

Seventeen of the Indian zoos that were founded during the colonial period are still open, but after independence this proliferated to in excess of 300 without control until the Indian Zoo Act was passed in 1991. The CZA (2009) currently states that:

> Since its inception in 1992, the Authority has evaluated 347 zoos, out of which 164 have been recognized and 183 refused recognition. Out of 183 zoos refused recognition, 92 have been closed down and their animals relocated suitably. Cases of the remaining 91 derecognized zoos are currently under review. The Authority's role is more of a facilitator than a regulator. It, therefore, provides technical and financial assistance to such zoos which have the potential to attain the desired standard in animal management. Only such captive facilities which have neither the managerial skills nor the requisite resources are asked to close down.

Walker (2001) goes on to argue that many of the zoos in India are problematic in terms of overcrowding both of animals and people, and argues for the need for the zoos in India to be privatised so that they might be run better, with less bureaucracy and with greater investment. Moreover, she further argues that India's zoos have so far failed to develop a single scientific breeding programme and have also failed to live up to their educational and conservational potential. She concludes that: 'perhaps Indian zoos should just concentrate on educating their public to protect its remaining habitat' (Walker, 2001: 290). However, both Walker and the CZA do not engage with the role of the contemporary visitor to India's zoos, which this chapter seeks to investigate.

Mumbai (Bombay) Zoo as a Heterogeneous Tourism and Recreation Space

The city of Mumbai has a current population of nearly 14 million people. It is geographically constrained being an island city and 50% of its population lives on just 8% of the land. Hence, the city has very limited green or recreational spaces except for a large urban forest and small park areas of which Mumbai Zoo is one (Zerah, 2007). Nijman (2006) notes that:

> This is India's commercial capital and largest city. It is sometimes referred to as "the City of Gold," a place where many have gone from rags to riches. It is a place, in other words, with plenty of opportunity for upward mobility and presumably a dynamic class structure. But Mumbai is also known as a city of extremes, of very rich and desperately poor, of a relatively large and prosperous "middle class", and as the site of the largest concentrations of slums in Asia. (Nijman, 2006: 759)

Indeed, these slums and the influence of organised crime in Mumbai were recently publicised in the Oscar-winning film, *Slumdog Millionaire*.

Mumbai Zoo, now called the Veermata Jijabai Bhosale Udyan Zoo after a locally famous Marathi woman, was originally founded as a botanical garden in 1873 and then renamed as the Victoria Gardens in 1889 and made freely available to the public. Walker (2001: 270) rightly suggests that this zoo is 'one of India's most problematic zoos because of high visitation, city pollution, and problematic administrative organisa-tion'. She also notes that in 2001, the zoo was in the process of renovation; however, as yet, this has clearly failed to happen. The following account is based on my (western, middle class) ethnographic observations of the zoo as a heterogeneous tourism and recreational space in January 2009 and is divided into two parts – as a space for visitors and as a space for animals. Both, of course, are entwined in terms of making Mumbai Zoo a contested heterogeneous space.

Spaces for visitors

Mumbai Zoo is located in the southern part of the city in a highly urbanised residential area called Byculla. On arrival at the zoo, visitors are met by a small shack that is used as the ticket office, with differential pricing for local and foreign visitors. Once inside the zoo, tourists are met with the wide vistas of a botanical garden and a welcome breath of space after the heat and congestion of the surrounding city. My ethnographic diary noted that:

> Many middle class male and female domestic tourists are present in the zoo with their families along with a few international tourists. The former seem relaxed and carefree as they stroll through the zoo, gazing at the few animals that can be seen and taking photos of their families at frequent intervals. The latter seem to be rather depressed by the zoo environment and take photos of the plight of the animals. There is little in the way of interpretation for tourists. Elsewhere, we can see a little used children's play park with slides and metal climbing frames. In the gardens in which the zoo is set we can see some Indian courting couples, talking chastely while sitting on benches and the grassed areas.

Spaces for animals

Since 2005, the animal rights organisation, People for the Ethical Treatment of Animals (PETA), has been lobbying for the closure of Mumbai Zoo: 'This zoo needs to be closed as the staff is unable to take care of the animals. They want to bring in more animals to get more visitors and money but who will take care of the animals?' (DNA, 2009). According to a 2006 inspection report by the Plant and Animal Welfare Society (PAWS), there are some 250 animals and birds kept at Mumbai Zoo in rusty, broken and rat-infested cages. This report also noted that visitors commonly feed and tease the animals in the zoo and fail to adhere to the zoo regulations in this respect (PAWS, 2006). Furthermore, my ethnographic diary noted that:

> We can see an elephant chained up and seemingly bored and disinterested. We are faced by many empty old cages which seemed to have once been spaces that enclosed primates of some kind. We then come across a somewhat stagnant pond which may or may not be home to some wildlife. Some mall enclosures for birds are next on the pathway before we come across a hippopotamus attempting to keep cool in its small water space. Here there is a simple board –

sponsored by the Rotary Club of India-that gives some identification to this species as "the third largest living land animal". A snake house comes next and holds a variety of snakes in small glass tanks – one has had a live chicken placed inside for its lunch and visitors crowd around waiting to see the spectacle if the snake will eat it, but the snake seems uninterested. Outside the snake house, some Indian cheetal or spotted deer can be seen trying to find something to eat in their dry enclosure watched by three middle class India women.

Conclusion

This chapter has sought to investigate Mumbai Zoo as a heterogeneous space for both visitors and animals. As a space for visitors, following Turley (2001), we can note that Mumbai Zoo is primarily a social recreational space, rather than an educational or exciting one, where the animals are very much a secondary attraction to the actual space itself away from the congestion of the city. As a space for animals, following Bostock (1993), we can note that Mumbai Zoo is an unpleasant, unfortunate and misguided space of confinement. After returning from Mumbai at the end of January 2009, I found that, following the death of a hippopotamus, new plans had once again been put forward to renovate Mumbai Zoo by 2012, which would include a new interpretation centre and a zoo hospital. The plans note that the zoo would be closed in phases to allow this work to take place (*Times of India*, 2009). However, many such plans have been in place since 2001 and little has so far actually been achieved to improve this heterogeneous space for both animals and visitors.

Chapter 10
Zoos as Tourist Attractions: Theme Parks, Protected Areas or Museums?

WARWICK FROST

Introduction

In order to understand zoos and the zoo experience, there is value in making comparisons with other tourist attractions. Three types of attractions – theme parks, protected natural areas and museums – have sufficient in common with zoos to deserve examination. At times in their history, these institutions have crossed paths and almost merged, at other times the distinction has been quite marked. Understanding their distinctive evolution allows us to make better sense of the paradoxical history of zoos.

A note of caution. In considering history, we must be careful to avoid taking a teleological approach. Just because zoos are the way they are now at the beginning of the 21st century, is no reason to believe that they were always destined to evolve this way. The same may be said for the other related tourist attractions. Rather than looking for a seamless path to the present, we need to look for the turning points and the box canyons in their evolution. We cannot see zoos as unique and separate institutions; rather there is value in considering them in relation to other tourist attractions. To borrow from James (1963) – we don't know about zoos if all we know about are zoos.

The Age of Revolution

Histories of zoos always start with royal menageries. As far back as classical times, rulers all over the world kept impressive collections of animals (Baratay & Hardouin-Fugier, 2002; Hancocks, 2001). This regal domination of the animal world was simply one of a number of ways in which monarchs demonstrated their superiority over their subjects. Numerous examples of this are given in the zoos literature, however, I will utilise just one to demonstrate the principle. In 1955, Grace Kelly, the American film star, was attending the Cannes Film Festival. The editor of *Paris Match* had an idea for a story – how about if the glamorous Kelly met Prince Rainier of Monaco. The 'playboy' Rainier was now at an age where he had to settle down and he needed to marry and have children, for if he was childless the principality reverted to France. The 'date' was arranged, but what were the celebrities to do? The prince took charge, leading Kelly into the grounds of his palace and to his private zoo: 'As camera shutters clicked, Rainier put his hand through the bars of the tiger's cage and nonchalantly patted the beast. Grace was impressed with his courage and his affinity for animals' (Spada, 1988: 172). Not only was the princess-to-be impressed, but so were the millions of readers who saw the syndicated photos.

Some royals also kept zoos because they were interested in science and, occasionally, some of these zoos were opened to the public (Rothfels, 2002). However, as the Age of Enlightenment slipped into the Age of Revolution, royal menageries increasingly became the focus of criticism and opposition. Symbols of absolute power, they demonstrated a divine right to dominate nature; just as the people were subjects of the monarch, so were the animals (Baratay & Hardouin-Fugier, 2002). When the French Revolution overthrew the monarchy, it also closed the royal menagerie at Versailles. After debating their options (with some arguing to simply let the exotic animals free), the revolutionaries decided to shift them to Paris, installing them in the Jardin des Plantes, which became, arguably, the first truly public zoo (Rothfels, 2002).

Elsewhere in Europe, zoos became symbolic of the increasing dominance by the bourgeoisie. Rapidly growing urban conglomerations demonstrated their political independence and economic importance by establishing a range of public institutions. These included parks, museums, libraries, art galleries and zoos. As David Friedrich Weinland, Director of Frankfurt Zoo, observed in 1862:

> Neither princes, nor scholars, nor pedagogues, nor ministers of education founded the zoological gardens of Frankfurt, Dresden, Cologne, Hamburg, Amsterdam, Antwerp, Rotterdam and Brussels. Rather they were created by the majority of the citizens of these cities. (Quoted in Rothfels, 2002: 18)

In Britain, zoos were established by societies and joint stock companies, drawing on the new middle classes for their subscribers and members. Professionals and businessmen dominated their management committees. The working classes were welcome to visit, for zoos were imagined as a cultural institution to encourage them to improve themselves (Baratay & Hardouin-Fugier, 2002). Zoos in Britain's colonies followed a similar model. In the USA, zoo establishment did not become widespread until the late 19th century. Nonetheless, here again it was tied to urbanisation and economic prosperity, seemingly zoos being a marker of progress. One distinction of the USA was that zoos were owned and managed by town governments (Hancocks, 2001).

With the shift to constitutional monarchy, royalty re-invented themselves as the paternal or maternal figureheads for the new nation states and zoos became a stage for highlighting this new role. William IV emptied the royal menagerie at Windsor Castle and the Tower of London to stock the new London Zoo. His niece, Queen Victoria, was a regular visitor with her children, giving a royal imprint to the attraction (Hancocks, 2001). In the 20th century, royalty took on the role of patronage, providing much needed publicity for fund raising and linking zoos with conservation. Thus, Prince Rainier and Princess Grace, whose romance so publicly started in a zoo, were recruited by Gerald Durrell as patrons of the Wildlife Preservation Trust International (Botting, 1999).

The growth of zoos in the 19th century is well documented in the zoos literature, but two key aspects are often overlooked. The first is that zoos were a direct result of economic and political changes. They occurred in towns and reflected major changes in the nature and organisation of urban centres. In the 18th century, menageries were symbolic of royal power, by the end of the 19th century they symbolised the power of cities and their citizens. The second aspect to note is that zoos were not alone in this role. A whole suite of new institutions came to prominence in this period. Parks, gardens, galleries, museums and libraries all proliferated, were enthusiastically embraced as symbols of urban status and became attractions for the new mass markets. At the beginning of the 21st century, we can see these same processes being repeated in Asia, with the governments of modern cities looking to zoos and other cultural attractions as symbols of their modernity. Accordingly, we are seeing a geographical shift in the re-imagining of zoos, exemplified by the success of Singapore Zoo (see Henderson, this volume) and the debate over the future direction of Mumbai Zoo (see Hannam, this volume).

Zoos as Museums

It has been suggested that zoos are 'a form of museum'. Both zoos and museums 'are essentially educational in purpose, have a professional staff, are frequently non-profit making, and own and conserve tangible objects that are exhibited to the public'. The major difference being 'that a zoo's exhibits are living' (Mason, 2000: 333).

In the 19th century, zoos and museums were often closely related. William Hornaday was a young taxidermist who worked for the National Museum in Washington and later for the Smithsonian Institution. On an expedition to acquire bison for a planned diorama, he was appalled to find that they were rapidly heading for extinction. Hornaday embarked on a campaign for a refuge for the bison and other endangered North American animals. This became the National Zoo in Washington, with Hornaday as its first director (De Courcy, 1995; Hancocks, 2001). In

Europe, zoo promoters combined them with museums, libraries and even conference centres in order to attract the widest range of potential subscribers (Baratay & Hardouin-Fugier, 2002). When Hagenbeck brought his animal show from Germany to the 1893 World Fair in Chicago, it was billed as a 'Museum and Menagerie' (Rothfels, 2002: 135). Even today, the distinction is blurred for many institutions, e.g. the bioregional zoo in Tuscon (USA) is the Arizona-Sonora Desert Museum.

The simple distinction between museums and zoos is that one keeps and displays live animals and the other does the same for dead preserved ones. However, there may be an overlap. Some museums display small numbers of live animals, usually as part of a larger ecosystem display. Thus, Melbourne Museum features a rainforest area with living trees and a number of captive and roaming birds, reptiles, insects and amphibians. Some major museums have gone as far as simulated animals. The Museum of Natural History in London displays animatronic dinosaurs, including a *Tyrannosaurus rex* and raptors. In Sydney, the Australian Museum utilises a life-like puppet of an *Allosaurus*. The Queensland Museum in Brisbane has animatronic versions of *Thylacaleo* and *Megalania*, while the visitors' centre of the Naracoorte Caves National Park in South Australia also features prehistoric megafauna. The temptation must be to move from robot versions of the extinct to the endangered.

How displays are presented and interpreted may also be different. In the 19th century, museums and zoos were often compared by the way their collections were grouped and ordered. Zoos, like museums, followed what was seen as a logical scientific rationale. Related species, e.g. monkeys, were grouped together in what was then seen as the optimal educational presentation. When zoos embarked on naturalistic exhibits in the late 20th century, it was then argued that they were consciously moving away from the museum approach. However, as zoos changed, so did museums, with many curators exploring new and different modes of exhibition.

The biggest difference between zoos and museums may be in how we view their place in society. Mullan and Marvin (1987) argue that museums and art galleries are commonly seen as places of 'high culture', critical for maintaining our civilisation. They are accordingly highly respected, seen as worthy of funding and support. By contrast, zoos are 'popular culture', an enjoyable experience, easy to digest, but with no higher purpose. As Mullan and Marvin (1987: 132) argue, it then becomes too easy to dismiss zoos as not important, for 'museums and galleries are adult institutions; zoos are not'. Clearly, this is a vision that many zoos would like to counter. It was notable that in 1975, when Seattle decided to redevelop Woodland Park Zoo, aspirations of a higher status led to it being branded as a 'Life Science Institution' (Mullan & Marvin, 1987: 62).

Zoos as Theme Parks

In 2007, members of TRINET (an online forum for tourism researchers) discussed the origins of theme parks. Broadly defined, theme parks are amusement parks that have a strong over-arching theme or image. Accordingly, the discussion was about when did amusement parks begin to market themselves with distinctive and attractive themes. Disneyland, established in 1955 by Walt Disney using characters and images from his movies, is often referred to as the first theme park. A number of attractions were suggested as predating Disneyland, e.g. Corrigan's Ranch on the fringes of Los Angeles. After the discussion had continued for some time, Peter Mason made a bold suggestion. Given the definition of a theme park as an attraction with a strong unifying theme, Mason argued that London Zoo, established in 1828, qualifies as the first theme park. In this section, I want to take Mason's idea even further and argue that zoos, such as London Zoo, became the template for future developments in attractions such as amusement and theme parks. To couch it in evolutionary terms, from this common ancestor, one family branch evolved as modern zoos, while another went in the different direction of theme parks.

Initially, London Zoo was conceived as a scientific institution, open only to learned members of the Zoological Society of London. However, guests could be signed in and there was a rapid progression to more and more days of general admittance. As its popularity grew, the animals were complemented with rides and entertainments. Formally, it was London Zoological Gardens, imitating the Jardin des Plantes in Paris (the shortened term 'zoo' was coined in a popular music hall song in 1867). From the beginning, this was an institution that combined animals and plants, and the extensive lawns and flower plantings were an important attraction.

London Zoo functioned as a pressure release valve for the rapidly growing city. On the fringe of the metropolis, it could be reached by walking. As London rapidly expanded, public transport networks tapped a huge market that was hungry for green space. A peak annual attendance of 3 million visitors was achieved in 1950 (Shackley, 1996: 116). Subsequently, increased car ownership and demographic changes (combined with changing tastes, competition from other attractions – particularly wildlife and safari parks – and growing concerns about conditions for animals) led to a decline in visitation. Currently, London Zoo attracts about 1 million visitors per year (Tribe, 2004: 37). London is an instructive case study, but it is important to see that it is not alone. There are quite a number of inner-city zoos, established in the 19th century, which are now struggling to be viable and relevant in the 21st century.

The problem is that zoos were expensive to establish and operate (Tribe, 2004). They required large areas on the urban fringe, ideally with some sort of transport access (just as theme parks would in the 20th century). As urban areas continued to expand, there was increasing pressure from housing on land values. Other capital costs were in visitor facilities, exhibits and the animals. Economies of scale applied, small zoos were constrained by limited revenue streams (see, e.g. the financial struggles of Healesville Sanctuary in Australia as outlined in Fleay-Thomson, 2007). One solution was to broaden their appeal as attractions. Developing and promoting zoos as pleasure gardens appealing to a broad market was important to attract subscribers and customers and to satisfy stakeholders, such as local government officials (Baratay & Hardouin-Fugier, 2002). Accordingly, for most of their existence, zoos have also featured concerts, restaurants, rides, conference venues and picnic facilities (Baratay & Hardouin-Fugier, 2002; Conway, 1991). These were features of the early zoos and they continue to be an important part of zoo operations today. In turn, a number of theme parks also feature live animals (Broad & Weiler, 1998).

The provision of rides was the most striking parallel with amusement and theme parks. In many cases, the rides seemed interchangeable, with no obvious linkage to animals (Figure 10.1). In the 1960s, Melbourne Zoo

Figure 10.1 A train ride in the zoo; but it could be at any attraction. (Photo: Warwick Frost)

featured a train ride snaking through its grounds with a replica of the modern diesel, the Southern Aurora. It still proudly maintains a working 19th century merry-go-round (or carousel). What was distinctive was animal rides, ranging from donkeys and ponies to elephants, camels and tortoises (De Courcey, 1995). In the modern mechanised world, these and petting zoo exhibits gave urban children one of their few chances to interact with animals.

A different approach to the same problem is to bring zoos into tourism precincts, where they can cluster with other attractions. While there are financial and logistical impediments to doing this with conventional large zoos, it is feasible for smaller operations, particularly aquaria, and this is a growing trend (Judd, 1999; Shackley, 1996; Dobson this volume). Accordingly, Fisherman's Wharf in San Francisco is the home of the Aquarium of the Bay. Sydney's Darling Harbour, another redeveloped dock area, hosts the Sydney Aquarium. Crocosaurus, an attraction focused on crocodiles, opened recently in the main street of Darwin, Australia. In Christchurch, New Zealand, Cathedral Square is the main tourism hub and it contains the Southern Encounter Aquarium and Kiwi House, accessible through the city's visitor information centre.

A penchant for fantasy architecture reinforces the image of zoos as theme parks. Disneyland was notable for creating a self-contained world, harkening back to earlier and simpler times, an 'architecture of reassurance' that allowed visitors to temporarily forget their modern woes (Marling, 1997). However, zoos went down this same path over a century before Disneyland. Influenced by Romanticism, 19th century zoos excelled in fantasy display houses, reflecting the architectural style of the countries where the animals came from (Baratay & Hardouin-Fugier, 2002; Hancocks, 2001; Hoage & Deiss, 1996). Thus, African animals at Antwerp Zoo (Belgium) were housed (and still are) in a faux Egyptian temple, while the antelopes were accommodated in a replica Arabian mosque (Figure 10.2).

The use of fantasy design is still widespread. Rainforests are now highly popular, even if some are entirely constructed of concrete and plastic (Hancocks, 2001). So ubiquitous are the rainforest exhibits that one can hardly be considered a modern zoo without one. Indeed, even Vancouver Aquarium in Canada has an attractive (indoor) tropical rainforest. This choice of emphasising rainforests illustrates how easily the concept of the 'architecture of reassurance' is adapted for zoos. With modern concerns about the environment and climate change (and indeed whether we should have zoos), these exhibits provide reassurance that rainforests are being valued and protected, albeit in a city tourist attraction. Nor has human architecture been forgotten, with many zoos looking to replicate human habitations to provide the right ambience.

Figure 10.2 Fantasy architecture: A faux Egyptian hut contrasts with nearby housing blocks. (Photo: Warwick Frost)

Thus, Seattle's Woodland Park Zoo has an African village and the Trail of the Elephants in Melbourne Zoo features a South-East Asian village and hawkers market.

National Parks and Other Protected Areas

Yellowstone, the first national park, was established in 1872 and it wasn't really until after the First World War that the idea spread beyond the similar settler societies of the USA, Canada, Australia and New Zealand (Frost & Hall, 2009). In many places, zoos substantially predated national parks. Germany, for example, was a crucial player in the development of zoos, opening one in Berlin in 1844, but did not establish its first national park until 1969. However, as both institutions have evolved, there has been some curious interplay between them. This is not surprising, given that both zoos and national parks have similar generic goals of nature conservation, education and entertainment. Indeed, they have, at times, been seen as substitutes.

Early national parks sometimes contained small zoos. These not only allowed tourists to see animals with minimal exertion, but complemented the idea of national parks being primarily for recreation. Of course, such developments stimulated opposition. Perhaps the most notorious was the zoo at Yosemite National Park. It was established in 1918 to house orphaned mountain lion cubs, victims of a programme to eradicate predators. They were then joined by a bear cub and a relocated herd of elk. Increasingly criticised as inappropriate, it was closed in 1932, with the mountain lions slaughtered to gain a bounty (Runte, 1990). In Australia, the Royal National Park (1879) and Belair National Park (1891) were established for the recreation of nearby urban populations and contained zoo enclosures (Frost & Hall, 2009). In 1908, plans for a National Park of Scotland included a wildlife reserve in the grounds of a stately home. Though eventually not designated a national park, it developed into a small zoo with a tropical birdhouse and baboons on display (Baratay & Hardouin-Fugier, 2002).

In 1954, Gerald Durrell began talks with Julian Huxley (founder of the IUCN) and Peter Scott regarding the establishment of a wildlife reserve cum national park, which could be used to breed endangered animals. Initially, Durrell's idea was to establish this in the West Indies, he then considered Cyprus. It was only after some time that he realised that it had to be more like a zoo than a national park, in that it had to be accessible to a sufficient potential market of paying tourists to be successful. His first attempt was at Bournemouth, UK, before moving to the island of Jersey (Botting, 1999).

Between the Wars, the success of African national parks, particularly Kruger National Park in South Africa, influenced a trend towards wildlife parks, such as Whipsnade in the UK (Baratay & Hardouin-Fugier, 2002). Here was a new type of zoo. Indeed, many were not even called zoos; instead names such as sanctuary and wildlife reserve signified their position somewhere between zoos and national parks. Located in rural areas, they could afford larger enclosures in which the animals could roam relatively free and they catered for the growing use of automobiles for day-trips and weekend holidays. Following the Second World War, high rates of motor car ownership further increased their appeal. For these wildlife parks, there were clear marketing benefits in not being identified exactly as a zoo, but rather something closer to a national park or other type of nature reserve. Thus, when David Fleay left Healesville Sanctuary in 1952, he established his own wildlife attraction on Queensland's Gold Coast, which he called Fleay's Fauna Reserve (nearby was Currumbin Wildlife Sanctuary, established in 1947). When he retired in the 1980s, his reserve was then purchased and subsequently operated by the Queensland National Parks and Wildlife Service (Fleay-Thomson, 2007).

Conclusion

The history of zoos has generated a substantial and fascinating literature. Much of it is concerned with the changes in how people relate to animals and the resulting developments in zoo exhibits and conservation programmes. In this chapter, I have taken a different approach to zoo history. My aim was to consider zoos as tourist attractions by comparing their evolution to those of similar attractions, particularly museums, national parks and theme parks. Taking such an approach is valuable, as it highlights both the differences and similarities between these various competing attractions. Zoos are neither museums, or theme parks or national parks, but by examining their parallel developments and influence on each other, we gain a better understanding of zoos and their future.

Part 3

The Visitor Experience

In recent years, there has been a decided shift from seeing tourists as passive observers of places and things to focusing on the active experiences that they engage in. Indeed, the use of the term 'experience' is now so widespread as to almost be a jargonistic cliché or buzzword and zoos are no exception to this trend.

Tourist experiences are best understood through three overlapping approaches. The first sees experiences as having profound effects on tourists. According to this view, tourist experiences have been variously described as 'extraordinary', 'memorable', 'meaningful', 'quality' and even 'life-changing'. Such descriptors elevate the tourist experience to a high and worthy plane, justifying tourism as an important catalyst for self-actualisation and improvement (see Ritchie & Hudson, 2009, for a detailed review of this literature).

The second approach is the 'experience economy', posited by Pine and Gilmore (1999). Whereas the previous paradigm was demand orientated, the experience economy is supply driven. It argues for a commodification of the experience, whereby canny businesses can value add, developing experience products that can be sold at a premium price. While initially developed in terms of the service sector in general, the experience economy is being increasingly applied to tourism (see, e.g. Morgan *et al.*, 2009; Oh *et al.*, 2007; Richards, 2001).

The third approach is taken by practitioners rather than academic researchers. This is the trend to market everything as an experience. This not only includes destinations, attractions and accommodation, but even mundane and functional services, such as airports and credit cards, are rebadged as experiences. Of course with such overuse, there is a very real chance that the term will quickly become meaningless.

It is important to note that the three approaches are overlapping and it is common to see them used in combination. For example, an approach marketing all tourism products at a destination as experiences may also suggest that there is something memorable and transformative about them and may even tempt suppliers to increase prices as they are now appealing to a higher status/income market segment.

If zoos have recently gone through a revolution, giving greater emphasis to conservation and animal welfare, then the swing to experiences might be viewed as a counter-revolution. In increasingly marketing a visit to the zoo as an experience, there is the danger of once again making zoos primarily about people and only secondarily about the animals and their needs.

There are five chapters under this theme. In the first, Frost and Laing consider how the notion of the experience economy has been taken up by zoo managers, leading to a range of higher-priced and value-added experiences. In their critique of the experience economy, they argue that zoo managers need to be mindful of the flaws and limitation of this concept.

The second chapter considers the food experience at zoos. Generally, zoos have a reputation for poor quality fast food at grossly inflated prices. Boksberger, Shuckert and Robinson argue that this need not be so and if zoo managers are serious about providing a quality experience, they can provide better food service. They illustrate this with a case study of recent changes at Zoo Zurich.

The third chapter examines the experiences of volunteers at zoos. Holmes and Smith argue that volunteer programmes are very popular in many countries and represent a sustained commitment by visitors. However, there is an interesting paradox, for zoo volunteers invoke costs and are subject to limitations, most particularly being typically restricted to visitor services and having no special interaction with animals.

In the fourth chapter, Cushing and Markwell examine the role of disgust in the zoo experience. Many animals, they argue, provoke a combination of fear and fascination. Using the case study of a reptile park, they look at how this shapes the experience. The final chapter is an empirical study of visitor expectations and satisfaction. Conducted by Crilley, it examines the nexus between expectations and satisfaction and the factors that influence satisfaction with visits to the zoo. He also provides valuable comparisons with similar studies of other attractions.

Chapter 11
Up Close and Personal: Rethinking Zoos and the Experience Economy

WARWICK FROST AND JENNIFER LAING

Introduction

The current trend in zoos is for providing *experiences* for visitors, rather than passive observation of animals in cages or enclosures. Zoos Victoria in Melbourne, Australia, for example, markets a series of 'Behind the Scenes Experiences' to visitors who are willing to pay for something out of the ordinary. At *Elephant Introductions*, available to a maximum group of six, one can 'get up close and personal with one of our beautiful Asian elephants. If you're there at bath time, you can even help give your elephant a scrub!' At the *Lion Encounter*, a group of up to six can 'meet our magnificent males and learn about their unique personalities and habits. Then enjoy... a training session with the keepers!' The *Tall Order* experience extols the fact that a visitor can 'see eye-to-eye with a giraffe as you hand feed these gentle giants from our special lookout'. At the *Vet Assistant for a Morning*, visitors can engage in role play:

> Join the team at Australia's premier wildlife hospital and be at the frontline of the action. As a Veterinary Assistant, you will meet our in-patients and be on hand to witness emergency admissions or gown up for in-theatre surgery. The experience is one like no other! (Zoos Victoria, 2008d: 14)

The zoo fantasy also extends to popular and even high culture connections. At London Zoo, schoolchildren take part in the *Amph Factor*, a specially produced show based on television's *X Factor* (Figure 11.1). Many zoos offer a series of musical performances, ranging from pop and jazz to classical, often in the evenings when they would usually be closed, in an atmosphere sometimes redolent of the Glyndebourne Opera Festival or concerts in Central or Hyde Park. The occasional noise of the animals reminds the concert-goer of their presence, but the zoo largely functions as a distinctive backdrop to the cultural event or activity. Melbourne Aquarium presents a show based on the cartoon *Teenage Mutant Ninja Turtles*. At the most extreme, some zoos offer visitors the opportunity of being frightened – a fantasy of being juxtaposed with the wild and dealing with one's worst nightmares. At Crocosaurus Cove in

Figure 11.1 The *Amph Factor* auditorium at London Zoo, right next to the gorilla exhibit. (Photo: Warwick Frost)

Darwin (Australia), tourists can choose between the *Swim with Crocs* and the *Cage of Death*. For the latter, up to two people are placed in a strong glass container, which is then submerged in a tank with huge saltwater crocodiles (Crocosaurus Cove, 2009). As with bungee jumping (and the market is very much the same), the experience is video-recorded for later playing to friends and relatives. Many aquaria now offer the opportunity to swim with sharks (Dobson, 2008).

What is the appeal of such experiences? A study of visitors to zoos and sanctuaries by Woods (2002: 355) has found that interaction with animals was regarded as an important element of these experiences, which she attributes to a desire for 'some sort of "connection" with the animals'. Opportunities are provided to touch and feed, and to look animals in the eye without intervening barriers. One can enact fantasies, take a 'safari', pretend to be a keeper for a day and even 'gown up' as a vet in surgery. Sternberg (1997: 951) notes that many tourist experiences draw on fantasies, 'either ones associated with the locality or others taken from the universal cultural domain'. Dann (1977) identifies two fantasy motivations behind tourism – *anomie* and *ego-enhancement*. The visitor attracted to a zoo experience may be looking to escape their normal lives and engage in activities or roles that would otherwise be denied to them or not accessible back home. O'Dell (2005: 17) describes the 'experiencescape' as a realm for imagining 'alternative lives and livelihoods'. This links with early conceptualisations of the tourist experience as distinctly different from 'the routine of everyday life' (Uriely, 2005: 203). There may also be an element of prestige or status associated with being allowed into a hitherto prohibited 'inner sanctum', or even conspicuous consumption in purchasing an expensive 'exclusive' experience.

The packaging and marketing of special experiences for visitors is common to many tourist attractions. Historical theme parks offer immersion programmes, where visitors can dress in historical costumes and even adopt historical characters (Edensor, 2001; Taylor & Shanka, 2008). At Stonehenge, in England, a special evening tour allows visitors exclusive access to go behind the fence and touch these prehistoric stones. However, it is zoos and aquaria, through the range and scale of their offerings, which have become so closely associated in the public imagination with experiential programmes for visitors. While popular, the offering of such experiences by zoos and aquaria raises many questions. How do they fit with the role of modern zoos as places of education and conservation? Are such experiences merely thrills or entertainment, dressed up as something higher and better than they really are? Do these experiences really change attitudes? And is the modern trend in offering zoos experiences more about increasing visitor yield and competing against other tourist attractions? This chapter explores these issues and how the zoo experience fits within the experience economy described by Pine and Gilmore (1999).

The Experience Economy

The concept of experiences has been widely popularised by Pine and Gilmore (1999). They argue that businesses need to attract customers with the promise of 'enjoying a series of memorable events that a company stages – as in a theatrical play – to engage [them] in a personal way' (Pine & Gilmore, 1999: 2). The metaphor of performance is used, where service is the 'stage', products are 'props' and staff are 'actors'. Experiences are thus seen as culturally and spatially organised and engineered phenomena: 'As sites of market production, the spaces in which experiences are staged and consumed can be likened to stylized landscapes that are strategically planned, laid out and designed' (O'Dell, 2005: 16). Memorable experiences can be designed based on a number of principles – creating a strong theme, reinforcing positive cues, the provision of souvenirs/memorabilia and engagement of the various senses (Pine & Gilmore, 1999; Hayes & McLeod, 2007). This emphasis on 'staging' or packaging tourist experiences suggests an element of control or contrivance that might ultimately affect perceived authenticity of and levels of satisfaction with the experience. Pine and Gilmore (1999: 96) even argue that surprises can be pre-planned, terming this 'staging the unexpected'.

Pine and Gilmore (1999) extol the contribution of companies such as the Ogden Corporation to the experience economy, with their American Wilderness Experience based at the Ontario Mills Mall in California and providing immersive experiences in

> nature scenes... inhabited by 160 wild animals, across 60 distinct species, including snakes, bobcats, scorpions, jellyfish and porcupines. Guests begin their journey with a motion-based attraction, called the Wild Ride Theater, that lets them experience the world through the eyes of various animals... and then tour live animal exhibits and enjoy nature discussions with costumed Wilderness rangers. (Pine & Gilmore, 1999: 23–24)

This can be followed by a meal in the Wilderness Grill and souvenir buying at the Naturally Untamed shop. This experience, while heavily staged or scripted within a retail environment, clearly has some elements in common with its zoo experience cousin, as discussed in this chapter.

Experiences have been conceptualised by Pine and Gilmore (1999) across two dimensions – the *level of participation* (passive through to active) and the *connection or relationship between the customer and the performance* (absorption through to immersion). This results in four 'experience realms' – entertainment, education, escapism and aesthetics. While Pine and Gilmore's ideas apply generally to services, they have been increasingly applied to tourism. Richards (2001) noted their relevance for cultural heritage, particularly in terms of staging and creativity. Oh *et al.* (2007) argued that it might be possible to develop a scale to measure experiences, allowing for benchmarking both within and across tourism sectors. Morgan *et al.* (2009) explored how these concepts were now being taken up by destination managers.

Pine and Gilmore's four *experience realms* can be applied to the zoo experience. There is clearly a desire to emphasise the educational component of these experiences, which marries with most zoos' mission to develop public understanding and support of the importance of conservation and the preservation of species (Beardsworth & Bryman, 2001; De Courcy, 1995; Smith & Broad, 2007; Smith *et al.*, 2008). Recreation or entertainment is, however, the main focus for many of the zoo experiences, with animals utilised that are popular or provide drama or spectacle. An example is the birds of prey show at Healesville Sanctuary in Victoria, which relies on the swooping of eagles, hawks and falcons past members of the audience to thrill and inspire. To a limited extent, escapism may be an element of some of the zoo experiences (Holzer *et al.*, 1998). Aesthetics are not, however, strongly identified with the zoo experience. Mullan and Marvin (1987: 132) refer to the aesthetic or emotional response to visits to galleries and museums and compare this with the less individual and reverential zoo experience, which 'seems to be something which is shared, the animals are spoken about, marvelled at or laughed at with others'. It is also often perceived by people as a 'childish' pursuit, rather than the more grown-up or sophisticated contemplation of art or artefacts (Mullan & Marvin, 1987) and the lack of children to take to a zoo is often a reason for non-visitation (Turley, 2001).

Pine and Gilmore (1999) argue that the most satisfying experiences occur in the 'sweet spot' of all four realms of experience, encompassing aspects of them all, and regard this achievement as accentuating the 'realness' or authenticity of the experience. They criticise the American Wilderness Experience as neglecting, to a degree, the educational aspects of the experience in favour of the other realms: 'Guests encounter no specially designed places set aside for curators to bring animals out into the open so children can examine and discuss them... Strengthening the educational element would make this already praiseworthy experience even better' (Pine & Gilmore, 1999: 40).

The development of experiences at zoos and aquaria is also related to two other well-known tourism concepts. The first is MacCannell's idea that tourists are seeking authenticity through going 'backstage' at attractions. He argues that modern tourists are motivated by 'the modern disruption of real life and the simultaneous emergence of a fascination for the "real life" of others' (MacCannell, 1976: 91). Accordingly,

> Sightseers are motivated by the desire to see life as it is really lived... [creating] a new kind of social space that is opening up everywhere in our society. It is a space for outsiders who are permitted to view details of the inner operation of a commercial, domestic, industrial or public institution. (MacCannell, 1976: 99)

Interestingly, the Disney experience is based on the idea that 'no one gets to see behind the curtain' (Pine & Gilmore, 1999: 37). In the context of zoos and aquaria, many of the new experiences are marketed as allowing people to go 'behind the scenes', with the special experience of the outsiders being allowed to view the details of the inner lives of the animals. Such experiences are promoted as more 'real' than merely viewing from the front of the display, yet how authentic is this space and is the visitor really privy to nature untamed? Is this just another example of tourism as a *performance* (Edensor, 2001), with the keepers in on the act? The animals could be argued to be turned into commodities by zoos, 'packaged and sold to tourists' (Cole, 2007: 945) and thus losing the authenticity they have to us in the wild.

The second concept is of encouraging mindfulness through inter-activity, variety and giving people control over their experiences. Moscardo (1996) argued that at tourist attractions, much interpretation could be dull, uninspiring and repetitive, encouraging 'mindless' reactions, where visitors took little in. Instead, attractions needed to encourage 'mindfulness' among visitors. Mindful visitors, she argued, were 'active, interested, questioning and capable of reassessing the way they viewed the world' (Moscardo, 1996: 382). To achieve this, effective interpretation needed to be 'multisensory... personally relevant, vivid or affectively charged... unexpected or surprising' (Moscardo, 1996: 384). This links with the assertion of Ooi (2005: 55) that tourism mediators, including guides, help to shape the tourist experience by directing the attention of the visitor towards certain artefacts or attractions and certain narratives or interpretation. This assists the mediator in transcending some of the differences between visitors. Modern zoo experiences could achieve this through providing close encounters with wildlife and provoking mindfulness and convergence of experience through inter- pretation that offered interactivity and stimulated the five senses, thus potentially making them more valuable as educational experiences.

Critiquing the Experience Economy

The premise of Pine and Gilmore – that experiences are economic opportunities, requiring design, staging and scripting – is open to criticism on five counts. These are discussed below, particularly in relation to zoos and aquaria.

The first is the need to script the visitor experience, in order to maintain quality through the repeated delivery of the experience. Is such scripting desirable (or even possible at a zoo)? Hom Cary (2004: 67) observes that memorable tourist experiences or 'moments' are often serendipitous and arise where there is 'a spontaneous instance of self- discovery as well as a feeling of communal belonging'. Ooi (2005) also argues against the packaging of tourist experiences, but on the basis that it is impossible for three key reasons. Firstly, tourists have vastly different interests and socio-cultural backgrounds. Developing a script that aims to delight or appeal to all visitors is a Sisyphean task. Secondly, experiences are 'multi-faceted', involving place, activity and social meaning, and thus individuals will undergo different experiences even when taking part in the same activity. Thirdly, experiences are personal and can be affected by the mood or emotion of the individual. This crystallises the challenge inherent in offering tourist experiences – the visitor is heterogeneous, not often predictable in their behaviour and may interpret or experience things in a very individual and sometimes perverse way.

The variability of the zoo experience from a cultural perspective is well demonstrated by Mullan and Marvin (1987). They open their exploration of zoos with four vignettes of panda displays – all observed in the same year. The first is at Beijing, where there are two unnamed pandas in a barred cage. A tour group of Americans excitedly take photographs. It is their only stop at the zoo. By contrast, the local Chinese are uninterested in the pandas. Their second example is in Washington. The exhibit is attractively glass fronted. The pandas are named and there are affectionate displays of Valentine cards and letters to the pandas. The third is Tokyo, where there are huge crowds, but they are displeased as they are not allowed to take photos. The final zoo is in Paris, where the panda is outdoors and no-one is looking at it (one of the authors of this chapter saw a similar scene in London in 1984). A further variation is that of pandas as a touring exhibit, somewhat akin to a tour by a rock star (Wilson, 1992). The point made by Mullan and Marvin is that while the animals are 'an experience', that experience is a human construction that varies depending on cultural differences. However, this leaves open the possibility that the increasing globalisation of culture may lead to a standardisation of the zoo experience; that nowadays, pandas would be afforded the same celebrity status (and their displays follow the same patterns) in all major zoos.

Nonetheless, applying Ooi's argument takes us further. His hypothesis is that individuals will have *different experiences*. This is not so much predicated by cultural standards, but by individuality: 'What a product tries to offer may be ignored because tourists have their own expectations and preconceptions... It is a challenge to get tourists to pay attention to things that they have imagined wrongly' (Ooi, 2005: 63). Chronis (2005) also makes this point with respect to visitors to a heritage site – they come armed with pre-established narratives and images that might be *co-constructed* with the assistance of a guide; an interactive and negotiated process. This again may be the role of the zoo guide in the experience – to find out what visitors already know (or think they know) and how they might jointly construct a narrative that is both meaningful to the visitor and achieves the zoo's objectives of education and conservation.

A second argument against the Pine and Gilmore approach is advanced by Florida (2002), who posits the growing importance of the 'Creative Class'. Creative, well-paid, modern, independent and culturally savvy, they are seen as the key drivers of economic growth. In tourism, they are seen as the most desired target market. However, their tastes are discerning. They seek multi-layered and intense experiences that are unique to them rather than what they see as old fashioned, mass, pre-packaged tours and products. These people 'prefer more active, authentic and participatory experiences, which they can have a hand in structuring' (Florida, 2002: 167). Similarly, they reject 'attractions that most cities focus on building – sports stadiums, freeways, urban malls, and tourism-and-entertainment districts that resemble theme parks'. They view these as 'irrelevant, insufficient, or actually unattractive' (Florida, 2005: 35–36). Accordingly, the danger with the experience economy approach is that in being scripted and mass produced, it might be perceived as inauthentic, lacking in personal engagement and unappealing. O'Dell (2005) labels the experience economy as the 'risky economy' on this basis, where successes are feted and failures rarely talked about or acknowledged.

The third criticism of the experience economy arises from its commodification of experiences. Pine and Gilmore (1999) argue that it is necessary to charge for experiences and the more that is charged the better the experience could be. They demonstrate this with the example of a children's birthday party – starting with the traditional home-baked cake, they move to a store-bought cake to, finally, a themed birthday party at an entertainment venue. At the first level, the cake ingredients only cost a small amount, the store-bought cake a bit more, but the themed party was much more expensive, thereby offering far greater potential revenue for businesses offering that service. Their argument is that the more expensive experience was better – after all, themed parties (and restaurants and other experiences) are growing, so there must be demand for them.

Such a paradigm sits uncomfortably with many. Are zoos – and other tourist attractions – purely about money? For zoos especially, there is the potential for conflict with their conservation role, making the animals just one ingredient in the commercial mix. Does commodifying the zoo experience downgrade its quality? Applying the experience economy to cultural heritage, Richards (2001) posed some telling questions. Were experiences that were free not really experiences? Did their cost somehow influence their worth? And what about experiences, such as walking down a street, that were difficult to charge for? Were they somehow no longer valuable?

Using the experience economy as a justification for charging high prices leads to a fourth criticism based on equity. As zoos move down the path of developing experiences with high price tags, there is a danger that they will be excluding large sections of society. Rationing by price is inherently unfair. Is that an approach that zoos would like to be associated with? This issue is well illustrated by the campaign of the member group Friends of the Zoo against a government proposal to have the theme park company Village Roadshow run the Werribee Open Range Zoo (Melbourne, Australia). In addition to complaints regarding the treatment of animals and the loss of education programmes, the campaign also used the equity argument:

> Community accessibility to Werribee Open Range Zoo is at stake. Village Roadshow charges entry fees of $66 for adults and $40 for children at its existing theme parks which compares to entry costs of $23 for adults and $11.50 for children at Werribee Zoo. Werribee will become unaffordable for many in the community under the proposal. (Dennis, 2008)

The fifth argument is that these are really old concepts. In the literature, the application of the concept of the visitor experience to zoos predates Pine and Gilmore (see e.g. De Courcy, 1995; Mullan & Marvin, 1987). Furthermore, historically, zoos have provided experiences to tourists that are comparable to those of today.

In the 19th century, personal contact with the animals was often possible. Many zoos sold food, such as buns, which could be tossed into enclosures. In some cases, a generous tip to the keeper would allow one to get up close and touch animals. A range of animals could be ridden for a fee – including camels, ponies and even tortoises – although elephants were the most common. At Melbourne Zoo, it was estimated that one elephant could provide rides for up to 500 patrons a day (Baratay & Hardouin-Fugier, 1998; De Courcy, 1995, Rothfels, 2002).

Performances were popular, particularly those involving primates in comedic anthropomorphic behaviour. Chimpanzees smoke, drank, dressed in costume, did acrobatics and laughed (in reality their fear grimace), as they did in Hollywood films (Cheeta, 2008). London Zoo was particularly famous for its daily 'Chimpanzee's Tea Party'. At Singapore Zoo, one could pay to have tea with an orangutan in one of the restaurants (De Courcy, 1995; Mullan & Marvin, 1987). At Artis Zoo (Amsterdam), visitors could pay an extra fee to watch the big cats being fed. The viewing space had a capacity of 30, although there were often 100 people in the queue. However, the zoo's director had put a stop to this, as he 'claimed that the show gave no useful information about the animals' (Mullan & Marvin, 1987: 6). Other performances were like those of a circus, where the animals performed tricks at the behest of their keeper-trainers. At a show at Barcelona Zoo, killer whales were trained to allow their keeper to put his head in their mouths. These are, Mullan and Marvin (1987: 19) argue, quite unnatural tricks. Killer whales do not behave this way in the wild, rather it is something invented by the zoo to provide cheap thrills for the spectators.

An Effective Experience?

The experience economy is a seductive idea, promising an appealing combination of higher revenue and satisfied visitors. For zoos, it is easy to be attracted by this and overlook the negative implications of the concept. However, it is possible that zoos have also overlooked the obvious, that they have already developed methods of providing effective experiences well before the commodification of the experience economy. We accordingly close this chapter with a short case study, based on an observation of a 'Keeper's Talk' on Chimpanzees at Taronga Zoo (Sydney, Australia).

Chimpanzees hold an unusual relationship with humans. Diamond argued that they were so genetically close to humans that they should be labelled *Homo pongoides* and he speculated on how we would feel if they were labelled as such in a zoo. For many of us, our knowledge of chimpanzees comes from film and television, where we have become conditioned to seeing their anthropomorphic antics (Cheeta, 2008). In the past, chimpanzees in zoos were often kept separated in small cages and presented as figures of fun. The chimpanzee exhibit at Taronga provides quite a different experience, for it is a large grassed area with in excess of 20 animals.

The Keeper's Talk aims to communicate messages about chimpanzee behaviour and social groups. It is constructed against a background of uneven knowledge held by the audience. Many of the audience are quite surprised to hear about their social groupings and pecking orders, when television presents them as solitary animals.

The keeper works through a range of predetermined points. However, it is not tightly scripted, nor could it really be, for there are many questions from the audience. There is no rush, the talk meanders. At one stage it is announced that the talk is over, but the keeper will stay and answer questions. Half an hour later, he's still there fielding questions. He doesn't have a lot of flair, there's no tricks and there's no contact with the animals. The keeper's engagement comes from his knowledge and enthusiasm, he clearly establishes a bond that allows him to communicate effectively and persuasively. It's not exclusive, the audience is over 100 people. And it's free. Following the conventions of the experience economy, it's wrong on nearly every level. However, it's a great experience.

Chapter 12

Feeding Time at the Zoo: Food Service and Attraction Management

PHILIPP BOKSBERGER, MARKUS SCHUCKERT AND RICHARD
ROBINSON

Introduction

In the opening scenes of the movie *Madagascar* (2005), viewers get
an insight into the zoo's food consumption phenomena. The animals
rummage in the rubbish bins for the remnants of pre-packaged convenience foods and steal the disposable cutlery of the unsuspecting visitors,
who complement their zoo experience on a seeming diet of takeaway-
style fare. As night sets in and the movie's hero, Alex, celebrates Marty's
birthday with his fellow inmates, stylised cloches are lifted to reveal
customised dishes and extravagant birthday cakes are presented to
highlight the occasion. Is this indeed representative of the visitor's and
the attraction's food service experience when visiting the zoo?

The aim of this chapter is to analyse if food service can create its own
experience value and therefore add value to the experience product. For
this reason, an empirical study in the context of Zoo Zurich in Switzerland was conducted. Hence, this chapter is organised as follows: first,
aspects of attraction management and food service are discussed; second,
the empirical results of the survey are presented and compared to the
theoretical debate within tourism and leisure research; and third, the
chapter concludes with some implications for the management of
attractions by outlining future research questions.

Attraction Management

Attractions have been viewed as new leisure trends etc means to fulfill
new leisure and tourism trends: they offer more quality for less, they are
safe and clean, their offers are multi-optional and time saving as well as
emotional and sense giving, and their visitation also meets the needs of
soft individualism (Fyall *et al.*, 2003). Moreover, these attractions can
satisfy the various needs of contemporary experience, economy-seeking
customers, including experience-intensity, life-hype, impulsive and fast
experiences (Pine & Gilmore, 1999). While Middleton (1989: 229) defines

an attraction as 'a designated permanent resource which is controlled and managed for the enjoyment, amusement, entertainment and education of the visiting public', the most cited definition states, 'attraction is a system comprising three elements: a tourist or human element, a nucleus or central element, and a marker or informative element' (Leiper, 1990: 371–372). In accordance with these definitions, a zoo can indeed be characterised as an attraction in the tourism and leisure market (Van Linge, 1992). An amended description of zoos as attractions includes not only the displayed animals and educational information as core products, but also augmented elements such as food services (Swarbrooke, 2002).

As Wanhill (2003) uses the term 'imagescape' to describe the total atmosphere of an attraction, it is the overall experience value of the attraction that is important for customers: 'while commodities are fungible, goods tangible and services intangible, experiences are memorable' (Pine & Gilmore, 1999: 11). These experiences evolve when customers engage with attraction services as the stage and attraction goods as props. According to Pine and Gilmore (1999), four possibilities exist as to how consumers can become involved or engaged in experiences. Thus, the combination of the dimension 'tourist participation' with the dimension 'environmental relationship' defines the four 'realms' of an experience, as illustrated in Figure 12.1. It is important to note that attractions are not just fun and pleasure, but also, and ever increasingly, educative (Martin & Mason, 1993). When visiting zoos, it is evident that the educational and epistemic motives are equally as important as the entertainment and aesthetics from a customer's viewpoint.

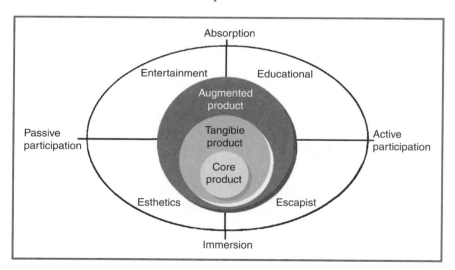

Figure 12.1 A taxonomy of a visitor attraction product in experience realms

Not surprisingly, there is considerable debate about how attraction management should respond to create these multiple experiences and to fulfill the dynamic expectations of their customers. For example, some advocate a focus on human resource management (Watson & McCracken, 2003), others emphasise the importance of marketing (Boyd, 2003), while there is also a recognition that particular priorities are pertinent to particular 'types' of attractions (Drummond, 2001). Much of the research on attraction management is based on a prescriptive approach and offering a list of success factors for the management of attractions (for an overview, see Pikkemat & Schuckert, 2007). The literature reveals three key drivers: factors affecting the supply side; factors triggering the market (customers); and factors that are set by the infrastructure and services (hard and software) within the attraction.

Now that these findings have been highlighted, it can be stated that not much attention or credit is given to augmented products in attractions. Indeed, investigating the food service at a zoo is something of an oxymoron. Animals, and arguably to a lesser degree plants, are the key attraction of zoological gardens (Conway, 2007; Turley, 1999). As Shani and Pizam (2008) observe, there are a plethora of ethical considerations concerning the commercialisation of animals for entertainment and amusement. That the food service in zoos should also be considered in this milieu seems logical. Indeed, caterers at some US zoos have incorporated ecologically conscious practices into their food service, which is documented in industry journals. These include the use of sustainable (organic) ingredients for menu items and recyclable consumables for service ware, such as cups and cutlery, although the all-encompassing adoption of these practices is compromised by the fast-food orientation of many of the attractions' outlets (Knaub-Hardy, 2008).

Yet, only fleeting references to the food service in zoos are apparent in the literature. In zoological settings, previous research has implied that the food service is limited to a hygiene factor from the perspective of the visitor (Jensen, 2007). This is not necessarily the finding of other studies in the broader tourism and leisure attraction literature. In the museum sector, McIntyre (2008) found that the food service was far from being an augmented product. Careful design and planning ensured that the food service can be an integrated component of the overall attraction's consumption experiences. It seems Jensen's (2007) inference is not congruent with professional practice either. Recent developments integrate the food service into the visitor experience, e.g. mimicked South-East Asian food vendors are incorporated into the Trail of the Elephant precinct at Australia's Melbourne Zoo (Frost & Roehl, 2008).

There are several potential benefits for investigating the food service in zoos. As outlined to this point, it may assist in maximising revenue potential, and given that zoos are often partly funded from the public purse, this is a highly attractive proposition. Furthermore, food service may augment the visitor experience, however, for zoos, specifically understanding the leisure market's consumption of food and beverage products has been previously identified as a means of segmentation (Kim et al., 2002). Finally, while much of the literature has focused on the ability of zoos to communicate key conservation and educational messages, carefully constructed food services may have the potential to support a zoo's core mission. Hence, to inform this current investigation, it is useful to more fully explore the generic food service literature as it applies to the tourism, leisure and attraction sectors.

Food Service

Food service within the tourism and leisure market has been a topic of much academic and industry attention. The food offered at a destination has a significant influence on the intention to visit destinations and even organises a visitor's daily itinerary (Kivela & Crotts, 2006). Various studies have also measured the food service expenditure of tourists. The general consensus is that upwards of 25% of visitor expenses are attributable to food and beverages (Correia et al., 2008; Hall & Sharples, 2005; Quan & Wang, 2004) and that this may be much higher in certain niche markets. But more than this, food consumption is not only a means of generating revenue, but also an integral part of the overall tourist experience (Hjalager & Richards, 2002). In this context, Rützler (2005) identified the following food trends:

(1) Nature food: Organic food is characterised by environmentally friendly production, animal husbandry and feeding that is appropriate to the species, and clear legal conditions concerning producing, manufacturing, marketing and labelling.
(2) Ethic food: The ethical aspect concerning the production and distribution of food is taken into account. This means that conservation, animal welfare and fair trade are becoming more relevant.
(3) Fast casual: This is the combination of the prolonged trends for fast food and casual dining, which is light and contains a lot of vegetables and only a little meat. Furthermore, it can be consumed anytime and fast, what is in the offer can be seen before ordering and it is possible to choose the portion (amount) by one's self. The presentation of healthy and fresh food has an important role and often it is prepared in front of the customer.
(4) Sensual food: The desire for a sensual experience while eating and drinking is increasing. People want to experience more intensive, special flavours.

(5) Anti-fat-food: Obesity is an increasing problem in industrialized countries. Suppliers of finished products are responding by changing their recipes to lower the amount of energy in the products, lower the portions, and by informing consumers with nutrition panels.

(6) Clean food: Because already 2% of the world's population suffers from allergies, with an upward trend, the demand for products free from allergens, additives, preservatives and hormones is rapidly increasing.

There is reasonable evidence to suggest that the provision of well-designed food products that respond to market trends can benefit visitor satisfaction through the creation of more distinct and memorable experiences (Beer, 2008). Leisure-based attraction providers, such as museums, gardens and zoos, primarily provide restorative, educational and enjoyable experiences for visitors. Even though many zoo food service facilities are strategically located to take advantage of the vista afforded by their surroundings, and menus are reported to be seasonally revised to reflect the seasonal changes (Detwiler, 2007), catering in such venues is seen predominantly as a secondary activity (Davis *et al.*, 1998).

From a marketing perspective, food in these leisure attractions is considered an augmented product (Kotler, 1994), or one that supplements and adds value to the core product, in this case the provision of environs and artefacts for the entertainment and enjoyment of visitors. This approach is clear in the catering strategy of many zoos. For instance, Columbus Zoo overtly endorses this approach by stating a policy of relying on brands in the selection of caterers (O'Brien, 2002). Although some customisation of a product is possible, there are limitations on how flexible the brands can be in the context of zoos. Research in this area has again focused on the potential revenue-generating potential of the food service to the attraction's overall visitor expenditure. Yet, little empirical research has been conducted to understand the contribution of food services to overall customer experience in attractions, despite evidence to suggest that visitors increasingly seek more than just catering: they expect a meal experience commensurate with the socio-cultural functions of the space within which it is offered (Flad, 2002). Thus, the food service incorporates the room, the meeting encounter, the product, and the management control system, which altogether result in the fifth aspect, which is the atmosphere (Edwards & Gustafsson, 2008).

Attractions have been investigated *vis-à-vis* the benefits of the food service to their overall business offering. Themed restaurants have long played a role in the total experience of visitors, e.g. at Disney's theme parks (Becker, 1987). Attractions are confronted with many of the same issues as hoteliers in their decisions as to whether they manage or outsource food service operations (Barrows & Giannapoulos, 2006). Indeed, Herbert (1994) explored the disconnection between contract caterers and an attraction's core mission, commenting that the food service providers rarely shared the educational and charitable objectives of their hosts.

The health and nutritional aspects of food consumption have also been investigated in the tourism and hospitality literature. Fields (2002) argues that health and nutritional concerns have increasingly become elevated in contemporary society due to the predominance of the human body in social discourse. Women, especially, are body image conscious and there is evidence that this awareness may impact food service purchase and consumption (O'Mahony & Hall, 2007). No matter, in the context of leisure-based attraction food service consumption, females not only make purchase decisions for themselves, but also for their families and companions (Lake *et al.*, 2006). Yet, there is a certain irony in the proposition that in the commercial world, tourism and leisure not exempt, consumption is geared towards *more*, but various media enshrine the body that is *less* – primarily a gendered concept. Indeed, previous research has identified this paradox (Williams, 1997). That some zoos appear to market healthy food options (Cavanagh, 2007) seems more a response by caterers to social trends, as identified by Rützler (2005), rather than a strategic decision to integrate food service practices with the zoo's overall mission. Thus, this chapter investigates the most suitable food service system for zoos, considering the zoos' philosophies and missions and at the same time the customers' eating habits in their leisure time.

Food Service at Zoo Zurich

Zoo Zurich was opened in 1929 and is a 365 days a year operation. In 2008, Zoo Zurich was home to 3731 individual animals (357 species) and welcomed 1.8 million visitors (Zoo Zurich, 2009). It is a cultural institute and functions as an intermediary between the human visitors, animal attractions and nature. Its main tasks are providing a recreation area, informing visitors and the general population, conservation of nature and research. The zoo's main purposes are, on the one hand, to display the indigenous and exotic animals in their various enclosures and, on the other hand, showcase Zoo Zurich's nature conservation programmes. A visit should stay in the mind as a recreational, entertaining and informative experience and should motivate visitors to practice responsible behaviours with their natural environment. Apart from awakening an interest in nature and environmental conservation, Zoo Zurich (2009) states in its mission: 'We create a worthy gastronomic experience'. Zoo

Zurich has two self-service food outlets and a designated picnic area. While the Siesta restaurant with its integrated playground is primarily for young families, the restaurant in the Masoala rainforest is higher priced and attracts more elderly zoo visitors and small groups.

In this context, and for the current study, visitors to Zoo Zurich were questioned about their general eating habits in their leisure time and the importance of healthy and organic options in food service as well as the relevance of atmosphere and cleanliness, to their food service experience. Between the period of 4–15 July 2008, 333 useable personal interviews were collected, utilising a self-administered questionnaire. Respondents were intercepted at the two existing food service outlets in Zoo Zurich.

The characteristics of the sample in terms of gender and age differences are reported first to identify the nature of the demographic patterns. The gender breakdown indicates that noticeably more females (62.5%) than males (37.5%) took part in this survey. The majority of the respondents are younger than 40 years, while 24% belong to the 25–34 year age group and 29.7% belong to the 35–44 year age group.

The survey also identified the visitor groups of respondents. Their composition reflects the gender and age of the respondent population with more than one third (37.5%) visiting Zoo Zurich with their family. Grandparents with grandchildren and school classes have been the second and third most common visitor groups, respectively. Since young families are the most frequent visitor group (Zoo Zurich, 2009) and females dominantly influence the food purchase decision within their family, at least in a domestic context (Lake *et al.*, 2006), this sample may be representative for a survey on the food service in a zoo.

A comparison of eating habits in relation to respondents' general leisure behaviour is reported next. The scores and rankings for the eleven selected food service options are illustrated in Figure 12.2. Noticeable differences can be reported in terms of healthy versus unhealthy food services. It can be stated that the respondents try to avoid any kind of fatty, heavy or fast food in favour of fruits and vegetables. However, this result may reflect what the respondents regard as an acceptable answer, rather than an accurate description of their actual eating habits. The worldwide success of fast food chains in general and the fast-food orientation of many tourism and leisure attractions in particular (Knaub-Hardy, 2008), suggest that there is a significant clientele for this type of food service.

Since healthy, nutritious and organic products have increasingly become a concern in our society, the respondents were next asked about the importance of these aspects in food consumption. Not surprisingly, the majority of respondents consider healthy food as important (45.6%) and very important (45.3%). However, less than half the sample (45.3%)

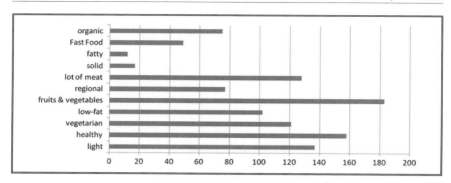

Figure 12.2 Preferred type of food in leisure time (note multiple responses)

is prepared to pay more for a healthy menu and would rather select the cheaper but unhealthier option. Similarly, more than half the respondents state that organic products are important (48.3%) and very important (9.6%) to them, respectively. Being asked about their willingness to pay more for an organically based menu, only 30% would do so. In line with the research of O'Mahony and Hall (2007) and Fields (2002), it can be stated that there is evidence of an increase in awarness of the health and organic aspects of food services. However, the impact on food service purchase and consumption in the leisure time of people at attractions seems to be marginal.

According to the literature (Edwards & Gustafsson, 2008), it is not only the menu that influences consumers' perception of food services, but also the type of catering, the service quality and the pricing. Strong support was found for the importance of a fast service, friendly personnel, cleanliness, reasonable prices, a comfortable atmosphere and child-friendliness (Figure 12.3). The preceding data analysis revealed that all these factors are important and very important to the majority of respondents. Interestingly, an authentically designed restaurant does not seem to be as important when visiting an attraction. The analysis of the qualitative answers to this question revealed that the respondents could not think of an authentic design for a restaurant in a zoo. When people have been asked about the importance of self-service or full service options, the results are interesting. Since full service includes everything from being seated at a table until leaving the place, it is more labour intensive than self-service, where food items are prepared in advance and guests are served at service stations or can choose the portions themselves from a buffet table. Therefore, full service is normally priced significantly higher than self-service, which, however, contradicts with the stated importance of a reasonable price-performance ratio by the respondents.

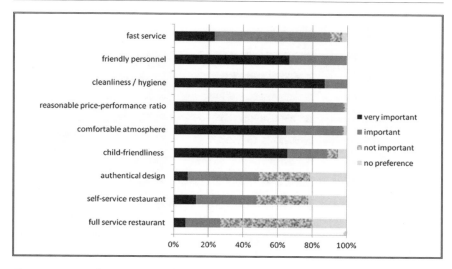

Figure 12.3 Influence factors in the food service system

For the purpose of completeness, and to address the issue of atmosphere, the following nine aspects of a restaurant design were examined as an extension (Figure 12.4). Similar to the results obtained from the analysis of the influence factors in the food service system, the respondents had difficulties in understanding the meaning of consistent design and appropriate decor in the context of a zoo restaurant. It can be stated, though, that overall these nine aspects are important in the design of a restaurant and, therefore, will contribute to the food service experience.

Conclusion

This research was initiated in response to a growing recognition that attractions are fundamental to the tourism and leisure industry. The contribution to the customer's experience of their augmented products, in general, and food service in particular, are however, under-researched. Moreover, food service systems are presently faced with a number of challenges that could, potentially, jeopardise their role in the management of attractions. In zoological gardens settings, in particular, there appear some unique contextual factors, including the paradox between offering a food service in a space where flora and fauna are the main attractions, and that the food service, as an augmented product, might serve as an agent for communicating the zoo's core environmental and educational objectives.

While the literature clearly identifies a societal change towards healthier nutrition, the vast majority of food outlets in tourism and leisure attractions offer burgers, French fries, sausages and chicken

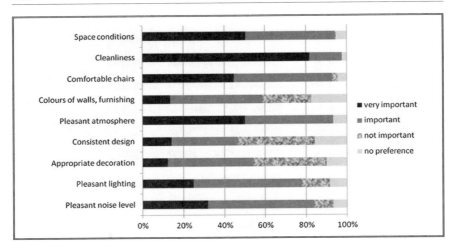

Figure 12.4 Optimal restaurant design

nuggets to families. In addition to the menu offerings, the predominant catering style is self-service in a functional design restaurant, devoid of atmosphere. Instead of making a contribution to the overall experience, the food service system might actually dissatisfy visitors. Indeed, previous research has identified that in leisure contexts, individuals' food consumptive attitudes shift from frugality, economy and health to release and treating (Williams, 1997), indicating that aligning an attraction's food service offer with domestic consumption habits might be incongruent with visitor expectations of a food service as an augmented product in an attraction.

Considering the results of this research, a number of recommendations for the restaurant in the Masoala Rain Forest at Zoo Zurich were elaborated (Figure 12.5). The Masoala Rain Forest was designed as a replica of the unique Madagascan landscape and opened in 2003. Visitors can stroll through this exotic paradise on unfenced paths, passing brooks, lakes and a 6-m high waterfall along their way. At present, 45 species of vertebrates can be observed in the dense forest of 17,000 plants, including lemurs, giant tortoises and flying foxes, and diverse species of birds, tomato frogs and coral fish. While the restaurant is directly adjacent and visitors can observe this unrivalled world of flora and fauna through a giant window while eating, the interior decoration breaks with the tropical surrounding. It has been suggested, for example, to play rain forest sounds in the background and to include some movable tropical plants in the dining hall. Offering traditional Swiss cuisine, Madagascan and other exotic menus should be included, featuring the Masoala theme. Similarly, the presentation of the food with tropical flowers will

Figure 12.5 The Masoala Restaurant at Zoo Zurich. (Photo: Boksberger *et al.*)

increase the food service experience. Besides the fact that purchased food should be convenient stage, it is crucial to provide healthy menu options. Focusing on children, the aim is to offer healthy, nutritious food that tastes good and is fun to eat. This goal can be achieved, for example, by cutting vegetables in the shape of animals, linking the kids menu to the diet of zoo animals, or presenting the food at an additional service station that is shaped like an animal and adjusted in height. In addition, these efforts need to be integrated into the marketing activities of Zoo Zurich. Supplying, and communicating through menu design, the use of free-range eggs, for example, may communicate a subtle message to the visitor about the overall values of a zoo. In other words, there is not only a need, but also a chance to harmonise a zoo's mission 'to educate' in between the core, tangible and augmented products.

However, there remains a need to continue this work in order to determine the depth of shared thinking around the contribution of food services to the overall experience of any attraction. More research is needed to understand the paradox between normal food preferences and consumption habits during special occasions (Williams, 1997) and to determine the primary decision maker in attraction food purchase (Lake *et al.*, 2006). It is only when this additional understanding has been secured that management's point of view will shift from a paradigm of predominantly revenue, yield and cost discussions, to consider food service as an augmented product with diverse values to an attraction.

Chapter 13
The Value of Zoo Volunteer Programmes

KIRSTEN HOLMES AND KAREN A. SMITH

Introduction

Volunteers assist at wide range of tourist attractions, yet the role of volunteers at aquaria, wildlife parks and zoos has rarely been explored in the academic literature, in contrast to the greater consideration of volunteers at museums, other heritage attractions, steam railways and in conservation. Exceptions to this are Caldwell and Andereck's (1994) survey of members of South Carolina Zoological Society, Holmes' (2009) analysis of the value of volunteering for volunteers at a range of tourist attractions including a zoo, and Holmes and Smith's (2009) review of volunteering across all tourism settings, including aquaria and zoos. Studies have also examined volunteer tourism programmes that involve wildlife, as these are among the most popular volunteer tourism trips (Ellis, 2003). However, these programmes rarely involve captive wildlife, usually focusing on conservation activities with wildlife in their natural setting. An exception is Broad and Jenkins' (2008) case study of tourists' motivations for volunteering at the Gibbon Rehabilitation Project in Phuket, Thailand, which features some captive animals. This chapter seeks to redress this imbalance by examining the role of volunteers at aquaria, wildlife parks and zoos and the contributions and costs of these volunteer programmes.

While there is a lack of empirical data on the recruitment of zoo volunteers, our own research attests to the popularity of zoo volunteering and that coveted roles can be highly competitive. This is in line with the popularity of volunteer tourism programmes involving animals, identified by Ellis (2003). Zoo websites clearly position their volunteering opportunities as desirable and in demand. Many carry statements that they are no longer accepting applications, e.g. Houston Zoo and Louisville Zoo (as of May 2009), suggesting aspiring volunteers should check back later in the year.

UK data show that wildlife parks and zoos frequently involve as many volunteers as full-time paid employees, with an average of 24 paid staff and 24 volunteers at each site (VisitBritain, 2007). The Australasian Regional Association of Zoological Parks and Aquaria (ARAZPA, 2008), which represents 75 zoos and aquaria in Australia, New Zealand the South Pacific, reports that its members have 3035 paid staff (full and part time) and 2189 volunteers. However, internationally, there is a significant variation in the numbers of volunteers involved at different aquaria and zoos. Seattle Aquarium, for example, involved 617 volunteers in 2008 through a range of adult and high school programmes and internships, compared to 74 full-time equivalent paid staff. Monterey Bay Aquarium (2007) involved over 1000 volunteer guides in 2007, whereas the Aquarium of Western Australia only has 70 volunteer interpreters compared to 90 paid staff members (AQWA, 2008). As many volunteers only offer their time on a weekly, fortnightly or monthly basis, many more individual volunteers may be needed compared to full-time staff.

The Role of Volunteers

Volunteers in aquaria, wildlife parks and zoos are overwhelmingly involved in visitor services. These are mostly front-of-house positions, such as guides and docents (a North American term for an unpaid educator or interpreter), and the role of volunteers as zoo interpreters has received some attention from researchers (Mony & Heimlich, 2008; Weiler & Smith, 2009). Volunteers also assist with special events and education programmes, including outreach programmes outside the organisation. A small number of individuals may volunteers at aquaria and zoos in order to gain work experience leading to paid employment within the sector. In North America, these volunteers are usually called interns and many aquaria and zoos operate separate internship and volunteer programmes.

These roles can be illustrated by London Zoo and its sister organisa-tion, Whipsnade Zoo, both operated by the Zoological Society of London. Volunteer roles are distinct from work experience or internship place-ments. Learning volunteers and outreach support volunteers assist with education, although the former are site-based and the latter involves assisting paid staff on visits to schools. Library, horticultural and office volunteers all assist paid staff in specialist areas. Membership volunteers are fundraisers who recruit new members to the Zoo's friends' scheme (Figure 13.1). None of the volunteers are directly involved in animal care. This situation is not uncommon, with the vast majority of zoo volunteers being predominantly in visitor services roles. The lack of direct animal contact needs to be clearly communicated to applicants, particularly as volunteers may be attracted to the aquaria or zoo because of the chance to work with the animals. Edinburgh Zoo, for example, includes a clarification on their volunteering information, stating that '[volunteer-ing] does not include working directly with the animals' (Edinburgh Zoo, 2009). Rather, their volunteers are involved in staffing touch tables,

Figure 13.1 A quiet day volunteering – membership kiosk at London Zoo. (Photo: Warwick Frost)

operating brass-rubbing activities and providing extra staffing and information at popular exhibits.

The nature of safari parks, as open spaces that visitors drive around, generally means that there is less need for visitor service volunteers, therefore safari parks typically only offer internship or work experience placements. These are similar to volunteer tourism internships, such as those at the Gibbon Rehabilitation Project in Thailand, where volunteers perform a number of duties, including education for visitors to the project (Broad & Jenkins, 2008).

Contribution of Volunteer Programmes

Volunteers make significant contributions to the operation of zoos. They are often the primary face-to-face contact with visitors on the ground, they provide additional visitor services such as interpretation and tours, they offer paid staff an extra set of eyes to monitor animal behaviour and free-up paid staff for other activities. Indeed, without volunteers, some smaller zoos would not be able to open and would certainly not be able to provide the visitor experience they would wish. The contributions of volunteers are often listed in annual reports and tend to focus on the quantitative measures of the volunteer programme, such as the number of volunteer hours, calculated as full-time equivalent staff and sometimes given a financial value. For example, Taronga

Conservation Society in NSW, which operates both Taronga Zoo and Taronga Plains Zoo, states in its annual report for 2008:

> Last year, volunteers at both zoos gave over 65,987 hours of dedicated service. This represents an estimated contribution of AUD$1.98 million based on average employment costs. (Taronga Conservation Society, 2008: 61)

While a useful and explicit indication of volunteers' time, the economic value of zoo volunteer programmes provides only a limited picture of the range of contributions made by volunteers. Programmes generate wider benefits for the volunteers, the organisations, their visitors and the community.

There has been considerable research on the benefits of volunteering for the volunteer, although only Holmes (2009) and Holmes and Smith (2009) have examined the benefits to volunteers at zoos, both in the wider context of tourism volunteering. Holmes found that the benefits to the volunteers included the opportunity to spend time in a special place, personal development (such as building confidence), the opportunity to meet people and a sense of achievement. These benefits concur with studies of volunteers at other visitor attractions. Researchers have identified subject interest, social contact, personal development and opportunity to learn as the main motivators for and benefits from volunteering in heritage attractions and museums (Edwards, 2005; Holmes, 2003; Smith, 2003). This is partly because volunteers at visitor attractions tend to be older, retired individuals rather than younger, work experience seekers.

Volunteering at visitor attractions has been described both as a form of leisure (Holmes, 2003) and as a form of serious leisure (Orr, 2006). Serious leisure volunteering involves pursuing a career as a volunteer, personal development, the occasional need to persevere and the development of a social world for participants (Stebbins, 1996). Zoo volunteers are usually required to make a regular time commitment to the zoo, which requires an obligation on behalf of the volunteer. For example, Vancouver Aquarium requires volunteers to commit four hours a week for six months or 100 hours in every six months. Zoo volunteers also need to participate in training programmes, the length of which varies depending on the volunteer role. A final benefit that zoo volunteering may offer participants is higher personal subject wellbeing. Volunteering has generally been associated with higher reported levels of personal subject wellbeing and as people frequently begin volunteering at times of change in their lives, such as retirement, marriage break up and migration (Holmes & Smith, 2009), volunteering may help them deal with these changes.

Zoo volunteer programmes usually offer some form of recognition to their volunteers in addition to their annual report. These rewards can include free entry into the zoo (when not on duty), long-service awards and an annual party. It is unlikely that volunteers are actually motivated to volunteer by these rewards, and Caldwell and Andereck (1994) found that these material rewards were rated the least important by members of the South Carolina Zoological Association. Intangible rewards, such as a sense of satisfaction and enjoyment from volunteering, can be more valuable to volunteers. Balancing the extent and value of rewards is an important part of planning and managing a zoo volunteer programme.

The benefits to aquaria and zoos of operating a volunteer programme have already been outlined above and include financial savings, assistance to visitors and to paid staff. Volunteers may also make donations to the zoo in addition to their gift of time or they may co-ordinate fundraising campaigns, as in the case of the Perth Zoo Docent Programme below. Holmes (2009) also found that volunteers can act as ambassadors for the zoo within the local community, both formally and informally. Formally, volunteers can be involved in outreach roles and giving talks to other community groups. Informally, volunteers can promote the attraction to their friends and family and also recruit further volunteers.

While there is limited empirical evidence of the benefits of volunteers to visitors, a number of studies have examined the impact of different forms of interpretation, including volunteer interpreters. Lindemann-Matthies and Kamer (2005) examined the impact of visitors' use of a touch table, staffed by both paid and volunteer interpreters and found that this enhanced visitor learning, which was retained up to two months later. Mony and Heimlich (2008) found that zoo visitors perceived docents to be an important source of information and interpretation and argue that visitors value human interactive forms of interpretation above other forms. This suggests that visitors appreciate the opportunity to access information from a volunteer interpreter even though they may not use this service during their visit. Lastly, Weiler and Smith (2009) established that zoo visitors benefitted from access to a range of interpretive media. The involvement of volunteers in interpretation can therefore enhance the visitor experience.

While discourse in English-speaking Western countries typically views volunteers as unpaid staff, the conceptualisation of volunteering as a form of leisure or serious leisure (Stebbins, 1996) can be used to argue that volunteers are clients as well as workers at their organisation. In the case of visitor attractions, this makes them part of the audience as well as part of the staff (Holmes & Edwards, 2008). Zoo volunteer programmes can be considered as an alternative way of engaging visitors, with zoo volunteers choosing to visit one zoo in-depth rather than several at a more shallow level. Indeed, Orr (2006) argues that volunteering offers visitor attractions, such as zoos, a means of engaging visitors in longer term and more in-depth relationships.

Researchers also argue that volunteer programmes generate benefits for the wider community, including increased social capital, which can lead to better education and health outcomes and lower crime levels for the community (Putnam, 2000; Musick & Wilson, 2008). It should be noted that these benefits could be generated by any volunteer programme, not necessarily one linked to an aquarium or zoo.

Costs of Volunteer Programmes

While volunteers bring many benefits, operating a volunteer programme is not without its costs. These include:

- Staff time in recruiting, training and managing the volunteers.
- Facilities for volunteers, such as a volunteer room and workspace.
- Training materials and instructors.
- Uniforms, if these are used.
- Volunteer rewards.
- Out-of-pocket expenses (e.g. travel).
- Insurance.

The costs vary depending on how the programme is administered, either in-house or through a membership association. These two models of managing volunteers are found in other visitor attractions, although the latter is less common at zoos (Mony & Heimlich, 2008). In the first case, the programme is administered entirely in-house by paid staff. The advantage of this model is that there is direct control over the programme and the staff who administer the programme are accountable to the organisation.

In the second model, the volunteer programme is administered by a separate but related organisation, such as a membership association or friends' group, as is the case at Perth Zoo below. The membership association will have its own constitution and the volunteer programme will be administered by members of the association, rather than zoo employees, although the association may also employ its own staff. The association will be governed by a committee elected from the members, so volunteers are managing each other. Membership associations charge a membership fee and are more likely than in-house programmes to try and recover the costs of a volunteer programme from participants. The advantages of the association model are that it can save the zoo money in terms of staffing, insurance and training. The disadvantage of this model is that the zoo may have less control over the membership association and therefore the volunteers, their recruitment and training.

The zoo will need to establish and maintain a good working relationship with their membership association.

Volunteering frequently involves costs for the volunteers. This is partly as the zoo or membership association seek to reduce their own costs by recovering these from the volunteers. In addition to travel to and from the attraction, volunteers may be required to purchase a uniform, pay for their training and training materials and pay an annual fee to belong to the volunteer association, if the programme is operated separately. The costs to volunteers can vary; for example, volunteers at Vancouver Aquarium pay CND$40 for their training, training manual and volunteer t-shirt. By contrast, a two-week internship, volunteering four hours each day at Buenos Aires Zoo costs US$1155. The internship does, however, include all accommodation, food and training for the duration. Ongoing research by the authors suggests that while not all volunteers are willing to pay for their costs (such as training or uniform fees), volunteers are more accepting of charges associated with the programme when it is administered by a voluntary association on behalf of the zoo, rather than by the zoo directly. Compared to other visitor attractions, zoos appear more likely to try and recover their costs from volunteers, although some successfully attract sponsorship for their volunteer programmes. The Zoo Friends Volunteers at Taronga Zoo, Sydney, have been sponsored by Clearview Retirement Solutions, for example, which reflects the predominant age of the volunteers.

The costs of volunteering can be a deterrent, with a survey by Volunteering Australia (2007) revealing that 1 in 10 volunteers had stopped or reduced their volunteering involvement in the past year due to the costs of participating. Good practice in volunteer management states that volunteers should not be left out-of-pocket by the organisation, although 88% of volunteers surveyed by Volunteering Australia (2007) incurred out-of-pocket expenses that were not reimbursed. The Chicago Zoological Society notes that in cases of financial hardship, the fees for the volunteer programme can be waived.

If volunteers are covering their own costs and giving their time, then they are making a double contribution to the organisation. It should be noted, however, that zoos will only be able to charge volunteers if the volunteers are willing to shoulder these costs. Some volunteers will view this as a further donation to the zoo, in addition to their time. This is common at other attractions where volunteers do not claim back legitimate out-of-pocket expenses, as they see this as an additional contribution to the organisation or cause (Holmes, 2003). It is also, perhaps, a testimony of the popularity of zoo volunteering that there are sufficient volunteers willing to pay their own expenses, although these costs may act as a barrier to some potential recruits. If existing volunteers are unhappy with the financial costs, then they may leave, even if other parts of their experience are positive.

Case Study: Perth Zoo Docent Association

Perth Zoo opened in 1898 and now houses approximately 1100 animals from 190 different species. The zoo attracts more than 620,000 visitors a year, predominantly from the Perth metropolitan area and the wider state of Western Australia. As with many zoos, the focus has changed since its inception, from entertainment to education and conservation, and the zoo is involved in significant scientific research and captive breeding programmes for threatened species.

Background on the volunteer programme

The Perth Zoo Docent Association was formed in 1982 and was inspired by the zoo's then chief executive officer's (CEO) visit to Washington Zoo in the USA, which had an extensive docent programme. This also explains the adoption of the American term 'docent' to describe the volunteers. The programme started with 54 volunteers, recruited in two cohorts; it was initially managed in-house and somewhat *ad hoc*. By the early1990s, the separate membership association model was adopted; this is described as a partnership approach between Perth Zoo and the Docent Association. The association now has approximately 300 docent members and membership is kept below 350 to ensure that every volunteer will be able to complete sufficient shifts to meet their commitment of two days a month and also maintain their interest. The Docent Association is managed by a committee, composed of officers elected annually from the membership for a maximum period of two years. The president and vice-president meet regularly with the zoo's delegated staff liaison and the zoo's CEO and also liaise with the visitor services team.

Who volunteers?

The volunteer profile is described as 'ageing', although this is in common with visitor attractions more widely. This is partly due to the demands of the volunteer role, as volunteers are needed on site during the week as well as at weekends, which is limiting for those in full-time work. Volunteers in flexible, part-time work or who are self-employed can fit volunteering around their paid work more easily. Many docents choose to start volunteering when they retire. Indeed, the decision to volunteer is frequently associated with a change in people's lives, including bereavement, children leaving home and retirement and the opportunity to do something for oneself, instead of work or the family.

One docent, for example, stated that volunteering was 'something I promised myself I'd do when I retired'.

Volunteer roles

The primary aim of the docent programme is to support the zoo by providing more 'bodies' on the ground, which not only enhances the visitor experience, but also relieves paid staff for other work. Docents' main roles are to:

- Staff the visitor centre.
- Take guided tours.
- Engage with visitors as they undertake their duties in the zoo.

Most zoo docents have little or no direct contact with the animals and this is specified on the Docent Association flyer, which states that 'If you are looking for voluntary work where you will have regular contact with animals, or can feed animals or clean enclosures, then becoming a Docent will not give you the job satisfaction you deserve'. There are other duties available to volunteers, including observing animals' behaviour for the keepers; assisting with special events; giving talks to outside groups (the Zoo to You programme); and some special duties such as walking the dingoes. These special duties involving animals are particularly popular. Docents are also involved in behind-the-scenes activities, including animal enrichment programmes, fundraising and maintaining the zoo archives.

Similar to other zoos, volunteer docents are recruited once a year as they must participate in a training programme. The training programme takes place once a week over a 10-week period and docents can miss a maximum of one session. This training programme is more onerous than at some other zoos, although as most individuals volunteer at the zoo because of an interest in animals, the training programme can be seen as an important motivator and reward. Volunteers admitted that the training programme was demanding, particularly the requirement to practice public speaking and give presentations in front of other trainees, with one volunteer describing the programme as 'stressful' and another saying 'the first four or five weeks of training is actually quite challenging'.

A potential problem with such an intensive programme is that it can raise the new volunteers' expectations of what their role will be once on the ground at the zoo. While docents give tours, some volunteers complained that they felt that they were often involved in little more than crowd control and giving directions to the toilets. An advantage of having only one intake of volunteers each year is that they complete a training programme together and build up a social world with their cohort, which makes the experience more enjoyable and can assist with retention. The average retention rate was described as between seven and eight years, although this varies across cohorts. For example, there are three volunteers from the 52 recruited in 1982 still active at the zoo over 25 years later. By contrast, only 11 out of 38 volunteers from the 2002 cohort are still involved.

Costs and benefits of the programme

The majority of the costs are born by the docents themselves and the Docent Association. Volunteers pay an annual membership fee, currently AUD\$40, a one-off fee of AUD\$75 to cover their 10-week training programme and manual and they also purchase their own uniform, although one uniform piece (their shirt) is provided by the zoo. The costs are explained at the start and are not hidden; one docent commented that 'nobody seems to mind' about the expenses, but these do not include lunch or travel costs either. In addition to these regular costs, members of the Docent Committee also bear costs such as telephone calls and travel associated with their committee role. The Docent Committee also take on substantial administrative roles, such as organising the annual training programme and the roster. In addition to the committee members, a number of docents also assist as coordinators for various parts of the volunteer programme, such as training. Scheduling the roster can be one of the most time-consuming jobs associated with a volunteer programme (Holmes & Smith, 2009), so the docent programme not only frees up staff time from dealing with visitors but also on the managerial side.

As noted above, a volunteer programme is not a free service. The costs to Perth Zoo for the docent programme are staff time (0.3 of the visitor services coordinator full-time position), administrative and strategic support for the Docent Association, and the Docent Lodge. As well as a members room, kitchen, toilet and shower facilities for on-duty docents to take a break while at the zoo, the Docent Lodge provides storage, an activity room and a committee room. Other direct costs associated with the programme include rewards and incentives, such as free entry to the zoo for all docents plus up to three guests, discounts in the zoo shop and cafeteria and other rewards throughout the year. Zoo staff also contribute to the docent training programme and the zoo pays the cost of police clearance checks for all docents.

The docents describe their role as one of partnership with the keepers, by acting as the public face of the zoo, and answering the more basic questions about facilities or animals. For example, 'where are the toilets?' 'has that animal had any babies?' and 'how long has it been at the zoo?' and the volunteers' role can be as much about welcoming visitors as providing a sense of security for lost children. The zoo docents also identified a range of personal benefits from their volunteering. They described arriving at the zoo, as escaping from their other commitments such as paid work and family: 'I walk into the zoo, it's a bit like going on holiday because the rest of your life drops away as you walk through the gate'. Overall, volunteers described their day at the zoo as physically tiring but in other ways, relaxing. The docents pride themselves on offering a professional service, which their wearing of a uniform contributes towards. However, the demands of the role can become onerous and some volunteers reported that they felt that the Docent Committee can make unrealistic demands on the docents, expecting them to put the zoo before their paid work and family commitments. This may be because volunteering at the zoo is more regimented compared to other volunteer programmes. The Docent Committee does, however, adhere to operating procedures as set down in their Procedures Manual, for which any changes are put to a vote by the Docent Association membership at the annual general meeting.

Evidence from the interviews with docents at Perth Zoo shows that while volunteering is demanding, e.g. during the initial training programme and in the expected ongoing commitment, volunteering is also an enjoyable activity, providing an escape from the demands of everyday life. As zoo docents, the volunteers build a different relationship with the zoo compared to everyday visitors, as they get to see 'behind-the-scenes', have access to the knowledge of paid staff, such as keepers, and can take part in special events, only available to docents. For example, docents sometimes have breakfasts at the zoo, which means they can visit the animals before normal opening hours and one of the volunteer rewards includes a raffle prize to be 'keeper for a day', a chance for a behind-the-scenes experience with animals and paid staff, which is rarely available for regular visitors.

The benefits to Perth Zoo are quantified in their annual report as contributing 42,418 hours of service in 2006–2007, equivalent to approximately 18 full-time paid staff for an organisation with 155 full-time employed staff over the same period. The Perth Zoo docents also fundraise for the zoo and in 2006–2007 raised AUD$45,500 to help build the new Sun Bear exhibit and bring two rescued bears to Perth (Zoological Parks Authority, 2007). However, there are significant benefits beyond the financial savings and fundraising efforts of the docents, with one volunteer summarising these as:

> We're there, we're out on the grounds, we answer the visitors' questions, we are there to notice things, we can report things to security or to [visitor] services and we generally provide information, we do animal watches so we help the keepers to a certain extent. We also raise quite a lot of money for them.

Summary of case study

The Perth Zoo Docent Programme is typical of zoo volunteer schemes where volunteers are involved in interpretation and visitor service roles, as well as behind-the-scenes. As with many zoo programmes, they clearly advertise the lack of animal contact, and when opportunities for direct animal interaction do arise, these are highly prized. Over 25 years, the Perth Zoo Docent Programme has evolved from an in-house to a separate membership association model. The Docent Association operates in partnership with Perth Zoo. While this transfers many of the operational elements of managing the volunteer programme to the association, zoo management and staff remain actively involved through regular meetings, contributions to training and supervision of volunteers. These are all costs to the zoo that must be set against the benefits volunteers bring to the organisation, its visitors and even the animals. New volunteers follow a demanding training programme, which requires motivation and commitment as well as a small financial investment in training and uniform. Ongoing costs include membership fees and other expenses, and these expenses need to be balanced by a range of personal benefits. Volunteers are expected and appear willing to bear the costs of volunteering; as one volunteer reflected: 'It is expensive to become a docent, competitive and hard work to stay one'.

Conclusion

Volunteers play a central role within many zoos. Volunteer interpreters, guides and docents are perhaps the most visible roles, but volunteers also donate their time to support the zoo behind-the-scenes, as well as offsite in outreach and fundraising roles. Despite their importance to zoos and the popularity of many zoo volunteer programmes, researchers have largely overlooked zoo volunteering, although it has parallels with volunteering in other types of visitor attractions. All volunteering should be a reciprocal and mutually beneficial relationship. Understanding the costs and benefits of volunteering to various stakeholders can help establish the relative value of volunteering to each. Each of these points has been illustrated with the case study of the Perth Zoo Docent Programme.

There is also evidence that volunteering at a visitor attraction is a progression from being simply a frequent visitor (Holmes & Edwards, 2008). The volunteer programme may therefore cannibalise other audience segments, rather than reaching new audiences. The research at Perth Zoo, however, found that few of the docents had been frequent visitors to the zoo before they became volunteers. Zoo volunteer programmes may also contribute to audience development by offering an alternative means for the public to engage with the zoo.

Importantly, this chapter has clearly demonstrated that volunteering is not 'free labour' and the zoo organisation and individual volunteers both bear costs to balance the various benefits of volunteering. Zoos can manage their volunteer programme in-house or through a partnership with a membership association, and in each model the costs of volunteering can be partly transferred to volunteers, although this has to be balanced and making volunteering too expensive can act as a barrier to participation and may limit the diversity of volunteers. The wider benefits of volunteering, to visitors and communities, are less well researched within a zoo context, but are important nonetheless and warrant further studies.

Chapter 14

I Can't Look: Disgust as a Factor in the Zoo Experience

NANCY CUSHING AND KEVIN MARKWELL

Introduction

On the typical zoo website, the viewer's gaze is returned by an endearing animal. Melbourne Zoo's website features an apparently smiling elephant; an entreating lemur is posted by the Bronx Zoo; at London Zoo, a red panda plays peek-a-boo with the viewer; and representing Singapore Zoo, an orangutan cuddles her baby. These images manifest the conventional emphasis in zoo marketing on animals, which evoke positive emotions in visitors. Amusement, empathy and aesthetic appreciation fit easily with an important motivation of most zoo visitors: experiencing a fun day out with the family. But not all animals in the zoo readily elicit positive emotional responses. Reptiles and many invertebrates, such as spiders, are commonly viewed as repulsive rather than attractive and yet reptiles, in particular, are often an important component of zoo collections. These animals play a distinctive role, expanding the opportunities for emotional responses to include squeamishness, disgust, revulsion, fear and aversion, thereby contributing to the pastiche of experiences that result in a memorable visit. However, the evocation of negative emotions must be interrogated to assess its impact on claims that zoos help to develop empathy and a conservation ethos within their visitors (Frost & Roehl, 2008).

The provision of opportunities for visitors to experience negative emotions has received little attention in the literature on captive animal displays. In this chapter, we focus on the emotion of disgust, especially as it is linked with reptiles and spiders, drawing on observation-based research conducted in a privately owned Australian wildlife park. The Australian continent is distinctive in that reptiles and spiders are the only indigenous terrestrial animals, apart from perhaps the dingo, which pose a real threat to human life. It may be the case that the disgust response to such animals in Australia is accentuated in comparison with that in other places because of well-founded caution with these animals based on personal experience and folk wisdom. However, as will be discussed below, disgust is not the same as fear and should not be confused with it. In addition, as Nussbaum has shown, disgust has considerable transcultural overlap (Nussbaum, 2004). The Australian experience holds relevance for the experiences of other nationalities, especially as zoos must take into account the tastes and sensitivities of local and international tourist markets in planning their exhibits and programmes.

Theorising disgust

Disgust is a basic emotion that is closely interrelated with other negative emotions, such as revulsion and aversion, and is specifically linked with animals and their products. Indeed, one definition of disgust is 'a shrinking from contamination that is associated with the human desire to be non animal' (Nussbaum, 2004: 74). The disgust response is intense and visceral, creating the bodily responses of creeping flesh, nausea, the wrinkling of the nose and drawing up of the upper lip. The disgusted person turns away from the offending sight or smell, driven by a desire to avoid all contact and to minimise cognisance of that which is perceived as disgusting. Disgust is an aversion not just to the physical touch of an entity, but to its essence. Objects of disgust are viewed as contagious, transferring their unwanted properties to things with which they are associated and affecting people through sights or smells and, less often, sounds. In one experiment, subjects who found spiders disgusting were unwilling to write with a pen across which a spider had walked (Woody *et al.*, 2005). This contamination effect means that disgust may well be a stronger factor in the zoo visit than fear (although not as strong as a phobia) because the measures put in place to secure the physical separation between people and animals neutralise the potential physical danger of zoo animals, whereas disgust operates independently of physical contact. Disgust is a powerful and essentially negative emotion, likely to have some evolutionary role that encourages humans to be both alert to and avoid substances like blood, mucus and faeces, or animals that could be harmful to them.

Disgust is paradoxical, however, in that at the same time as we are repelled by the object of disgust, it fascinates us. Disgust makes us super vigilant, watching carefully for disgusting traits in ourselves and others; surreptitiously studying these traits when we do identify them. We look away, but then cannot help but look again. The attraction of the repellent could be inherent. Nussbaum (2004) speculates that the culturally determined disgust response could have evolved precisely to warn humans away from things that are attractive but could be dangerous. Alternatively, the fascination could be a product of certain objects or actions having been deemed disgusting and therefore forbidden. As Miller (1997: 17) argues, 'Disgust shocks, entertains by shocking, and sears itself into memory'. The engaged observation that zookeepers wish to promote in their visitors can be delivered by a disgust response.

The use of disgust as a means of engaging the interest of the zoo visitor is rarely discussed in the literature. While emotional responses are increasingly displacing the focus on didacticism in zoos, it is the positive emotions that bond people and animals that have received most attention. Of disgust and its fellow negative emotions, much less is written. This is not surprising. Even Miller (1997), the legal historian whose book, *The Anatomy of Disgust*, firmly established the topic of disgust within the Humanities, included a justification of his scholarly interest in the topic as it was so often perceived with discomfort among his family and his peers. Another factor specific to the zoo context may be that zoo staff do not share the disgust response of visitors. One study of the impact of feeding lions and tigers live fish or carcass meat, in this case whole horse leg bones, claimed that this dietary enrichment would enhance the visitor experience because the animals exhibited more hunting behaviours (Bashaw *et al.*, 2003). However, this study offered no discussion of the potential disgust response in visitors to viewing these meals. Through repeated exposure, an understanding of the biology and behaviour of the species in question and their own personal commitment to animal welfare, animals' waste products, sexual activity, feeding habits and bodies do not offend those who interact with them on a daily basis.

Disgust in the animal viewing experience

Although few seem to want to admit the role of disgust in the zoo context, its paradoxical appeal is openly harnessed elsewhere in contemporary society. This appeal of the disgusting is evidenced by the flowering of disgust-evoking images and scenarios deployed in feature films, news reportage and reality television (Miller, 1997). Dark or thanatourism similarly serves to evoke disgust among other negative emotions as it taps into a curiosity about, and at some level, enjoyment of a range of sites that have been the location of some form of human atrocity or tragedy. As one visitor in his review of the London Dungeon commented, 'At the London Dungeon you will experience the *thrill of disgust* at the true horror London can offer' (Virtual Tourist, 2005; emphasis added).

Looking specifically at disgust responses linked with animals, the film genre opens a range of possibilities. Many of the first films of animals in the early 20th century featured the killing of animals in cock fights, slaughter houses and on safari (Horak, 2006). More recently, there is a wealth of evidence of disgust's effectiveness for creating interest on the video-sharing website, YouTube. These videos are generally either excerpts from documentaries that have been made for television or privately produced 'home videos'. Videos posted on YouTube show graphic and gruesome fights between all manner of animals, such as 'mother cougar vs grizzly bear' (4,266,167 views – all views listed here are as of 19 May 2009), 'crocodile fight to the death' (933,470 views) and 'crocodile vs tiger' (625,241 views). Fights between invertebrates were also popular, such as 'giant centipede vs tarantula' (1,277,016 views). Snakes swallowing other animals appear to be another popular 'genre' and so, for example, 'snake swallows a hippo', which showed a large python harried into regurgitating a baby hippopotamus, recorded a staggering 7,619,982 views; 'snake eats boy', in which animation was incorporated into a video showing a young boy with his large pet python, attracted 5,224,617 views. A series of videos features the feeding of live mice, rats and chickens to captive reptiles, including, e.g. 'python eats bird alive' (853,343 views). Many of these videos have elicited strongly worded negative reactions, manifesting disgust, from viewers. For example, these are some of the 10,654 comments associated with the video 'python eats bird alive':

- You can still hear the chick chirping from the inside! How fucking sick.
- Stop whining about that someone filmed this... It's just how the world looks like and you can learn something from this vid.
- Cruel bastard.
- TO EVERY ONE WHO DOESN'T LIKE THIS VIDEO...WHY THE FUCK DO YOU CLICK ON A VIDEO NAMED 'PYTHON EATS BIRD ALIVE'?

The recorded number of viewings shows that there is a large audience for videos that feature actions involving animals, which are construed by many as being in bad taste, disgusting or revolting. The contradictory nature of disgust is shown in the critical comments left by viewers who elected to watch the video, characteristically named in a highly unambiguous way, perhaps anticipating that they would indeed be disgusted by what they saw. People are attracted to what also revolts them.

YouTube provides a 21st century setting for a practice with a long history. From its beginnings in Ancient Egypt, the desire to look at wild animals in captivity has been strong and enduring (Kisling, 2001; Baratay & Hardouin-Fugier, 2002; Hanson, 2002; Rothfels, 2002; Bulbeck, 2005), but this enduring desire has not been based solely on an appreciation for and empathy with the animals on display. Indeed, it could be argued that such empathic emotions are relatively recent and that other emotional responses, such as domination, control (Tuan, 1984), revulsion and disgust, formed the basis of this long-lasting attraction. As human societies became more ordered, civilised and subdued, animals were used as a register of progress. Just as disgust between humans is used to elevate the self above those of lesser status in terms of class, gender, caste or race (Miller, 1997; Nussbaum, 2004), the observation of animals performing acts that humans no longer carried out in public, allowed humans to reaffirm their superiority and distinctiveness from beasts. Europe's commercial menageries of the 18th and 19th centuries did not turn their profits on animals that looked soft, caring or vulnerable, but on those that triggered the most negative emotional responses, such as fear, revulsion and disgust. Wild and exotic animals, such as big cats and elephants, were exhibited alongside malformed domesticated animals, such as two-headed calves and human 'freaks' (Preece, 1993; Kisling, 2001). The mobilisation of negative emotions continued unabated well into the 20th century in the sectors of live animal displays, which were overtly orientated to entertainment. Circuses harnessed the power of fear when they dramatised the ferocity of their lions and the bravery and skill of the lion tamer who dared to risk putting his head between their jaws.

While it persisted in animal entertainment, disgust was submerged in the zoological gardens of the 19th century as the increasing rationality of the Victorian era was applied to the viewing of animals. Haphazard arrangements were replaced by presentation by scientific nomenclature with captive animals as living exemplars of the natural order. In keeping with this scientific frame, animals were displayed in minimalist and easily cleaned concrete cages with metal bars, feeding took place behind the scenes and animals were housed individually or in pairs to avoid unwanted interactions (Hanson, 2002; Bulbeck, 2005). Instead of building disgust or fear of animals, anthropomorphic treatments, such as chimpanzee tea parties, and anthropocentric activities, such as elephant rides, encouraged visitors to think of animals as part of a natural order ruled over by more highly evolved human beings. Vining (2003) argues that the rise in the keeping of pets and animal welfare movements of the same period similarly reflected the idea that superior humans had the duty to treat animals humanely, that is in a human not an animalistic fashion. An element of the superiority of human beings was the ability to control animals' capacity to disgust.

As the 20th century proceeded, zoos once again reorientated themselves, this time to simulations of the natural and we posit that disgust began its revival. In imitation of Hagenbeck's arrangement of his zoological garden outside Hamburg, Germany, in 1907, animals were positioned within zoos by their continent of origin within enclosures designed to mimic their native habitat. In these naturalistic settings, there was an increasing emphasis on encouraging natural behaviours in the animals and consequently exposing visitors to them. Social animals were permitted to live in groups that interacted in animal-like ways, including aggressively and sexually. Feeding was brought into the open and objects introduced to enrich the experience of animals, leaving enclosures littered with toys and uneaten food. In effect, visitors were increasingly permitted entry into the private space of animals, the space humans keep to ourselves, where we eat, groom ourselves, pass wastes and have sex. This violation of the usual rules of privacy leads to a disgust response for some visitors: averting eyes from the heaps of elephant dung dotting their enclosure or moving on when the kangaroos become amorous, while for others it leads to a fascinating opportunity to observe aspects of life that are taboo among humans. According to Weller (1998: 119), 'the lewd antics of the orangutans enable us to affirm and confirm our humanness'.

Reptiles and Disgust

Rather than allowing disgust to operate only on this passive level of covert observation of quotidian animal behaviour, some captive animal displays mobilise this emotional response in deliberate ways. Reptiles have proven to be very suitable for this purpose. Even the word reptile or reptilian when applied to humans suggests grovelling, mean or malignant behaviour. Snakes in particular are commonly regarded with a revulsion that goes well beyond the fear of the capacity of some of them to do actual harm through their venomous bites. People recoil from snakes; tell tall tales about them; kill them and display their bodies as trophies. Snakes are often assumed to possess many of the traits that Miller (1997) lists as most likely to elicit disgust: they are viewed as slimy, sticky, slithery, wriggly, oily and viscid. Irksome to many when viewed singly, the disgust response is heightened when they are seen en masse in the seething unruly throng of a snake pit.

Reptile shows continued to profit from disgust even when rationalism ruled the zoo. Reptile handlers, known as 'snakeys', travelled Australian show circuits in the late 19th and early 20th centuries, thrilling viewers with their bravery in handling venomous snakes and often attempting to sell snakebite cures (Cann, 2001). Snake shows continued in more permanent snake or reptile parks, like the Snake Park in Adelaide, opened in 1927. Visitors were entertained by snake handling demonstrations, and could watch, at 4.00 every afternoon, as 'the giant python [was] offered its substantial meal' (Anon, 1927), no doubt evoking feelings of disgust and fascination within the audience. Opened to the public in 1959, the Australian Reptile Park at Gosford on the NSW Central Coast became the leading reptile attraction in Australia. The expressions on the faces of visitors to the Reptile Park as they watched its founder, Eric Worrell, milk venom from a large, writhing snake were captured in photographs that provided the inspiration for the writing of this chapter. Worrell milked the snakes for the Commonwealth Serum Laboratory in Melbourne, where their venom was used in the production of antivenom. Worrell could easily have carried out the whole process behind the closed doors of his own laboratory, but he recognised the power of disgust to attract and hold visitors. While it drew a weekly crowd of rapt onlookers, this showmanship possibly worked against his other aim of increasing the acceptance of snakes as an important part of Australian ecosystems.

As he built up the park, Worrell introduced other species that could be used to entertain his visitors. Starting with a few individuals presented as a gift by Taronga Zoo director, Edward Hallstrom, a large collection of American alligators was established, including two very large animals christened Edward and Edwina. A performance based on the hand feeding of the alligators was held on Saturday afternoons during spring and summer from the early 1970s. This dramatic event involved the keeper being chased around a small island by the two hungry alligators with mouths agape while he threw fish in their direction. The sound of the jaws snapping shut was surprisingly loud and added an extra dimension to the drama of the performance. Next, the keeper entered a large enclosure to feed upwards of 40 alligators, ranging in size from just over 1 metre to 3 metres. The construction of a feeding 'jetty' in the early 1980s not only increased the safety aspects for the keepers involved, but also enhanced the viewer appeal of the performance as the alligators leaped out of the water, mouths open wide and bodies thrashing as they sought the morsels of fish and chicken being offered to them. With little or no information provided about the biology, ecology or conservation status of the alligators, such performances were explicitly entertaining and evoked a range of emotions in onlookers, including disgust and revulsion, at the appearance and behaviours of the alligators as they chomped through the eviscerated bodies of fish and chickens.

The need to attract visitors by offering entertaining spectacles saw the spread of such performances to public and private zoos in the 1980s. Trying to focus on serious scientific and conservation endeavours while keeping paying visitors coming through the gate posed a challenge for the zoo industry and many feared the idea of following museums down the route to Disneyfication and inauthenticity as they introduced membership schemes, sought sponsorships, expanded retailing and opened themselves up for new activities, such as weddings, birthday parties and concerts. Harnessing disgust simply by showcasing certain aspects of animals' natural behaviours offered a solution, because visitors could be entertained without expensive interventions or the need to make animals behave in uncharacteristic ways.

Zoos have been creative in repackaging their collections to induce a wider range of emotional responses. 'Zoo sex' tours have become a feature of the educational programmes of some zoos, such as the Australian Reptile Park (Australian Reptile Park, 2005) and San Francisco Zoo (Yollin, 2006). A common means of engaging visitors and one related to the disgust response is the feeding of carnivores. Feeding offers sights and sounds that are disgusting for visitors, who rarely witness the 'uncivilised' bone crunching and flesh ripping consumption of a wild animal. While the big cats serve as the archetype of such displays, the smaller but pugnacious and vocal Tasmanian devils provide a spectacular feeding show at some Australian zoos. At one park, visitors gasp and contort their faces as blood sprays from euthanised rats fed to these animals. The same park also offers the devils whole legs of road-killed kangaroos that are tied to a rope suspended from a log in the enclosure, thus requiring the devils to tug, yank and tear the flesh away from the skin and bone. At a Tasmanian conservation park, visitors can observe devils fighting over their food at a feeding station four times a day, with the devils 'snarling and doing what they do best, crushing up bones and generally being, well, devilish' (Tasmanian Devil Conservation Park, 2009). Such displays of carnivorous animal feeding, show the power and strength of the animal and give visitors a better understanding of the ecological role that these animals play. The animals' behaviour might be perceived as disgusting, yet it is fascinating and informative.

Disgust is a powerful force and there are legal and ethical limits on its application to live animal displays. The feeding of live vertebrates to captive animals, for example, is illegal in some countries, although fish and rodents are sometimes exempted and the practice is considered more acceptable when carnivores are being prepared for reintroduction to the wild. A visitor survey in the UK found that most respondents would find live feeding objectionable unless it was limited to invertebrates. The significance of disgust in the construction of this opinion was evident from visitors' statements that they would have fewer objections to off-exhibit use of live prey, signalling that it was their own reaction, not concern for the welfare of the prey animals, which determined their attitude (Ings, 1997). The response to allegations that some Chinese zoos offer visitors the opportunity to watch as lions attack and feed on cows or goats or to buy live chickens to feed to tigers (McDermott, 2006), is indicative that such a scenario would be unacceptable on several grounds, including disgust, in western zoos.

Managing Disgust

The mobilisation of disgust is a dangerous game. On the one hand, disgust is a basic human emotion that cannot be fully excluded from the zoo experience and it can be an effective tool in encouraging engagement with animals. This was noted in an observational study at the Australian Reptile Park. During 26 hours of observation time over a five-week period in the summer of 2007/2008 (Markwell, 2009), the reptile with the longest 'viewing time' was a large reticulated python, with an average viewing time of 37 seconds ($n = 63$). The python elicited the most audible and observable response in visitors, depending in part on how it had arranged itself in its enclosure. When it was positioned with its enormous girth and long length observable and its large head visible, it prompted exclamations of disbelief, amazement, revulsion and disgust. Indicative comments included, 'Holy hell, look at the size of it!', 'Oh my godfather!', 'OH MY GOD!' or 'That's just disgusting, that over there'. Another animal that elicited strong, often negative, emotional responses was a large alligator snapping turtle, which many would regard as grotesque in appearance with its large hooked beak-like mouth containing a worm-like lure to attract passing fish. Visitors who commented about the animal to other members of their group generally remarked that the animal was 'disgusting' or 'revolting'. The feeding of dead mice and rats to the snakes also provoked strong reactions from visitors. While no systematic count was made, a large proportion of these reactions was negative and frequently the word 'disgusting' was employed. While some of those who were clearly disgusted quickly moved on to another exhibit, many in fact stayed to watch the snakes swallow their prey. The experience of disgust and revulsion, for at least some visitors, creates a thrill and contributes to satisfaction with the experience. Detachment, boredom and apathy are not consistent with feelings of disgust. It is the type of charged moment of heightened awareness when deep learning can occur (Dirkx, 2001), and indeed, according to Tilden (1957: 9), effective interpretation must incorporate some form of provocation: 'the chief aim of interpretation is not instruction but provocation'. Uzzell and Ballantyne (2005) have also argued for interpretation to embrace the affective domain and not to shy away from topics that might evoke strong emotional responses in visitors.

Among these emotional responses, disgust can heighten awareness and trigger deep learning, but this learning is likely to be negative. Muris *et al.* (2008) cite numerous studies that have shown that the triggering of a disgust response can be linked with the development of anxiety, fear and even phobias about the object of the disgust, especially when that object is an animal. Nussbaum (2004) shows that disgust is used as a means of oppressing vulnerable individuals or groups in society by associating them with disgusting characteristics, such as foulness, bad smells and decay. Animals that are regarded with disgust generally occupy a similar position as expendable vermin or enemies of humans that should be killed on sight. In the case of the reptile exhibition described above, some visitors, particularly men, expressed negative views. One thought the snakes 'looked mean', and a few mentioned how much they 'hated these bastards'. Some men recounted stories of having killed snakes that wandered into their backyards. These in-grained attitudes seemed to be confirmed rather than challenged by close observation. What this means for the zoo mission of encouraging caring about animals and their ecosystems is untested – there are few studies of relationships between caring and emotion in the context of zoos (Vining, 2003), but clearly emphasising the elements of animals that evoke a disgust response, without appropriate and sensitive interpretation, will not encourage visitors to develop a sense of fellowship with them or become advocates for their cause. Visitors are unlikely to extend their circle of moral responsibility to include animals if what they are shown of them induces disgust.

This issue has been grappled with by the Australian Reptile Park in the case of their collection of spiders. Disgust, revulsion and even fear are common responses to spiders; and according to Gerdes *et al.* (2009), spider phobia is the most common animal phobia (Figure 14.1). Their study found that spiders cause much more pronounced negative responses in respondents than insects do, such as bees that envenomate humans more frequently. They attribute this response to a range of causes, including an evolutionary bias to spider avoidance, culturally transmitted ideas about spiders and disease transmission and spiders' unpredictable and un-controllable movements. Such negative perceptions might also be under-pinned by the fact that the body of the spider, like the body of the snake, is so *unlike* the body of the human (Desmond, 1999), and that this bodily difference positions these animals as alien, threatening and, indeed, disgusting. The Reptile Park has held a large number of Sydney funnel web spiders since the 1960s in order to supply venom to the Common-wealth Serum Laboratory. The initial funnel web exhibit emphasised the

Figure 14.1 Tarantula exhibit at Victoria Bug Zoo, Canada. (Photo: Stephen Frost)

threat that these deadly spiders posed to human life and the involvement of the park in the life-saving work of helping to produce an antivenom. More recently, the park has acquired an impressive array of other native and exotic spiders. Instead of the usual naturalistic presentation, when developing a display in the late 1990s, park management chose to show the spiders in a somewhat theatrical setting that would challenge the negative emotions many visitors display towards spiders.

The entrance to this 'Spider World' is enlivened by a rap-singing animatronic funnel web spider, called 'Syd', who encourages visitors to overcome their reluctance to enter a spider exhibit with a song beginning, 'Welcome to my parlour. Won't you come a little farther?' The exhibit deliberately employs an anthropomorphic approach in engaging the visitor's interest and attention. It mixes displays of live spiders with a 3-metre high representation of a funnel web spider that rears up periodically to the accompaniment of claps of thunder and lighting. Humour and whimsy are the keystones to the exhibit, although the serious business of maintaining and milking the venom from Sydney funnel web spiders is counterpoised against the more playful elements in the exhibit.

Spider World is an expensive addition to the Australian Reptile Park and will be retained for many years. More accessible measures are also available to captive animal displaying institutions that want to engage with the issue of disgust. While dramatic shows of feeding or snake milking heighten the disgust response, intimate keeper talks and handling of animals can help to overcome the disgust response. Morgan and Gramann ([1988] cited in Woods, 1998) explored this challenge in the case of snakes and found that attending a presentation in which a keeper demonstrated his or her own confidence with snakes and allowed visitors to touch snakes produced more positive attitudes towards them than simply looking at them in an exhibit. Examining the effects of Steve Irwin's public interactions with Australian reptiles, Lunney and Moon (2008) argue that his respect, even love, for these animals helped to rehabilitate them from their low status, persuading many to view them as both legitimate Australians and creatures of interest and value in their own right. They argue that his highly dramatic style, what Clive Hamilton called a 'freak show' and David Suzuki labelled a vulgarisation of environmental issues (quoted in Lunney & Moon, 2008), evident in both his television series and his live performances with animals, drew in an audience who paid little attention to nature documentaries like those of David Attenborough with their slower pace and greater detachment.

Conclusion

There is a case to be made that in order to engage a broad cross section of society with conservation issues, a wide range of communication techniques needs to be employed at captive wildlife exhibits. When used with caution, disgust is one emotion that can be harnessed for the purposes of leveraging educational value from it. In his study of how disgust operates, Miller (1997) argued that the relaxation of the disgust response signified intimacy, duty and caring between individuals. In other words, the closer people feel to others, the less disgusting they perceive the other and his or her bodily functions or waste products to be. To translate this into human–animal relations, the closer people feel to animals, the more we should accept their appearance or behaviour, no longer insisting on sharply differentiating ourselves from them and no longer perceiving them as disgusting. This effect can be seen in those who work most closely with animals, whether domestic or wild and also in attitudes to domestic pets. Even for those who are unable to overcome their disgust, the outcomes can be positive. Caring is multidimensional and can encompass a wide range of emotions (Vining, 1993). While we might be disgusted by changing a baby's nappy, the drive to nurture the next generation prevails and we complete the unpleasant task (Miller, 1997). Disgust, then, does not preclude caring. By harnessing the paradoxical attraction of the disgusting, zoos can evoke the strong emotional responses that provide the basis for affective and cognitive engagement with the objects of disgust, whether they are grotesque turtles, giant pythons or deadly spiders.

As an alternative to disregarding disgust or using it in an exploitative fashion, zoo staff need to acknowledge the existence of negative emotional responses in the visitor experience and recognise that for many visitors, some animals or aspects of their behaviour will bring about a disgust response. While powerful, these responses are neither inevitable nor immutable and through careful planning, zoo staff can use them to their interpretive and educational advantage. Contemporary demonstrations of snakes and other reptiles, carnivore feeding and spiders provide the possibility for a skilled and talented interpreter to harness the strong emotions elicited by these animals to establish a rapport and a more sympathetic appreciation of them.

We believe that more research needs to be focused on the relationships between negative emotional responses, such as disgust and revulsion to animals in captivity, in order to better understand the complex, multi-dimensional and often contradictory ways by which human visitors come to know and experience non-human animals. As we have shown, if zoos are to take their conservation role seriously, visitor feelings of disgust and revulsion should be used to help inform interpretive strategies and responses rather than being ignored or exploited for simple entertainment value.

Chapter 15
Visitor Expectations and Visit Satisfaction at Zoos

GARY CRILLEY

The Sleeping Elephant?

Given the number of visitors to zoos in developed countries, it is appropriate, if not ironic, to claim that they could be termed collectively as the 'sleeping elephants' of the biodiversity conservation movement. As an example, the Australian adult population visits zoos at similar levels to libraries, major sporting competitions and botanic gardens, but well in excess of visits to galleries, museums, theatres and pop concerts (ABS, 2007). So what are zoo visitors' motivations and expectations, particularly compared to services and visitor service? This chapter reports on recent empirical data of zoo visitors' perceptions of service quality, their profiles and their intended future behaviour. This chapter also highlights the levels of visitor awareness of key zoo roles, especially conservation and education. It concludes by examining how zoo staffs may apply information for decision making in targeted marketing, staff training and development, event programming, and specific education and engagement strategies as these relate to visitor segments and visitor services.

Bentrupperbaumer (1998) provided an excellent summary of the phenomena best referred to as the apparent innate human need for contact with plants and animals. In this text, clearly focused on viewing animals in the wild, the psychophysiological benefits from the human affiliation with animals, often referred to as the biophilia hypothesis, is argued to be most effective when experiential and in nature, as opposed to vicariously through artificial media.

Tomas *et al.* (2003) claimed that their report of service quality measures in the context of a zoological park was, to the best of their knowledge, the first such report. They may have been only partly correct, at least for a journal publication in English, given that Tian-Cole *et al.* (2002) dealt with a similar study of visitors to a wildlife refuge. However, in 1998, Bartos and Kelly (cited in Tribe, 2001) also claimed a paucity of quality evaluation information relating to the effectiveness of research projects. In a similar vein to Tomas *et al.* (2003), Fredline (2007) stated that no research had occurred in Australia regarding the motivation of so-called 'wildlife tourists' or satisfaction levels with their experience. In this study, 17% of respondents to a telephone survey ($n = 1356$) reported that their wildlife encounters had occurred in a zoo, this ranked second to 44% of reported encounters in a national park (the largest of eight response categories).

Zoo Visits and Visitors, Customers and Service

So what is important to visitors, what motivates them, what do they expect, do and say about their zoo visits and service? The Tian-Cole *et al.* (2002) study involved a theoretical model of relationships between (1) the quality of (service) performance, (2) the experience quality with (3) the overall service quality and (4) overall satisfaction, with future behavioural intentions. The key findings of Tian-Cole *et al.* (2002) included:

- Visitors' intended future behaviour was influenced by quality of performance, quality of experience, overall service quality and overall satisfaction.
- Quality of performance (on service attributes grouped as domains or factors) had the strongest total effect on behavioural intentions.
- Overall satisfaction had the second strongest effect on behavioural intentions.

Crilley and March (2003) used a similar study framework at Adelaide Zoo to explore visitor services. For service quality, 22 attributes were found to make up four underlying factors, subsequently titled 'viewing opportunities', 'staff', 'services' and 'engagement'. The ratings of importance of these dimensions by visitors, on a six point Likert-type scale from 1 (disagree) to 6 (very strongly agree), are presented in Table 15.1.

In the study by Tomas *et al.* (2003), additional emphasis was placed on the inclusion of benefits sought from a zoo visit. Among the findings of this study were:

- The two most important service quality attributes were the 'health of the animals', and 'access to viewing the animals'. These were two of the four items in the 'Wildlife' domain, one of seven domains (derived from exploratory factor analysis of 28 items).
- Visitors rated the 'Education' domain lowest in quality of performance, along with similar ratings in importance and expectations.
- There is a disconnection between the zoo's mission and the priorities of the visitors, namely, a desire for more 'family togetherness opportunities' and the 'entertaining transfer of educational material' to visitors.

This concern with the motivations of visitors, or the net benefits from their visits was also included in the Crilley and March (2003) study.

Table 15.1 Summary for adult service quality ratings, by dimensions

Dimensions of service (attributes paraphrased)	Importance
Viewing opportunities	
Ease of access	5.0
Physical comfort and pleasantness	5.1
Physical layout	5.1
Wide variety of animals	5.0
Animals appear healthy	5.4
Stimulation for animals	5.1
Displays resemble natural habitat	5.1
Staff	
Staff are friendly	5.2
Staff are responsive	5.2
Staff presentable and identifiable	5.2
Staff experienced and knowledge	5.2
Feeling of safety	5.3
Keeper talks	5.0
Interactive opportunities	4.9
Services	
Built amenities	5.2
Value for money	4.7
Food and drink facilities	4.8
Kiosk value for money	4.4
Engagement	
Learning opportunities	5.0
Informative signage	5.1
Information available	5.0
Clear directional signage	4.9

Source: After Crilley and March (2003)

Table 15.2 Desired levels for benefits

Benefits domain or dimensions	
1. Relaxing, calming and getting away from the stresses of life	5.1
2. Enjoying time with family and/or friends	5.3
3. Improving physical health	4.0
4. Learning more about nature and how to help	4.8
5. Being more productive at work/home/school	3.8

Source: Crilley and March (2003)
Note: The scale used for this part of the questionnaire ranges from 1 ('very low') to 6 ('very high').

Visitors ($n = 393$) were asked to rate their desire for a range of benefits as listed in Table 15.2.

That many zoo visits by adults are not primarily about education and conservation is evident in the range of activities visitors engage in during zoo visits. Figure 15.1 and 15.2 represent the range of activities at two Australian zoos; Adelaide Zoo in 2003, and Melbourne Zoo in 2007.

The similarity of diversity of activities undertaken at these Australian zoos, and of the similarity of findings on benefits sought by adult visitors in the Tomas *et al.* (2003) study is interesting. In their findings at Fort Worth Zoo, they found them similar to related studies in that the main benefits sought by zoo visitors were recreation, informal learning, interaction (with others) and comfort. This acknowledgement of the social element and, in particular family groups, being dominant at zoos is reflected in Figure 15.3.

Is there Satisfaction, and if so, How does it Matter?

Within the broader range of sites, events and attractions that adults visit as a recreation or leisure experience, there remains keen interest in the theories and prediction levels of a visitors' future behaviour. This is often based on the quality of service they received, the quality of the experience, the level of benefits attained from a visit, their overall satisfaction and variations of these key concepts (Crilley, 2008; de Rojas & Camarero, 2008; Tian-Cole *et al.*, 2002).

Knowing the future intentions of customers from their visit can be critical for service providers or site managers. Positive recommendations, for example, are often regarded as the most influential information affecting a potential customer's decision making (Howat *et al.*, 1999). Crilley (2005) reports that visitors' advocacy intentions for Adelaide Zoo show that 96% of respondents to the survey were willing to recommend

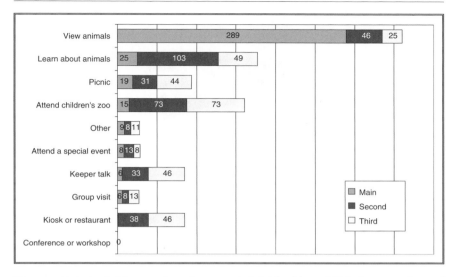

Figure 15.1 Activities undertaken at Adelaide Zoo, 2003, by number of visitors surveyed. (*Source*: Crilley & March, 2003)

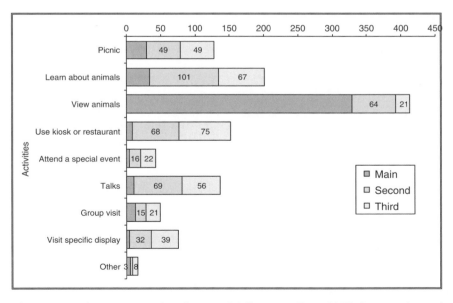

Figure 15.2 Activities undertaken at Melbourne Zoo, 2007, by number of visitors surveyed. (*Source*: Crilley *et al.*, 2007)

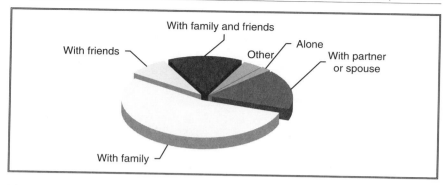

Figure 15.3 Visitors at Melbourne Zoo, 2007, for 'who did you come with?' (*Source*: Crilley *et al.*, 2007)

Table 15.3 Customer recommendations

Levels of recommendation	Adelaide Zoo (%)	Botanic Gardens (%)	Campers in protected areas (%)
Strongly recommend	45	72	63
Recommend	51	26	33
Undecided	3	2	1
Not recommend	0	1	2
Strongly not recommend	0	0	1

Source: After Crilley (2005)

the zoo to potential users (Table 15.3). Of the total number intending to recommend, 45% would 'strongly recommend', an important qualifier compared to an overall level of recommendation (such as 96% in this case). Comparative data in Table 15.3 are from studies using very similar protocols and instruments to that used in the zoo study. These studies are reported in Crilley (2005) and although comparisons need to be made with caution, this is a valid action given that each of the sites provides popular free choice recreation and learning activities.

In addition to needing to know what visitors intend to say about their visit, is the need to know if they were satisfied with the visit and the services they received. This is where the overall satisfaction scale is often used, and sometimes abused. The satisfaction with the 'what' question needs to be dealt with, be it about perceived service quality or the overall experience. Additionally, there needs to be an appreciation of how complicated the experience is for many people, given their mood state and aspects affecting them at the time of the visit, including the people with them. These influences may or may not be accounted for in the capturing of data and, therefore, the evidence needs to be interpreted with caution, assuming causal relationships. In a number of studies in Australian zoos and botanic gardens, the variation of visitors' ratings of their 'overall satisfaction with their visit', explained by a suite of service quality attributes (usually from 16 to 22), has varied considerably from 16 to 25% (Crilley & March, 2003; Crilley *et al.*, 2007). Major contributions to these relationships between service attributes and satisfaction or recommendation levels within the zoo studies have been from attributes concerning *viewing opportunities* and *stimulating activities for the animals*.

In a similar vein to the comparison of service levels across zoos and competitor sites or opportunities, is the principle of meaningful benchmarking as an input to quality management. A similar study by the author has compared the zoo visitors' level of awareness the role of zoos in educating about animal conservation. This question is not only important to people interested in the effectiveness of programmes and interpretation at zoos, but does the reported result reflect your studies, or similar? Is there something to learn from the comparison between this zoo's experience and similar studies in botanic gardens?

If visitor education is about conservation as a key role for the zoo, it is best for the visitors to know this. Visitors also need to consider the zoo's messages concerning this role and, preferably, engage in supportive behaviour informed by the messages. To not monitor, measure and compare these levels of awareness and actions is poor management and zoos could run the risk of being perceived as falling short of meeting their own objectives.

This argument for meaningful comparisons to aid good management is supported by the need to support or improve the underlying conceptual model articulated by Tian-Cole *et al.* (2002) of the relationship between service quality, benefits and future behaviour. The results in Table 15.4 clearly highlight the stronger results from zoo respondents compared to botanic garden visitors surveyed at six capital city gardens in the same year.

Further analysis of the zoo results, however, found that *unaware* males explained approximately 64% of the significant difference between the genders. Although the effect size for this result is small, further analysis indicated that *unaware males* under 30 years of age contributed most to the difference between these groups. In effect, this could be a key target group if education or branding, incorporating zoo conservation roles, is critical for the zoo.

Table 15.4 Awareness level of education and interpretation of animal/ habitat conservation as a role of the zoo and botanic gardens

	Zoo (%)	*Botanic gardens (%)*
Yes, aware	88	76
No	7	15
Unsure	6	9

Source: Crilley *et al.* (2009)

Implications for Zoo Managers and Researchers

Staffs of zoos, regardless of their roles, will normally claim that animals are their core concern. Increasingly, they are discussing the relationship between animal conservation, *in situ* and *ex situ*, and visitors to zoos. Zoo visitors, be they direct or vicarious (such as web site browsers), are fundamental to the success of the modern zoo. Their direct support through fees or membership, or indirectly through public institutions fiscal and social policy is fundamental to zoos viability.

The study of zoo visitors and, in particular, their individual characteristics, their motives for engaging with a zoo, their service expectations, their overall experience with that engagement and their future behaviour, needs more systematic and regular monitoring. These collective monitoring processes will provide input to major decision making in a wide range of local operations, from product and service provision, to marketing and staffing, to strategic policy options that include the broader scientific, social and cultural public at local and international levels. The small number of studies noted in the English literature and used in this short contribution is an encouragement for more studies to be done, and widely shared.

Part 4
Media

Media provides a wide range of images, ideas, scenarios and messages that shape tourists' expectations of zoos, other attractions, destinations and experiences. This 'image formation' may be split into two categories (Gartner, 1994). The first is 'induced', where tourism managers deliberately create and disseminate media to influence tourists' decision making. The most common example of this is an advertising campaign. The second is 'organic', where the media is created by other parties. Examples include film, books, blogs and social networking sites.

These two categories invoke conflicting notions of control and trust. Induced images are completely under the control of the tourism manager who created them and can be skilfully produced to communicate a clear and persuasive message. By contrast, organic images are created by others, tourism managers have little or no control and they may even communicate negative messages. However, potential tourists are more likely to trust and rely on organic images, reasoning that as they are independent, they are more reliable (Gartner, 1994).

In a competitive attraction marketplace, zoos rely on the media to attract visitors. Their media marketing strategies combine both induced and organic methods. The latter are particularly important as a way of stretching marketing budgets and developing engagement and trust with the public in a way that conventional advertising may not be able to achieve. In such a strategy, zoos are little different from other attractions, but they have developed quite successful tactics for gaining publicity in the media. Three methods stand out. The first is celebrity animals, particularly baby animals (a good example is Knut the polar bear, charismatic enough to make the front cover of *Vanity Fair*). The second is the celebrity zookeeper, such as Gerald Durrell, Steve Irwin and Dixon Bainbridge, charismatic (perhaps eccentric) adventurers journeying to exotic places and communicating with the public through books, television and video. The third is the increasing use of zoos as locations for reality television shows. In all these, we see the stretching of the notion of organic image formation through the cooperation of zoos with media producers in the creation of these products.

While baby animals are a sure way to get on page one of the newspapers, zoos have also been disappointed to find that stories of animal mistreatment may just as easily catapult them into the media spotlight (Hancocks, 2001 and for examples of such newspaper articles see Millar & Houston, 2008a, 2008b). In such cases, there may be heavy coverage for a short period, before some other issue gains attention (Hall, 2002; Mason *et al.*, 2005). For zoo managers, there is a paradoxical relationship with the media, often friendly and supportive, but at other times savagely critical.

There are three chapters in this section. The first by Mason examines how zoos are represented on television. Mainly focusing on 'reality' shows on British television, Mason argues that there is an interesting balancing act occurring. The aim of these productions is primarily to entertain, but they also quite regularly engage in deeper examinations of some of the issues facing modern zoos.

A similar conclusion is reached by Frost in a study of fictional media involving zoos. Starting with Winnie-the-Pooh and childrens' literature, he moves on to look at three recent feature films. His argument is that the producers operate at two levels, firstly aiming for entertainment, but secondly also attempting to apply a more critical lens to the keeping of animals in zoos and the experiences offered to visitors.

Both these chapters examine organic images. In the final chapter, White looks at induced image formation through the marketing strategies of Zoos Victoria. Operating zoos at three locations, this organisation aims to develop quite distinct badging and identity for each zoo. White also considers how Zoos Victoria (and other zoos) has recently moved into the marketing of conservation campaigns. Examples include the linking of mobile phone recycling to gorilla conservation and the campaign to change food labelling laws so that consumers may choose to help orang-utans by not purchasing products containing palm oil.

Chapter 16
Zoos and the Media

PETER MASON

The Changing Roles of Zoos

Modern zoos were founded in Europe in the middle of the 18th century and by the mid 19th century major zoos had been established in Paris, Vienna, London and Berlin (Jamieson, 1985). These zoos were similar to today's zoos in that they contained a mixture of local indigenous animals and some exotic species. Modelled largely on the European concept of a zoo, the first American zoos were set up in Cincinnati and Philadelphia in the 1870s (Jamieson, 1985). By the early 21st century, there were in excess of 10,000 zoos worldwide with most in Europe, North America and Australasia.

Shackley (1996: 114-115) suggested eight specific, yet related roles of zoos, as follows:

(1)   educating people about animals;
(2)   conserving endangered species;
(3)   safeguarding the welfare of visitors;
(4)   entertaining visitors to generate revenue;
(5)   providing visitor facilities, such as catering and merchandising;
(6)   breeding animals to halt the decline in the wild;
(7)   re-introducing captive breeds into the wild;
(8)   carrying out zoological and veterinary research to improve animal welfare in the wild and in captivity.

Bostock (1993) and Jamieson (1985) concur largely on the roles of zoos. As Jamieson (1985) indicates, there are four roles of zoos: amusement, education, scientific research and species preservation. To a great extent, these are a summary of the roles suggested by Shackley (1996). This chapter initially considers the roles of zoos based on the categorisations of Shackley (1996), Jamieson (1985) and Bostock (1993) and discusses these zoo roles in detail under the following headings: the educational role, the scientific role and the entertainment role. The chapter then considers the tourism role of zoos under the heading of 'zoos as visitor attractions'. The nature of the relationship between zoos and media is then discussed.

The Educational Role of Zoos

Zoos can be considered to be a form of museum and are similar to other types of museum in that they are essentially educational in purpose, have a professional staff, are frequently non-profit making, and own and conserve objects that are exhibited to the public (Alexander, 1979). As Alexander (1979: 99) stated, a zoo contains a collection of labelled animals to be 'studied while incidentally providing enlightenment and enjoyment'.

Shackley (1996) indicated that a major role of zoos is to provide educational experiences. Shackley claimed that a zoo's educational appeal is particularly strong among children, and children, of all visitors, often show the greatest interests in animals, but are least able to see them in their natural setting. Despite the increasing numbers of tourists who are able to travel to locations where exotic wild animals are indigenous, Shackley argued that there are still many parents who are unwilling or unable to transport their children to these places as they are generally distant from the home of the children. Under these circumstances, in which the visitors cannot be taken to the animals, then the animals have to be brought to the tourists.

Broad (1996) argued that zoos may be perceived as having a specific educational role, which can be characterised as the process of gaining knowledge about animal species. Broad suggested that zoos also have a wider educational perspective. She suggested that zoos can develop awareness of major ecological issues and hence a zoo's role is education concerned with conservation. This wider educational role is also echoed by Mason (2000) when he claimed that zoos could be viewed as significant ecotourism attractions. As Mason (2000) stated, although ecotourism has not been defined to everyone's satisfaction, for a tourism activity to be labelled in this way, key elements are that it is nature based or natural resource based, focuses on learning about nature, should contribute to conservation, is small scale, low impact and is locally orientated (Fennell, 1999). Mason (2000) argued that it is the important educational role of zoos, particularly in terms of ecological education, that makes them potentially important in terms of the aims of ecotourism.

The Scientific Role of Zoos

Zoos have a number of related scientific roles. Bostock (1993) suggested that these are as follows: taxonomic, observational, reproductive, physiological, veterinary, genetic and behavioural. Bostock indicated that zoos are also important in terms of the scientific research that they conduct. This research in zoos will be under one or more of the following headings: to add to biological knowledge, to assist care and breeding of zoo animals; to assist management and conservation; and to assist in the solution of human medical problems (Bostock, 1993).

With growing concerns for the welfare of animals in captivity, it has frequently been the scientific role of zoos that has been seen as controversial (Jamieson, 1985). The way that animals have been kept in captivity in traditional zoos has led to mounting pressure to improve conditions (Durrell, 1990). Also, some of this concern is similar to that directed at institutions using 'wild' animals in experimentation. For such people, the term 'scientific research on animals' has usually implied, from their perspective, that animals will be abused. Hence, some such people have equated animal experimentation in laboratories with animal breeding in zoos (Jamieson, 1985). Nevertheless, by the early 1990s, it was more fully understood that some zoos were involved in the conservation of severely endangered species and without them, certain animals would already be extinct and others very close to extinction (Woods, 1998).

Broad (1996) suggested that a zoo's scientific role is closely compatible with its educational role. She linked the two roles when suggesting that zoos have the capability of explaining the nature and value of ecosystems and the importance of bio-diversity. She also linked the roles when arguing that zoos can provide a very effective learning environment.

The Entertainment Role of Zoos

Bostock (1993) argued that most visitors go to zoos to be entertained and a zoo's entertainment role is its most important. Certainly, the earliest zoos were little more than menageries that provided entertainment for visitors (Mason, 1999, 2008). Here, the entertainment factor was often enhanced by official guides, or the visitors themselves, instigating 'dangerous' wild animals, who were safely behind bars, to act as they would in the wild. Hence, provoking big cats to roar and strike was very much part of the entertainment for the 19th-century zoo visitor.

As recently as the late 20th century, Shackley (1996) reported that 'big cats' are the main attraction for zoo visitors in the UK (particularly for males), which she argued is a hangover from these earlier attitudes. She claimed that entertainment for wealthy 19th-century men would include the use of rifles to shoot these animal species in the wild. Today, cameras may have replaced rifles, but zoos still provide a location where 'dangerous' wild animal, despite being tamed and kept behind bars, can be approached closely, and provide excitement for visitors. It is this proximity to a real 'wild' animal that provides the opportunity for entertainment and as Birney (1988) claimed, living animals generate excitement and enthusiasm.

Despite zoos containing 'dangerous' wild animals, or perhaps because of this, they tend to attract families (Ryan & Saward, 2004). Oduro *et al.* (2001) indicated that a very high proportion of visitors to zoos are children and Turley (2001) argued that children are a major influencing factor in parents' decision to visit a zoo.

Zoos as Visitor Attractions

As stated earlier, it is becoming increasingly common for zoos to be regarded as museums (Mason, 1999, 2008). Hence, in the way that a traditional museum conserves and exhibits cultural artefacts of value, it can be argued that a zoo, as a form of museum, exhibits objects (in the form of living animals) of cultural heritage value, and more specifically natural heritage value (Mason, 1999). As Hediger (1968) claimed, wild animals can be regarded as having cultural value as they are part of human heritage. Zoos can therefore be considered as major cultural visitor attractions (Hunter-Jones & Hayward, 1998). Hence, when wild animals are kept in zoos, then this place becomes a repository of living objects with cultural value.

Until the post Second World War era, the majority of traditional zoos were located in urban locations. Some zoos have become major urban visitor attractions, attracting significant numbers of tourists as well as local visitors (Mason, 2008). Copenhagen and Rotterdam Zoos attracted more visitors in the first half of the 1990s than any other urban-based attraction in each of these cities (van der Berg *et al.*, 1995). Berlin Zoo was one of the major zoos of Europe with over 2 million visitors per year in the period from 1990 to 1994, with a high percentage of non-local visitors (Shackley, 1996). Zoos are also important visitor attractions in the USA and probably the best known example internationally is San Diego Zoo (van Linge, 1992). At the end of 20th century, zoos were, in fact, the most frequently visited type of museum in the world and also had a broader cross section of visitors than any other form of museum (Kotler & Kotler, 1998).

During the latter part of the 20th century, with growing concerns about the relationship between animals and humans, traditional zoos were frequently in the front line of this concern. A major consequence was the emergence of non-traditional forms of animal attractions. By the last decade of the 20th century, there was a broad range of attractions exhibiting wildlife. In an attempt to classify this range of attractions, Shackley (1996) used the concept of 'mobility restriction' and created a scale from 'complete confinement' at one end to 'complete freedom' at the other. She indicated that safari parks and nature reserves are located near the 'complete freedom' end of this scale, aquaria and butterfly parks are near the 'restricted' end of the scale, while traditional zoos are located roughly in the middle.

Despite the increase in non-traditional forms of animal attractions, and competition from the rise of other day-visitor attractions in the past 30 years or so, zoo visitation remains a significant leisure pursuit (Beardsworth & Bryman, 2001). However, as new forms of animal attractions have emerged, and attitudes to animals have changed, some traditional zoos have re-evaluated their role as visitor attractions. Hence, it has been argued that zoos could offer themselves as either ecotourism attractions (Mason, 2000) or as a relatively easily accessible substitute product for ecotourism (Ryan & Saward, 2004).

The Multiple and Controversial Role of Zoos

Although zoos have a number of roles, these roles are, in reality, linked. Broad (1996) indicated that the roles are often interwoven and, in her study of Jersey Zoo, suggested that although most visitors were well educated, they reported gaining more knowledge of the conservation work of the zoo from their visit. Visitors felt that the most important learning process was watching the animals, but they also learned about conservation and specific scientific work at the zoo from displays and keeper talks.

However, zoos have provoked much criticism because they contain live exhibits in captivity and these exhibits are animals that are found naturally in the wild (Bostock, 1993; Jamieson, 1985). This led Jamieson (1985) to suggest that the different roles of a zoo are, in fact, incompatible and he argued that the supposed educational and conservation roles in relation to wild animals in captivity are very difficult to defend. He claimed that zoos teach us a false sense of our place in the natural order. As he argued:

> The means of confinement mark a difference between humans and animals. They are there at our pleasure, to be used for our purposes. (Jamieson, 1985: 117)

Within the context of the UK, where zoos are not generally supported by the state, Huxley (1981) indicated that they depend for their existence on paying visitors. Huxley was concerned about the potential conflict between the commercial and scientific roles of zoos. A major dilemma, Huxley (1981) claimed, is that zoo managers would prefer to run their zoo without admitting any members of the public at all, or only those genuinely interested and in sympathy with non-commercial aims. Hence, the problem is that zoos have to serve two masters; their scientific god and their gate-money mammon (Huxley, 1981).

Swarbrooke (1999) discussed the future of zoos and suggested that they cannot be considered sustainable tourism attractions. He argued that, on ethical grounds, zoos cannot be considered sustainable because of the way they treat animals, and that they do not appear to have a sustainable future owing to changes in consumer taste, where other types of visitor attractions have become more popular.

Despite the significance of traditional zoos as visitor attractions, their popularity seems to have declined in the past 20 years. Zoos are also probably unique in tourism in that people may object to their very existence as attractions (Turley, 1999). In a zoo, an animal is out of context and without this, the animal loses much of its meaning and information content (Robinson, 1989). The conditions in which animals are kept may even deter visitors and there is currently some evidence to support this. Turley (1999) conducted a small-scale survey, which nevertheless had national coverage, of latent visitors to zoos in the UK in the late 1990s, in which 40% of respondents' associated traditional zoos with bars and unnatural conditions, while over one third (35%) indicated that not liking to see animals in captivity was a reason for not visiting.

Zoos and the Media

Research studies of the media portrayal of tourism-related themes have tended to be crisis focused and concerned on an international or even global scale, such as tourism and natural disasters (see, e.g. Faulkner & Vikulov, 2001), tourism and terrorism (see, e.g. Hitchcock & Dama Putra, 2007), tourism and human diseases, e.g. SARS (Mason *et al.*, 2005) and the effects on tourism of animal diseases, such as the UK Foot and Mouth outbreak (Ritchie *et al.*, 2004). In the case of the media concern with tourism and crises, the 'issue attention cycle' (Downs, 1972), in which a major media story emerges, rapidly takes up several pages of a newspaper and then, over time, gradually fades away, as revealed by movement from the front page and a reduction in coverage space, to be replaced eventually by another story, has been applied. Such media coverage has often been criticised for being sensationalist and/or trivialising (Hall, 2002; Mason *et al.*, 2005).

However, zoos appear not to be primarily one-off media topics, but feature more regularly, although perhaps intermittently in the media. Therefore, stories concerned with zoos tend not to be linked to a major global crisis. The approach and tone of particular stories about zoos may therefore be different on each occasion, although a sensationalising approach may not be that uncommon. For example, a newspaper may run a controversial story, such as that reflecting concern with the conditions animals are kept in at a specific zoo. This same newspaper will be attempting to provoke a rather different emotional reaction when it focuses on an animal birth in a zoo, particularly if it is an endangered species in the wild, or has previously proved difficult to breed in captivity. Although different in tone and content from each other, unlike media tourism-related crisis topics, such stories are likely to be more locally focused and be found on the inside pages, rather than the front page.

However, almost all human experiences involving wildlife, other than direct contact at, e.g. zoos, or in the wild itself, are via some form of media. It is generally accepted that the media has a central role in influencing public opinion (Hall, 2002). As Wood and Peake (1998) claimed, public perceptions of the relative importance of a topic, or issue, is largely determined by the news media. This is mainly the result of the amount of attention given by the media to the issue (Hall, 2002). The media also plays a major role in influencing consumers' images of visitor attractions (Hall, 2002). This is not just a direct process of the media communicating with potential consumers, but it also operates indirectly through 'word of mouth' information and advice given by friends and relatives (Swarbrooke & Horner, 1999).

In past generations, the cinema, newspapers and magazines made frequent use of wildlife images and these forms of media still commonly feature images of wildlife. However, by the 21st century, the major way that humans engaged with the wild was through television (Beardsworth & Bryman, 2001). Nevertheless, as Beardsworth and Bryman suggested, the images that television produces are, in fact, highly processed, involving careful editing. Hence the 'wild' and 'natural' as represented on TV (and also film), are largely in the form of 'staged' images, although these may be combined with 'natural' footage. It is these highly mediated electronic images that now dominate the way the wild is 'created' in contemporary western cultures, according to Beardsworth and Bryman.

Wildlife images have been used to influence public thinking about a range of issues. As Newsome *et al.* (2005) argued, wildlife images, and particularly those presented on television, are a very popular way of communicating information about the natural environment and developing public awareness and environmental consciousness. Such images can also be used in a particularly poignant way to illustrate habitat loss or destruction and ecosystem collapse (Reser & Bentrupperbaumer, 2000). Champ (2002) goes so far as to claim that wildlife images have made a significant contribution to a shift in public opinion, from animals being seen as merely serving the purposes of humans and being exploited accordingly, to a more protectionist view of wildlife.

Since the 1970s, there has been mounting concern for animal welfare. Some of this concern has been directed at animal conditions in zoos. This has not only led to new forms of animal attractions, such as safari parks, where animals are kept in more 'natural' settings, but it has also contributed to traditional zoos re-examining the ways in which they present animals, and hence their approach to entertaining visitors.

A major factor contributing to this re-examination of the ways that zoos present their exhibits to the public, according to Beardsworth and Bryman (2001), has been the influence of the American theme parks created by the Disney media organisation. Beardsworth and Bryman (2001) suggested that this 'Disneyisation' of traditional zoos has led to the theming of exhibits. This has meant the creation of, for example, Jungle World at New York's Bronx Zoo, London Zoo's biodiversity exhibits and Adelaide Zoo's nocturnal house. In these themed presentations, an attempt is made to entertain visitors with a simulation of the natural habitat of the animal exhibit and hence the context also assumes importance. One reason for theming is the growing concern with animal welfare and it can be viewed as an attempt to make animals more comfortable with their surroundings than in the traditional zoo (Tarpy, 1993; Beardsworth & Bryman, 2001). However, it has been argued that this provision of a 'naturalistic' context for the animals has more to do with making the visitor feel comfortable about the ways in which animals are being kept in captivity (Anderson, 1995).

Of concern in this process of Disneyisation is that animals can be more easily anthropomorphised (Beardsworth & Bryman, 2001), to the extent that during presentations to entertain visitors, they are attributed human motivations and characteristics. Under these conditions, attempts to entertain are likely to trivialise and frequently sentimentalise animals' actions (Mason, 2000). This may be the case particularly when a large proportion of the visitors are children (Turley, 2001). Newsome *et al.* (2005) also argued that the anthropomorphised portrayal of wildlife is a widespread form of media presentation. They suggested that this can take the form of caricatures and cartoon characters. This portrayal can appear to be relatively harmless, as can be epitomised in such phrases as 'cuddly koalas' or 'cunning snakes', but as Bentruppenbaumer (1998) argued, this anthropomorphising may provide very ambiguous and even entirely incorrect messages about particular animal species. An example to illustrate this point is the portrayal of bears, such as the cartoon animals 'Winnie the Pooh' and the bear called Baloo in Disney's 'Jungle Book'. Clearly, these cartoon characters have little in common with real wild bears.

Nevertheless, it should be of little surprise that the World Wildlife Fund (WWF) has used the panda as its logo. Clearly, this animal is likely to evoke a much warmer and more sympathetic response from an audience when conservation messages are presented or attempts are being made to raise money for the organisation. It is much easier to generate an anthropomorphised response to a panda, than to a large hairy tarantula!

Theming in such animal attractions has meant that it has become easy to commoditise the 'wild' in zoos (Beardsworth & Bryman, 2001). Consequently, the threatening aspects of the wild have become sanitised in the modern zoo and have been rendered virtually harmless, largely to provide entertainment for visitors. However, commoditisation of the 'wild' in zoos may also lead to questions of authenticity in the minds of some visitors. In the traditional zoo, with clearly visible cages and bars, visitors will need little reminding of where they are. In the themed, commoditised, modern zoo, visitors may desire 'staged authenticity'. Under these circumstances, to entertain visitors, zoo animals will be expected, according to Beardsworth and Bryman (2001), to play their part in creating the illusion of a 'jungle' or 'the polar environment'. This may contribute to the enjoyment of visitors and even scientific knowledge may be gained, but it is also likely to pose a significant ethical dilemma of the appropriateness of treating captive animals in this manner. Of particular concern here are the likely effects on the traditionally most popular zoo animals, the big cats and our nearest relatives among the primates (see Mason, 1999, 2003, 2008).

The Disneyisation of zoos also means that they become more similar to other forms of attraction, hence losing their distinct identity to the point that they are almost indistinguishable from other themed attractions (Beardsworth & Bryman, 2001). However, zoos may benefit, in terms of visitors, from this blurring. The most extreme example of this loss of distinct identity, according to Beardsworth and Bryman, is Disney's Animal Kingdom. This is a zoo in the midst of a themed attraction, Walt Disney World, which includes a water park, a theme park, six golf courses, 20 hotels and numerous restaurants.

This discussion of the way that the Disney media organisation presents images of wildlife reveals another aspect of the relationship between zoos and the media generally - the media does not just passively *reflect* images of wildlife (including wildlife in zoos), but is involved in the *creation* of these images. In this way, the media can be seen to potentially have a powerful influence on public opinion and views about controversial topics, such as the conditions animals are kept in zoos, endangered species and captive breeding in zoos.

It is clear that the images used on television and in film are also being supplemented and perhaps even superseded by internet images of wildlife. Although internet technology makes it possible for continual monitoring of animal behaviour via e.g. webcams, which may provide more 'naturalistic' images, it seems probable that many of these images available on the internet have been subjected to the same form of 'staging' and editing as those that are used on television and in film.

A Brief Analysis of Selected Media Portrayal of Zoos

The amount of space available means it is not possible to offer a detailed analysis of the media portrayal of zoos. Nevertheless, a small-scale study of specific zoo-related media coverage is provided here, to indicate a technique for analysis and the nature of the audience as well as the messages contained within this coverage. It is also hoped that this brief study will act as a spur for those who may wish to conduct more in-depth research.

As Beardsworth and Bryman (2001) have indicated, the most significant source of media images of wildlife in the early 21st century is television. Thus, a number of television programmes form the focus of this analysis. The major concern of this analysis is the way that television portrays the roles of zoos today and, in particular, how the aforementioned roles of education, science, and entertainment are presented, as well as consideration of zoos as visitor attractions, in these programmes. Here, the content analysis is primarily focused on the intended audience and the message of the television programme, with reference to the presentation format (e.g. with a presenter on camera or some other format such as the use of cartoon images) contained within the programme and, in particular, how this relates to the roles of zoos.

This analysis is confined to television programmes in the UK, concentrating mainly on the terrestrial channels (although there is some attention given to satellite/cable television and other broadcast media) and the period of analysis was initially intended to be just one month and March 2009 was selected. The initial approach was to investigate any series of animal/zoo-related programmes that were being shown for a significant proportion of the year and to view the episodes being shown during this month. However, a study of several months' TV listings indicated that there was also a number of one-off programmes, as well as a short series that had taken place in the previous year up to the end of March 2009. Therefore, episodes of programmes in series formats being shown in March were analysed as well as series and 'one-off' programmes shown between April 2008 and March 2009. Satellite/cable channels were also considered, although these were not included if the programme was a repeat of a programme previously shown on terrestrial channels. The following discussion is a summary of the main findings of this analysis.

During March 2009, all of the five major UK-based terrestrial television channels (BBC 1, BBC 2, ITV, Channel 4 and Channel 5) had at least one programme concerned with wildlife, and a number of these focused specifically on zoos. There were several animal-related regular series, such as the BBC 1 programme 'Animals 24:7', as well as one-off documentary programmes with an animal focus. One of these animal-focused programmes, 'Animal Park', shown on BBC2 during this period was concerned with the Longleat Safari Park, in South West England - a modern competitor to more traditional zoos. Another similarly focused programme also shown on BBC 2 was 'Roar'. This series studied Woburn Safari Park in Bedfordshire, a similar type of attraction to Longleat. These programmes were shown between 6.30 and 7.30 pm in the evening. The presenters of each of the programmes were also regular hosts of other television programmes, particularly children's programmes. The presenter of 'Animals 24:7' has also previously presented programmes on zoos. In terms of content and format, both these programmes gave significant amounts of time to what the keepers did and used the keepers' comments about the animals for which they were responsible.

One of these animal-related series was specifically zoo focused. Channel 5 showed a regular weekly programme entitled 'Zoo Days', featuring Chester Zoo and Colchester Zoo in the UK. This series purports to show day-to-day activities in both zoos and reports incidences as if in a chronological sequence. A large range of animals featured in this programme, including 'favourite zoo animals', such as primates and big cats (see Mason, 2008; Shackley, 1996) and perhaps lesser known ones, such as fruit bats as well as birds and reptiles. A frequent theme was the birth of young and the relationship between the mothers and the young animals. This programme was shown early in the evening, between 6.30 and 7.30 pm.

In terms of the intended audience, the time that they were shown suggests that the target audience was primarily children. In fact, the presentation format, with the use of cartoon images on occasions, used in conjunction with more conventional approaches to presentation, language, tone and general content confirmed that those up to 11 or 12 years of age were the likely intended audience.

The messages broadcast in each of the programmes referred to above, also suggests that children are the primary audience. Conservation messages regarding specific endangered species as well as breeding programmes featured in each programme. A major message of the 'Zoo Days' episodes was that zoos are places where specially trained people, keepers and vets, can help make 'sick' animals better. However, the episodes of 'Zoo Days' did not indicate whether or not incidences of illness in the animals were related to them being kept in captivity. Nevertheless, both the conservation and their related education role (Broad, 1996) were prominent in this programme.

In terms of the way in which the key messages were delivered, anthropomorphising (see Beardsworth & Bryman, 2001) was common in these programmes. For example, in 'Zoo Days', young were frequently referred to as 'babies' and a young hippopotamus was reported by the presenter to be 'reluctant' to go into its refurbished enclosure, but after a few days was said to be 'now happy' with its new surroundings. Likewise, one of a group of young lions was initially referred to as demonstrating 'naughty behaviour', but a few days later as 'getting along famously' with its siblings.

Zoos were not presented or discussed overtly as controversial, in terms of containing captive animals, in any of these programmes. However, there was discussion of animal behaviour being different in captivity - such as less wariness towards humans than in the wild, as well as a number of references to habituated behaviour, which can occur in certain species such as elephants in zoos. These issues were mentioned, but not specifically referred to in terms of the potentially negative consequences of wild animals in captivity.

Although not shown in March 2009, at other times of the year there are other zoo-focused programmes that use 'celebrities' as presenters. One such celebrity is Michaela Strachan, who has been a children's television presenter in the UK for over 20 years. Her programme, 'Michaela's Zoo Babies', shown on Channel 5, has a very specific focus, as can be gathered from its title, and has presented stories concerned with captive zoo breeding and attempts to return endangered species to the wild.

The use of celebrities, the focus on particular types of animals and their behaviour, such as chimpanzees, the young offspring of animals such as big cats and bears as well as concern for 'sick' animals suggest that providing entertainment, as well as education, is a key role of these programmes and by implication the zoos/animal attractions presented as well.

Regular wild animal/zoo-related series are frequently shown on cable/satellite television as well. Often, these programmes, such as 'Zoo Vet' shown on Sky in the UK, are very similar to those discussed above in terms of intended audience, presentation format and message. There are also other types of animal/zoo-related programmes, including Sky's 'Lion Man'. This programme focuses on one individual, (although there has been more than one 'Lion Man') who is based at Whangarei Zoo, New Zealand, and works with lions in enclosures at the zoo. This differs from the television programmes referred to above as it focuses on one species (although other big cats feature also). It also concentrates much more on one individual - the Lion Man - who attempts to train animals to perform. The programme, through its narrator and images used, seems very much to be promoting the feelings about wild animals that early Victorian zoos were attempting to provoke - that is, both fear and awe (Bostock, 1993; Jamieson, 1985). The programme also attempts to gain the audience's admiration and sympathy for the Lion Man as he 'bravely' faces the 'wild' animal. It would also appear that this programme is much more concerned with entertainment than education or science.

The programmes discussed above are regular series. In addition to these series, which are aimed primarily at children, in 2008, the BBC featured a series about a zoo that was targeted at viewers other than just children. In early 2009, Channel 4 screened a one-off zoo-focused programme. Each investigated a specific, but different zoo, but the programmes had in common that each zoo was an old traditional zoo, with declining visitor numbers, in need of modernisation, and this was occurring under new ownership. These programmes were both shown at a slightly later time in the evening than the regular series programmes referred to above.

'Ben's Zoo' was filmed in the style of a documentary and was concerned with why the journalist, Ben Mee, and his family bought a dilapidated zoo in the South West of England and the challenges of establishing what they called 'Dartmoor Zoological Park'. The Channel 4 programme, 'Chaos at the Zoo', was also mainly in documentary form but was a one-off programme featuring a celebrity - Anna Ryder Richardson, known for her input to a number of house 'make over' programmes in the UK - who with her husband bought a run-down zoo in Tenby, South Wales. Like the series 'Ben's Zoo', this programme was concerned with the rationale for the purchase of the zoo and how Anna and her family helped restore it.

In both cases, a number of significant issues concerned with the role of zoos emerged. The rationale for keeping animals in captivity as well as the actual condition of wild animals kept in captivity were important related themes in 'Ben's Zoo', particularly in relation to big cats, such as lions, tigers and cheetahs, and a number of critical comments were raised and discussed. In the television programme, Ben Mee was interviewed and indicated that he tried to stop the big cats becoming bored and gave them challenges such as placing the carcass of dead livestock that the zoo uses as replacement for the natural prey a big cat would capture, high in the branches of a tree in the tigers' enclosure. 'Ben's Zoo' also considered the importance of the animals in zoos, particularly endangered ones, as breeding stock. Ben Mee has also written a book about his experiences at the zoo and in this he indicates his awareness of the controversial nature of zoos:

> there are many complicated arguments for and against zoos, from those extremists who think that all captive animals should either be released back into the wild or killed, to those who see no harm in any kind of containment for entertainment. (Mee, 2008: 211)

For him, it is the conservation argument that is the key reason for the continued existence of zoos, with, as he claims, a long history of species saved from extinction by zoos.

In each of these programmes, the owners had young children and the relationship between zoo animals and pre-teenage children was a focus, particularly the educational role, but also the entertainment that children obtain in a zoo context. However, unlike the episodes of programmes discussed above, both these programmes were also very much interested in the viability of zoos as visitor attractions. The need to prepare a business plan, conduct risk assessments, complete complex paperwork, undergo a zoo inspection and obtain a zoo licence, all featured in both these programmes. The day-to-day running of a zoo as a visitor attraction and the financial implications of 'gate receipts' in relation to the provision of the animals requirements for food, shelter and good health, as well as meeting staff salaries were significant issues.

However, another form of media, radio, via BBC Radio 4, presented during 2009 a particularly significant input to the discussion of the role of zoos in modern Britain. This programme entitled 'The Point of Zoos' has the obvious disadvantage of a lack of visual images, but compensated for this through a detailed discussion of the often controversial aims of modern zoos. The programme, broadcast in early June 2009, used extracts from interviews with both opponents and supporters of zoos. The writer and presenter of the programme, journalist Quentin Letts, indicated the pleasure of experiencing through a variety of senses, in a zoo, what would be a dangerous animal in the wild, but did not shy away from commenting on the living conditions of animals, such as chimpanzees, elephants, lions and tigers, in some zoos. However, in his concluding comments, the presenter suggested that for him, zoos are far less places for learning about animals, but much more locations to learn from animals. As he put it: 'In a zoo we can meet the neighbours and as a result acquire greater self knowledge'.

Conclusions

Many different types of media make use of animal and wildlife images and these images are used for a variety of purposes. In general, the media like to use animal stories and animal images, including those concerned with zoos.

As Beardsworth and Bryman (2001) argued, the major media source for images of zoos in the early 21st century is television. Television shows focusing on wildlife, including those concerned with zoos, are popular programmes in the UK and are frequently shown on television at prime time as well as at other times. Many of these programmes are targeted primarily at children. The content of such programmes, many of which are long running series about specific zoos, involve education and scientific topics - both these areas are related to major roles of zoos. However, such programmes tend to anthropomorphise animals in zoos and in their attempt to provide entertainment as well as education for the audience, there is a danger that they may trivialise important topics. Some programmes, such as 'Lion Man', seem to hark back to an earlier era where wild animals in zoos were there largely to be goaded and provoked by keepers to entertain visitors. Such a programme can be accused of sensationalising, as well as trivialising the relationship between humans and animals.

However, there is evidence that British television can provide documentary-style programmes that are aimed at adults to not only entertain them, but also inform them about the various roles of zoos, including the challenges confronting new owners trying to establish their zoo as a visitor attraction. British radio also appears to provide evidence that this type of media can offer an opportunity for a rational discussion of issues about zoos, including controversial topics such as the treatment of animals in captivity and endangered species breeding programmes, as well as the pleasure of a face-to-face experience with a rare wild animal - here, there are obviously no visual images that can be used to make the blood boil, or conversely tug at the heart strings!

Chapter 17

Zoos Victoria: Branding, Marketing and Designing Multi-Location Zoos

LEANNE WHITE

Introduction

This chapter will examine the branding and marketing of the organisation known as 'Zoos Victoria' in 2009. Zoos Victoria is the umbrella brand that comprises 'three great zoos' in the state of Victoria, Australia. Melbourne Zoo is located 4 km from the city of Melbourne and provides a good sample of the world's wildlife. Healesville Sanctuary is located one hour from Melbourne and displays much of Australia's unique wildlife. Finally, Werribee Open Range Zoo is located 30 minutes from the centre of Melbourne and aims to provide an 'African adventure experience'. With more than 1.6 million visitors annually, together the three zoos are Victoria's biggest tourist attraction.

Recent studies in tourism have considered the role of tourist attractions, such as zoos, in assisting with the creation of an identity for a city. Rojek (1997: 58) argues that 'most tourists feel they have not fully absorbed a sight until they stand before it, see it, and take a photograph to record the moment'. Morgan *et al.* (2004: 4) argue that travel for the purpose of leisure is 'a highly involving experience, extensively planned, excitedly anticipated and fondly remembered', while Urry (1990: 12) argues that when tourists gaze, they effectively become semioticians 'reading the landscape for signifiers of certain pre-established notions or signs derived from various discourses of travel and tourism'. Finally, Pitchford (2008: 98) argues that tourism promotional materials 'speak to tourists in a language that creates a set of expectations about a destination'.

Marketing collateral produced by Zoos Victoria along with photographs that visitors take (often then posted on social networking sites such as Facebook) constitute an important form of promotion and have become key elements in the marketing mix. An astute marketing strategy for a major destination (or in the case of Zoos Victoria – a set of three destinations) must be critically aware of the key messages it communicates to all stakeholders and, particularly, potential visitors. Zoos Victoria's marketing team would also be wise to assess and evaluate the ways in which visitors engage with the destinations and talk about their experiences of the visit with others.

Branding Zoos Victoria

Zoos Victoria has a grand vision to be no less than 'the world's leading zoo-based conservation organisation' by building 'enduring relationships between people and wildlife' (Zoos Victoria, 2009). The Zoos Victoria logo (Figure 17.1) was designed by advertising agency, SAE Creative. Part of the job of designing the logo for Zoos Victoria was creating a style guide to ensure that brand consistency was achieved every time the words and logo were reproduced.

Applying a semiotic analysis to the logo, the colours orange, green and blue represent warm, cool and cold colours. While the words 'Werribee' and 'Healesville' might not necessarily register with the international tourist, the three zoo destinations are immediately connected and it is clear that the main attraction (by virtue of both the central positioning of the logo and the green association with the main heading 'Zoos') is 'Melbourne'.

Figure 17.1 Zoos Victoria logo
Source: Leanne White

As one might expect, the Werribee Open Range Zoo (opened in 1996), which displays African wildlife such as the zebra, lion, giraffe, rhinoceros and hippopotamus, is displayed in orange – consistent with the warm habitat in which the animals usually live. The green of the Melbourne Zoo logo is indicative of the jungle canopy that surrounds the great apes and also sends a conservation message (further reinforced by the green heading 'Zoos'). The great apes and their offspring have been a significant visitor drawcard for Melbourne Zoo over a number of years and, as will be discussed later, were given added emphasis in 2009. Healesville Sanctuary (opened in 1934) is essentially an Australian wildlife park and displays more than 200 species of Australian native animals, including the koala, kangaroo, emu, wombat, Tasmanian Devil, and one of Australia's most unusual animals – the platypus. As the natural habitat for this monotreme is water, the Healesville logo is blue. The animals in the Zoos Victoria logo are evenly balanced with two zebras, three gorillas and two platypuses presented. The black band with white writing between the large word 'Zoos' and the three images below reinforces to the visitor that all three attractions can be found in the state of Victoria.

The idea of three concepts or images being presented in the one logo was a relatively new concept at the time, perhaps stemming from the marketing of the Sydney 2000 Olympic Games. The Australian Tourist Commission (ATC: now known as Tourism Australia) made it clear that it saw the Sydney 2000 Olympic Games as an opportunity to shift tourist attitudes regarding Australia. The ATC wanted to use the Games to remove the 'Crocodile Dundee' image of Australia (Rivenburgh *et al.*, 2004). In 1995, the ATC embarked on a new way to promote Australia – known as 'Brand Australia'. In this campaign, a unified and cohesive image of Australia was developed for the major markets – Asia, Europe and the USA. Australia's personality was presented as youthful, energetic, optimistic, unpretentious and genuine. In their cross-cultural study of foreign attitudes towards Australia before, during and after the Sydney Games, Rivenburgh *et al.* (2004: 13) argued that 'the ATC saw the Opening Ceremony as an opportunity to sell Sydney and Australia to the world' and to get Australia recognised as an exciting and desirable travel destination.

For the Sydney Games, Australian native animals were used as the official Olympic mascots. De Lange explains that this was the first time more than one mascot had been selected for a Summer Olympic Games and that the choice of these 'three relatively unknown creatures' made for 'a weird and wonderful blend' of mascots (De Lange, 1998: 150). The three mascots were: Olly (Olympics) a kookaburra, Syd (Sydney) a platypus, and Millie (Millennium) an echidna. Furthermore, the three native animals represented earth (the echidna), wind (the kookaburra) and water (the platypus).

The natural elements also played a key role in the Sydney Olympic Games Opening Ceremony. The connection of the natural elements to the mascots is outlined in the ATC's information booklet, *Sydney Australia Towards 2000*:

> These native Australian animals representing the land, air and water, will team up to tell the Sydney 2000 Olympic story. Each will have an individual role in the years leading up to the Sydney 2000 Games. (ATC, 1998: 16)

Apart from representing earth, wind and water, the Olympic mascots were also promoted with their own distinct personalities. Promotional material attempted to make the mascots come to life by explaining that:

> These animals capture the essence of Australia; a land of contrasts and easy going, friendly, sporty and optimistic people. Syd is a team player and natural leader by example. He is focused, dynamic, enthusiastic and captures the vigour and energy of Australia and its people. Millie is a born optimist and information guru whose eye is firmly set on the future. A confident young woman, she is a sharp and witty observer who is always taking notes and coming up with new ideas. Olly is gregarious, honest, enthusiastic and open hearted. He embodies the Olympic spirit of generosity and universal friendship. (Thinkquest, 2000)

Taking its lead from the Olympics, the Zoos Victoria logo has achieved a good deal of brand recognition among its target audience. Commenting on research undertaken about Zoos Victoria advertising by the *Herald Sun* newspaper, Misha Horsnell, Brand and Portfolio Manager for Zoos Victoria said, 'It is very reassuring to know our brand communications are having the desired effect on our target audience, and we are also seeing these claimed visit intentions coming through in our actual visitor numbers' (*Herald Sun*, 2009).

Melbourne Zoo: Past and Present

Melbourne Zoo is Australia's oldest zoo and has been operating at its current site since 1862. The Melbourne Zoo entrance reveals hints of the binary opposites – old and new. Binary oppositions, a concept central to structuralism, transpire when meaning is generated by the relationship between two opposing and different signs. The term was first developed by French anthropologist Levi-Strauss. In binary oppositions an explicit quality exists in one of the pair and not in the other. It is essentially the non-existence of a particular quality in one half of the pair that

Figure 17.2 The main entrance of Melbourne Zoo
Source: Leanne White

contextualises and thus creates greater meaning in the other. Thus, meaning is produced as a direct result of what is present and what is absent. Some common binary oppositions include: black/white, rich/ poor, old/young, high/low, nature/culture, dead/alive, good/evil and past/future.

Above and to the left of the word 'Zoo' is a statue of a polar bear, while a statue of a kangaroo is located on the right (Figure 17.2). In front of the more ornate entrance is a modern façade (built in 1996), which displays both old and new features, such as the formal title of the location – 'The Royal Melbourne Zoological Gardens' and the Melbourne Zoo logo featuring the gorilla.

Before the visitor to Melbourne Zoo enters through the main gates, the past and present have been made evident. The theme is reinforced again as the visitor walks down the main path and comes across one of the zoo's original enclosures (Figure 17.3). While many may simply walk past and casually observe the caged enclosure, others will stop to read the signs and thus be further exposed to the zoo's message. A sign headed 'Our Past' reads:

> Built in 1927, this Victoria style enclosure was designed to house orang-utans. Restored in 1992, it is one of our last iron-barred cages, built in an era when animals were objects of curiosity and displayed in cages which paid little heed of their true needs. Now surrounded

Figure 17.3 An original enclosure serves as a reminder of the past
Source: Leanne White

by native date-palms, flower beds and a Peter Pan statue, this significant building is a permanent reminder of our history.

To reinforce the message of cruelty, the photograph below these words is that of a crouching orangutan unhappily clinging to the bars and avoiding the gaze of the crowd of curious onlookers. Melbourne Zoo's vision for the future is much more optimistic. The sign 'The Future' reads:

> It is no longer acceptable to keep animals in unnatural surroundings simply for public amusement. The Zoo's master plan will ensure that animals live in re-created habitats, like our Gorilla Rainforest. The aim is to help you know and think about the links in nature between people, other animals and their habitats.

In terms of the way in which Zoos Victoria, and Melbourne Zoo in particular, market themselves, emphasising the close link between animals and people is a key feature. Jenny Gray, Chief Executive of Zoos Victoria says, 'Everyone is interested in the animals and what we are doing. There is a real passion, a real connection' (Dean, 2009). Given that the connection between animals and people is a central plank of the zoo's marketing, it is no wonder that the great apes are a key feature of Melbourne Zoo marketing and conservation campaigns. The zoo is also quick to emphasise that gorillas share 98.4% of their genes with humans, and orangutans are 97% human.

The Year of the Gorilla

The United Nations declared 2009 the 'Year of the Gorilla' (Figure 17.4). Gorilla populations are declining and their main threats include loss of habitat and being hunted. As a result, it was not surprising that the look and feel of both Melbourne Zoo and many of its marketing efforts in 2009 were firmly focused on this animal. The main entrance of Melbourne Zoo was lined with large posters of its popular gorilla family. A brief content analysis of the posters displayed down the main path of Melbourne Zoo reveals 20 large banners. All are gorillas and many display gorillas with human-like characteristics or behaviour patterns.

Melbourne Zoo currently has eight gorillas – four male and four female. Rigo (born overseas in 1970) is the oldest male. The first gorilla

Figure 17.4 The Year of the Gorilla – 2009
Source: Leanne White

ever born in Australia was Mzuri (born in 1984). Mzuri is now based at Jersey Zoo and is part of an international breeding programme for Western Lowland Gorillas.

Some of the ways in which Zoos Victoria worked to highlight the plight of the gorilla in 2009 included: large onsite posters of gorillas, a school banner competition, an animal adoption programme, and a mobile phone recycling campaign entitled 'They're Calling on You' (Figure 17.5). The title of the campaign was a clear call to action designed to make humans feel that they needed to do something to assist their helpless 'distant relatives'. When promoted at Melbourne Zoo, the campaign information was presented on a blackboard and as such, the visitor who encountered the blackboard essentially received a lesson.

Visitors to the three Zoos Victoria properties or those who logged on to the Zoos Victoria website were informed that as their mobile phones contained the metal coltan, mined from gorilla habitat, sending back

Figure 17.5 'They're Calling on You' mobile phone recycling campaign
Source: Leanne White

phones would reduce the need to mine for the metal as the coltan-coated capacitor could have a second life. Another positive outcome would be that fewer phones would end up as landfill. The mobile phone campaign saw the return of more than 7000 phones with $9000 donated to the Jane Goodall Institute and the Dian Fossey Gorilla Fund to help protect gorillas from poachers (Dean, 2009).

Not to be forgotten in the Year of the Gorilla was the possibly less popular, but even more endearing, orangutan. Melbourne Zoo has built the 'Make a Difference' pavilion so that visitors can learn about the endangered plight of this acrobatic ape (Figure 17.6). The 'Don't Palm Us Off' campaign is another overt call to action. Explaining how the orangutans tug at the heart strings, Zoos Victoria CEO, Jenny Gray, explains, 'You just look into their eyes, and instantly there is a connection. They talk to you and ask for help' (Dean, 2009). Gray also points out that a review of Zoos Victoria's activities identified the various ways in which

Figure 17.6 Orangutans are the man of the forest, 97% human and threatened with extinction
Source: Leanne White

the organisation could play a larger role in the promotion of conservation issues (Sheridan, 2009: 7).

The campaign is designed to firstly raise awareness about the destruction of forests, which are being cleared for palm oil plantations. Palm oil is found in many fast-moving consumer goods, such as biscuits, chocolate, noodles, desserts, detergent, shampoo and toothpaste. It is estimated that Australians consume an average of 10 kg of palm oil annually with only 1% being produced in a sustainable manner (Sheridan, 2009: 7). The second goal of the campaign is to lobby the federal government for the proper labelling of the ingredient so that consumers can choose whether or not they wish to buy products containing this ingredient. Currently, manufacturers who use palm oil normally list it simply as 'vegetable oil', as food labelling laws in Australia and New Zealand do not require them to be any more specific.

Zoos Victoria staff argue that the harvesting of palm oil is resulting in the deaths of about 50 orangutans each week. In keeping with communicating with their target market, the campaign video can be viewed on YouTube, fans can join a dedicated Facebook group and the latest information about the situation of the orangutans can be followed via Twitter. Television commercials promoting the issue used slogans such as 'Palm Oil: All Day, Every Day. Not OK'! At Melbourne Zoo and in promotional literature, orangutans are presented in a highly personal manner with as many human parallels as possible (Figure 17.7).

For Zoos Victoria, social awareness campaigns, such as 'We're Calling on You' and 'Don't Palm Us Off', cleverly promote a conservation issue as opposed to the destination itself. This shift in focus marks a significant change in the marketing strategy and allows the zoo to showcase its actions under the all-important banner of corporate social responsibility. In 2009 (and to coincide with the opening of the 'Wild Sea' enclosure at Melbourne Zoo), Zoos Victoria launched another environmental awareness campaign about the responsible disposal of fishing lines.

Baby Elephants: A Drawcard

Another significant drawcard at Melbourne Zoo is the new $6 million elephant enclosure known as 'Trail of the Elephants', which was opened in 2003. The previous elephant enclosure had long been an embarrassment for the zoo. Former Chairman Donald Hayward said, 'the living conditions of the elephants are unsatisfactory and are far from a source of pride' (Zoological Parks and Gardens Board, 1997: 3). With a much bigger enclosure to share, the zoo's male and female long-term resident elephants, Bong Su and Mek Kapah, were joined by three new females in 2006. Num-Oi, Kulab and Dokkoon are the names of the

Figure 17.7 The point that orangutans are 'almost human' is emphasised by the zoo's display of family portraits
Source: Leanne White

three female elephants and two of them soon became pregnant. After a 22-month pregnancy and close monitoring by world elephant experts, the first calf was born on 16 January 2009. Dokkoon's baby was eventually named Mali (meaning jasmine in Thai) after a public competition from a short list compiled by the zoo keepers. Mali was the first elephant to be born in the 147-year history of the zoo. The second calf was born in September 2010. The exciting developments and resulting media coverage have created increased visitation for Melbourne Zoo as it remains uncommon for elephants in captivity to become pregnant.

The Trail of the Elephants allows the visitor to journey into a tropical garden setting and Asian village, to eventually stumble on the 'Elephant Village Community Hall', displaying elephant-related information, a hawker market, photographs, living quarters and artefacts before walking through four large, secured, elephant paddocks. It is at the hall where the relationship between nature and culture is deliberately emphasised.

Making the most of the award-winning exhibit, the zoo operates functions at what is known as Mek Kapah Terrace (which can cater for up to 500 guests) and the Bong Su function room (for up to 200 guests). Other function venues at Melbourne Zoo include the Carousel Park Marquee, the Rainforest Room and the Lakeside Room and Terrace. Wedding receptions, corporate functions and other events held at Melbourne Zoo add to the all important revenue (above and beyond the entrance fee) that Zoos Victoria need to raise to continue their work.

Maximising Earnings and Experience

All three Zoos Victoria attractions – Melbourne Zoo, Healesville Sanctuary and Werribee Open Range Zoo charge the same admission price – $24.40 for adults and $12.10 for children. Various concession, family and group discounts are also available. However, in order to undertake the conservation, education and animal care work that they do, the organisation relies on state government funding and raising funds through other means.

Consequently, extra programmes are marketed to maximise visitation and encourage visitors to pay more to have a value-added experience with the animals, such as a 'behind the scenes' encounter or a 'photo experience'. Behind the scenes experiences available at Melbourne Zoo are marketed as: 'lion encounter', 'elephant introductions', 'trunk art' (where for $300 per person, a couple can watch an elephant paint and take home the art work), 'tiger territory', 'gorilla games', 'reptile house' and 'tree kangaroos and koalas' (where visitors can pat a koala and capture the memory of the encounter for $70). Melbourne Zoo created the opportunity for tourists to get 'up close and personal' with the cuddly koala as it was something that many international tourists felt they needed to do to reinforce, contextualise and emphasise their connection with Australia. All of the encounters (except for those with the elephants) are priced at $70 with a maximum group size of four or six people.

Melbourne Zoo also conducts a number of events over the Summer with the 'Zoo Twilights' concert programme being a significant attraction. An opportunity for visitors to spend the entire night at the zoo is the 'Roar 'n' Snore' programme, where campers dine in a former elephant barn and are given a guided tour of the premises at night. Similar to any well-planned tourist attraction, the souvenir shop is positioned directly next to the exit. The shop sells toys, clothes and other souvenirs of the zoo experience, such as mugs and ornaments (Figure 17.8).

Figure 17.8 The mugs provide an ongoing reminder of the zoo experience
Source: Leanne White

Conclusion

Zoos Victoria's vision to be 'the world's leading zoo-based conservation organisation' (Zoos Victoria, 2009) may well be on its way to being achieved. The Zoos Victoria logo has achieved a good deal of brand recognition among its target audience. Further integrating both the individual and separate location logos with the actual visitor experience at the venue should further strengthen public recognition as the positive zoo experience will be better connected with the brand.

When visiting Melbourne Zoo, the only encounters with the brand logo were found at the main entrance, on the uniforms of most zoo employees and on mugs found on the bottom shelf of the souvenir shop (Figure 17.8). Signs around Melbourne Zoo varied enormously in design, colour, size and font and nowhere in the zoo could a sign that incorporated the brand be found.

This chapter examined the branding and marketing of Zoos Victoria in – what turned out to be the United Nations Year of the Gorilla – 2009. With its multi-location logo in particular, Zoos Victoria has embarked on a relatively solid IMC campaign that appears focused and reasonably consistent. However, when one visits the locations and walks around a Zoos Victoria 'campus' and encounters the many types of signs, symbols and communication messages, the branding is much less obvious and virtually non-existent. As the brand is still relatively young, this situation is likely to change in the future.

Chapter 18

From Winnie-the-Pooh to Madagascar: *Fictional Media Images of the Zoo Experience*

WARWICK FROST

> This zoo is some sort of whacked-out conspiracy. (Skipper the Penguin, *Madagascar*)

Fictional media provides a valuable tool for understanding society's perceptions of the zoo experience. This chapter considers four case studies. The first is Winnie-the-Pooh. Based on a Canadian army mascot abandoned to London Zoo, it combines the twin themes of anthropomorphism and the trade in zoo animals. The second is the film *Fierce Creatures*, which posits (but ultimately rejects) that successful zoos need fierce predators to attract visitors. The third is Michael Crichton's *Jurassic Park*, which imagines a Walt Disney-type entrepreneur creating a futuristic zoo aimed at high-yield tourists. The fourth is *Madagascar*, a recent animated feature film that also highlights issues of the ethics of keeping animals for entertainment.

In recent years, there has been growing interest in the relationship between fictional media and tourism (e.g. Beeton, 2005; Herbert, 2001). Initially, this interest was in how films, television and novels attracted tourists, turning the locations used into tourist destinations. More recent research has probed deeper, relating fictional media to motivation, expectations and the tourist experience. Furthermore, fictional media has long been seen as a lens used to view and reflect on human behaviour, and this is increasingly being applied to tourism and tourists. For example, fictional media, such as the book and film *The Beach*, are used to help our understanding of backpacker tourism. It is this latter approach that is used in this chapter. My aim is to use fictional media set in and about zoos to explore some of the themes about zoos and tourism covered in this book.

Winnie-the-Pooh

Zoos are a common theme in children's books, providing inspiration for storylines and characters. The utilisation of zoos dates back to the

19th century, when animals first began to feature in children's literature (Baratay & Hardouin-Fugier, 2002). Books aimed at British children provided a combination of moralising, education and imperial values (De Courcey, 1995). In the 20th century, the focus was on anthropomorphising zoo animals, encouraging children to see them as fellow children. This section will focus on Winnie-the-Pooh, perhaps the most famous of such fictional adaptations.

Winnie-the-Pooh was the creation of A.A. Milne. A successful dramatist, Milne began producing children's verse and stories after the birth of his son Christopher Robin. Much of this highly popular output concerned his young son's experiences, particularly with Winnie, his toy bear come to life. Initially featuring as an unnamed bear in *When We were Young* (Milne, 1924), he graduated to lead character in *Winnie-the-Pooh* (1926).

The name Winnie was taken from a black bear at London Zoo. In 1914, Winnie had been brought to England as the mascot of a Canadian regiment. The name Winnie was a shortening of Winnipeg, the home city of Harry Colebourn the Canadian officer who had bought the bear en route. When the regiment was posted to active service in France, the tame cub was deposited with London Zoo. After the war, it was formally donated to the zoo, where it lived until 1934 (Thwaite, 1992).

The connection between the young boy Christopher Robin and the real zoo bear has been the subject of mythologising. In interviews, A.A. Milne was careful not to be too specific and interviewers often embroidered the tale. The bare bones of the story are that the writer and his son went to the zoo for a children's birthday party and saw Winnie. The legend is that the children were allowed inside the cage, either through the offices of a friend who was on the zoo's board or through the common expedient of tipping a keeper. In the cage, they may have patted or fed the tame bear. One version of the story came from an interview of Milne conducted by a young Enid Blyton, who wrote *The Zoo Book* (1924). This interview improbably had Christopher Robin playfully wrestling with the bear (Thwaite, 1992). A widely reproduced photograph of Christopher Robin with the bear in its cage (see Thwaite, 1992: 75) reinforced the story of close contact, though it is probable that the photo was a later publicity shot. In 1981, London Zoo erected a plaque commemorating Winnie, though it no longer has any black bears on display.

We need to take care with such stories. Both the zoo and Milne gained publicity and were under no obligation to allow the truth to get in the way of a good story. A similar myth surrounds Dr Seuss (Theodore Seuss Geisel). He grew up in Springfield, Massachusetts, where his father was a commissioner for the local Forest Park Zoo. Many accounts of Geisel's life credit his boyhood roaming the zoo and behind-the-scenes access as the source for many of his later ideas. However, there is a catch in such a romantic story. Geisel's father did not take up a position with the zoo until the boy was in his late teens. He probably was a regular visitor, but had no privileged access (MacDonald, 1988).

The real story of Winnie the bear illustrates two important issues. The first is the long-standing tradition of direct interaction with zoo animals being facilitated by extra payment. This was not confined to just London Zoo, nor to just the 1920s, rather it has been a common facet of the zoo experience across time and around the world. Small payments, often solicited by underpaid keepers, enabled visitors to feed animals, pet them through the bars and even enter enclosures (Baratay & Hardouin-Fugier, 2002; De Courcey, 1995; Mullan & Marvin, 1987; Rothfels, 2002). Indeed, it continues today in the form of behind-the-scenes encounters and special feeding sessions.

Such personal interactions also feature in one of Milne's poems – *At the Zoo* – included in *When We were Young* (Milne, 1924). A short poem of three verses, each of four lines, it describes a small child's visit to the zoo. With faux misspellings, the various animals are catalogued. However, these animals are diminished by each verse ending with the real highlight of the trip: 'But I gave buns to the elephant when I went down to the Zoo!' (Milne, 1924: 46–47).

The second issue concerns the acquisition of zoo animals. Harry Colebourn buys Winnie to be a pet, but within 6 months he is no longer able to keep him and loans him to the zoo. The cub's mother was shot by hunters, who were fully aware of the sale value of a young specimen. Many zoos acquired animals in this way, conveniently forgetting the slaughter involved. As William Hornaday, Director of Bronx Zoo, cautioned Carl Hagenback in 1902:

> We must keep very still about forty large Indian rhinocerous being killed in capturing the four young ones. If that should get into the newspapers, either here or in London, there would be things published in condemnation of the whole business of capturing wild animals for exhibition. There are now a good many cranks who are so terribly sentimental that they affect to believe that it is wrong to capture wild creatures and exhibit them, – even for the benefit of millions of people. (Quoted in Rothfels, 2002: 67)

Such concerns did occasionally make it into children's literature. For example, *Raffy and the 9 monkeys* (Rey, 1939), starts with

> Raffy, the giraffe, was terribly unhappy. There had been a big hunt and all her family and friends had been caught and carried away to a Zoo. Raffy had escaped because she had the longest legs and ran faster than all the others. But now she was all alone in the wider desert. She felt so lonely that she cried and cried. (Rey, 1939: 3)

Fierce Creatures

Fierce Creatures (1997) is a light romantic comedy set in a small English zoo. Marwell Zoological Park in Hampshire was used for location shooting. Rod McCain (Kevin Kline) is a New Zealand media baron who has just acquired the zoo as part of a takeover of a group of companies. Rod, a thinly veiled caricature of Fox's Rupert Murdoch, insists that all his assets make a 20% return on investment and the zoo will be no exception. If it fails to achieve that benchmark, he will close the zoo and sell the site for housing.

Rollo (John Cleese) is put in charge, even though he has no previous experience of running zoos. To increase attendance, he adopts a strategy that his zoo will only feature fierce creatures. People, he reasons, like to be frightened and they only come to zoos to see the predators, such as lions and tigers. Accordingly, he decides to get rid of those animals that can't provide cheap thrills. The staff engages in a number of schemes to foil Rollo's plans. Finally, Reggie (Ronnie Corbett) stages a showbiz-style performance in the sea lion enclosure, which draws in large crowds. Rollo is now convinced that visitors can be attracted by gentler animals (though the fact that sea lions are predators is conveniently forgotten).

Meanwhile Rod's feckless son Vince (also played by Kevin Kline) is trying to demonstrate his usefulness to his father. He too seeks ways to increase zoo attendance figures. His first plan is to have celebrity sponsorships of the animals. This only fails when the celebrities refuse to sign up. Vince then unveils a new attraction – a giant panda. Rollo and the staff are impressed and agree this will boost attendances and profile. It then turns out that the panda is actually an animatronic robot. The clueless Vince argues that if visitors don't know it's fake, they will still be highly satisfied.

The underlying theme of this film concerns the increasing commodification of zoos. Management has decided that the zoo must be profitable, that it must have the same return on investment as a range of completely different business ventures. To survive, it must be commercially successful. To draw in the required increased attendance, four strategies are trialled and they are represented as having differing levels of success and/or desirability. Fake animatronic robots are shown as being the most ridiculous innovation. An emphasis only on fierce creatures is quickly dismissed. Yes, people do like savage carnivores, but there's also an expectation that a zoo will contain a wide range of animals. Celebrities sponsoring animals is portrayed as having some merit; after all, corporate sponsorship is widespread in the modern zoos. This idea only fails due to Vince's poor execution. The fourth idea, of a showbiz-style performance, is also, of course, quite common in zoos. The key point seems to be that the staff can't have the idyllic zoo that they have had in the past. Zoos are now about entertainment. The commercial imperative will force them to change and become more focused on marketing and performance.

Jurassic Park

Michael Crichton's novel *Jurassic Park* imagines a zoo containing genetically engineered dinosaurs. The zoo has been specifically created as a money-making venture, pushing the boundaries of the visitor experience. This idea of fantastic theme parks is common in much of Crichton's work. In *Westworld* (Crichton 1973), a feature film he wrote and directed, the characters in history-themed attractions are robots programmed to satisfy the visitors' every whim. In his novel *Timeline* (Crichton, 1999), time travel is used to create an authentic medieval theme park.

The novel *Jurassic Park* emphasises the zoo theme more than the film (Crichton, 1993) and the discussion below draws mainly on the novel. John Hammond (Richard Attenborough in the film) has perfected a means of creating living dinosaurs by extracting their DNA from fossil bones and amber. As in *Westworld* and *Timeline*, the entrepreneur sees that the most profitable way of exploiting this technological break-through is via tourism. Keen to avoid US government regulations, Hammond constructs his zoo and associated resort on an island off the coast of Costa Rica. He is particularly worried about animal rights and cruelty legislation, even arguing that as they are his creations, they have no rights. He also plans to build Jurassic Park Europe and Asia, again on off-shore islands under the sovereignty of governments with little interest in regulation.

Hammond's market is rich tourists who will happily pay for the experience of seeing extinct animals. His resort is exclusive and he monopolises transport and accommodation. To maximise his profit, Hammond is fanatical about reducing labour costs via automation. Visitors are transported past the exhibits in a mock safari landrover. Centrally controlled, it has no driver, follows a rail and all interpretation is provided by a pre-recorded commentary. In tests of the prototypes, visitors complain that the dinosaurs are hard to see. The ambush predators, particularly the *Tyrannosaurus rex*, are adept at hiding themselves. Hammond ponders the old paradox of how best to combine naturalistic enclosures with visibility. The pre-recorded commentary is particularly banal and lacks any flexibility or interactivity.

Opposed to Hammond are three scientists brought to the island by his backers, who are worried that the project might not work. These experts are palaeontologist Alan Grant (Sam Neill), palaeobotanist Ellie Sattler (Laura Dern) and Chaos theorist Ian Malcolm (Jeff Goldblum). Malcolm is the leading critic of the park, predicting that the dangerous animals will escape. Increasingly frustrated that Hammond won't listen to his scientific arguments, Malcolm finally explodes 'I'll tell you what's wrong. You took this knowledge and you used it. But you didn't work to get it, you paid for it. You had no discipline and no responsibility'. It's an interesting outburst – featured in both book and film – and worth a deeper look. On the surface it might just be that Malcolm is complaining about Hammond's commercial use of science. That makes little sense. An entrepreneur exploiting discoveries he paid for, but didn't actually make, is common place, hardly worth commenting on. However, if we take an alternative interpretation, that Malcolm is raging against Hammond's use of technology to stock his zoo, then we do have a powerful moment in the book and film.

Conventionally, zookeepers work hard to build up their collection. This can be done through collecting expeditions to dangerous and exotic locales (think Gerald Durrell or Steve Irwin) or through painstaking breeding programmes. Hammond circumvents these usual paths. He acquires his zoo by genetic engineering. Conservation is irrelevant for Hammond. He gets his extinct animals from the laboratory. They can be modified for desirable characteristics (Hammond argues with his staff about their ferocity, his technicians want tamer, easier to manage animals, Hammond wants them ferocious and attractive to visitors). Nor does he need to worry too much about their well being, if they die he can make more. Hammond can even make completely new animals; he has a tiny elephant, no bigger than a household cat. None of this is too different to animatronic displays. Hammond points to a future of made-to-order zoos, where conservation is not required.

The sequel film *Jurassic Park II: The Lost World* inverts the concept of Hammond's zoo. Hammond has lost control of his company to his nephew Peter Ludlow (Arliss Howard). Ludlow proclaims to his investors that Hammond has got it all wrong, 'you don't bring people to where the animals are, you bring the animals to the people'. His plan is to build a dinosaur zoo in San Diego, which has the advantage, he says, of already having a destination image linked to zoos. Accordingly, Ludlow mounts a collecting mission to the island (the technology has now been lost, he cannot make animals, only collect them). This is foiled by ecowarrior Nick Van Owen (Vince Vaughan). The film ends with Hammond back in control, trying to establish the island as a protected area rather than a zoo.

Crichton's chief interest is the adventures that arise when the dinosaurs escape. However, there is also an underlying theme of zoos as commercial theme parks. The attraction combines elements of theme parks and of zoos. There are live animals with habitat exhibits, but there are rides and merchandising, with a strong dose of safari park paraphernalia. In short, Jurassic Park is very much like many modern zoos.

Like Rod McCain in *Fierce Creatures*, owner Hammond is chiefly concerned with his return on investment. Similarly, in *Jurassic Park II*, Ludlow is also motivated by the potential profits of tourism. Of course, in both films these are counterpoint devices. McCain, Hammond and Ludlow must have these mercenary instincts to be set in opposition to the heroes. The entrepreneurs are looking to marketing gimmicks and have no real feel or empathy for the animals under their control. By contrast, our heroes (Rollo, Van Owen, Grant, Sattler and Malcolm) lack the commercial smarts, but are genuinely captivated by the animals they encounter. They provide a perspective for the audience that zoos are wonderful places, but we must put the animals before profits.

Madagascar

An animated feature, *Madagascar* (2005) is widely used by zoos for marketing. Indeed, modern glass-fronted exhibits are ideal for framing and presenting animals in a way similar to film and television (Figure 18.1 and 18.2). In *Madagascar*, Alex (Ben Stiller) is a lion in Central Park Zoo in New York. Nicknamed 'the King of New York', he is a popular star of the zoo, performing every day for large crowds. Alex is portrayed as a self-obsessed performer, preening and prancing for the crowds. The zoo provides performances similar to the shows on nearby Broadway. About to perform, Alex whispers 'It's Showtime' to himself, and at the end of the day, zoo staff usher out the crowds with 'Show's Over'. Alex loves the attention and loves his life in the zoo.

By contrast, other animals are dissatisfied. Marty the zebra (Chris Rock) dreams of visiting the 'wild', only known to him through a mural painted on the side of his enclosure. The penguins are planning an elaborate escape and return to Antarctica. When the opportunity comes, the chimpanzees also seize their chance to escape. An unsuccessful mass escape convinces the public that zoo animals have no place in New York. It is decided to repatriate the animals. However, an accident leads to Alex and his friends being washed up on the shores of Madagascar.

The film plays with the question of whether or not animals are happy in the zoo. Alex certainly is. His has an idyllic existence with mass adulation and plenty of food. His friends are also reasonably happy, but doubts gnaw away at them. They wonder if there is a better life in the wild, but they don't know (only Alex is specifically depicted as having been born outside the zoo). Their ideas of life outside the zoo are sketchy. Marty thinks the wild might be in Connecticut. When the penguins finally reach Antarctica, they are so disappointed ('well this sucks') that they immediately turn around to return home to New York. Shipwrecked

Figure 18.1 Modern glass-fronted exhibits provide close-ups (and even a TV-like frame) of the stars of *Madagascar*. (Photo: Warwick Frost)

Figure 18.2 Modern glass-fronted exhibits provide close-ups (and even a TV-like frame) of the stars of *Madagascar*. (Photo: Warwick Frost)

on Madagascar, the animals believe the jungle is some sort of naturalistic zoo exhibit. They assume they must be in San Diego.

Madagascar is firmly in the cartoon tradition of anthropomorphic representations of zoo animals. Their characters, personalities, foibles and expectations are all human. In essence, it utilises the old notion of a secret life of animals after closing time (an idea also central to *Night at the Museum*). During the day, the animals are only acting as animals, they are performers putting on a show for the benefit of the paying customers. Alex has the top billing, excelling in his act as the King of the Jungle/ New York.

Conclusion

The four fictional stories examined here are a subjective selection, but they well illustrate some of the issues surrounding zoos and how we see them in society. It is important to note that film makers and writers operate on two levels. First, they aim to be popular and achieve good sales, thereby allowing their creators to continue producing similar works. However, there is also a second level, in which film makers and writers see their work as art, providing comments and insight on the world. Like zoos, they seek to create a balance between multiple objectives.

Accordingly, films and stories about zoos operate at two levels: entertainment and artistic/critical analysis. The entertainment angle typically relies on anthropomorphism. The animals are represented as people, ranging from the childlike Winnie-the-Pooh through to the neurotic New Yorkers of *Madagascar*. Such confections are aimed at children, who are also a key market for real zoos. While this premise is squarely in the realms of fantasy, it does reflect that many zoo visitors also see the animals on display through some sort of anthropomorphic lens. An alternative entertainment subject is the adventure of animals escaping. Again, such entertainment is a fantasy, animals do not escape en masse and when individuals do break free, they are often terrified by the experience. Nonetheless, such fiction plays on the conceit of humans trying to subjugate wild animals and what happens when that goes wrong.

The artistic and critical analysis that writers and film makers engage in might not be so obvious. Indeed, the artist might take pride in hidden messages and clues that only the knowing reader or viewer will pick up. Furthermore, producers of entertainment for children often include storylines and messages that are explicitly aimed at the different markets of the children and the parents.

From the fictional stories considered in this chapter, at least three key issues are presented. The first is that zoos are attractions, institutions clearly designed to attract paying customers and generate revenue. In *Fierce Creatures*, the zoo is but one of a suite of businesses that McCain has just taken over and which he demands must make the same 20% return on investment as all his other holdings. In *Jurassic Park*, entrepreneur John Hammond sees a zoo as the most profitable way to exploit the new DNA technology. Later, when his nephew wrests control of the company away from Hammond, he too plans for a zoo, placed appropriately in San Diego, a destination that is already linked with a zoo. Central Park Zoo, as depicted in *Madagascar*, is a mass visitor attraction.

If zoos are businesses, it then follows (as the second issue) that they are profitable through providing some sort of entertainment or a show for the visitors. No one is satisfied by just looking at the animals. In *Fierce Creatures*, visitor yield is ultimately improved by the introduction of a razzle-dazzle sea lion feeding show. Jurassic Park is conceived as a theme park with faux safari rides and banal interpretation. At Central Park Zoo, Alex is the consummate performer starring in his own show. While he loves to perform, it is a performance staged by humans for humans.

In all the works, the human reaction to the performances is uncritical. No visitor turns to the camera or reader and declares that 'this is corny' or utters any simile for mediocre. And yet, the film maker or author is often giving a knowing wink. They know that the audience is in on the joke. Zoos are mass-market, low-brow entertainment. As Mullan and Marvin (1987) argue, art galleries and museums are high culture, zoos are simply popular culture. In *Fierce Creatures*, the joke is extended to the concept of authenticity. The buffoonish Vince scores a big success with a giant panda. The crowd and his colleagues love it until he tells them that it is animatronic. In an uncharacteristic moment of insight, Vince complains that everybody was really happy when they thought it was real, so what's the problem with fakery?

The third and final issue is that these fictional works underscore the idea that zoos are not about animals, they are about people (as argued by Mullan & Marvin, 1987: xiv; Rothfels, 2002: 7). These works critique the zoo visitor experience, particularly its entertainment dimension. Conservation and education are hardly considered. The animals are stage-managed for human consumption. Indeed, they are quite disposable. Both *Jurassic Park* and *Fierce Creatures* countenance the destruction of inconvenient animals, a sorry chapter in past zoo histories (see, e.g. the shooting of Chumley the Chimpanzee at London Zoo in the 1950s in Botting, 1999: 203). Again, I suspect that the filmmakers and authors are giving their audience a knowing look and posing them the question of how they feel about this part of the zoo experience.

Chapter 19
Zoos and Tourism in a Changing World

WARWICK FROST

Introduction

In this concluding chapter, my aim is to draw together the themes and issues examined within the chapters and to consider future research directions. In order to frame this summary, it is useful to begin by reflecting on recent developments both in zoo management and research into zoos and tourism.

The view from last century

Zoos have long been the poor second cousin of nature-based tourism. They predated national parks, but have often been over-shadowed by them. While zoos reached peak attendances with the Baby Boom of the 1950s, the rising environmental consciousness of the 1960s and 1970s quickly reduced their market. Deemed no longer worthy or relevant, zoos were forced to change, to again be hit by a growing competition from other leisure and tourism options. In the 1990s, the growing trend of ecotourism included a component of wildlife tourism. Characterised by small groups being expertly guided into remote areas with minimal impact, this new type of tourism activity seemed far preferable to those provided by old fashioned zoos. Experiencing animals in the wild seemed far more attractive than visiting enduring relics of a past age.

This decline in favour is well illustrated in Shackley's (1996) *Wildlife Tourism*. She argued that there was a strong growth in wildlife tours catering for high-income Westerners. The destinations were into the developing countries, particularly Africa, now easier and cheaper to reach through developments in air transport. The focus was often national parks, with tourism services developed by new public–private partnerships. Tourists were attracted to this as a form of *alternative* or *special interest* tourism and were motivated partly by 'ethical questions about the keeping of animals in captivity' and 'ways of using tourism revenues for conservation species' (Shackley, 1996: 11–12).

By contrast, zoos were a low-status, second best option. Only those who found that 'expensive wildlife watching holidays' were 'not financially possible' and long haul travel (to say Africa) was unsuitable

227

for families with children, still needed zoos (Shackley, 1996: 97). Furthermore, zoos were beset by controversies about their treatment of animals and accordingly demand declined. Shackley noted that of the top ten captive wildlife attractions in the UK, seven were recording declining attendances (1996: 102). She reported on a survey that found that 27% of zoo visitors believed that zoos should be abolished (Shackley, 1996: 104). These difficulties faced by zoos were illustrated by the near closure of London Zoo in 1992 (Shackley, 1996: 116–117).

Shackley's book was one of a number published around the turn of the century that questioned the role and existence of zoos. Some focused on the ethics of keeping animals (Bostock, 1993). A number took a historical approach, reflecting on past ill-treatment and hopefully (although almost apologetically) looking to a better future (Baratay & Hardouin-Fugier, 2002; De Courcey, 1995; Hoage & Deiss, 1996; Rothfels, 2002). Some emphasised that given that zoos were primarily for humans, they were accordingly interested in the sociology of their visitors (Mullan & Marvin, 1987; Rothfels, 2002). Perhaps most influential was David Hancocks, formerly of Seattle's Woodland Park Zoo, who argued that justifications of zoos on the basis of recreation, conservation or education were suspect. Rather his view was:

> we should not accept zoos as they currently are. My proposal is to *un*invent zoos as we know them and to create a new institution, one that praises wild things, that engenders respect for all animals, and that interprets a holistic view of nature. (Hancocks, 2001: xv)

Balancing the multiple roles of zoos

The argument that zoos have multiple roles in conservation, education and entertainment runs through much of the literature and is indeed often used by zoos themselves. At its heart is a difficult balancing act. Entertainment (or recreation, leisure or tourism) is not by itself a sufficient argument to justify zoos. For zoos to be acceptable in modern society, they need to make a worthy contribution to conservation and education. However, this argument often founders due to two problems. The first is that zoos have had a poor record in conservation. Only five species have been saved from extinction by zoos (Hancocks, 2001: xvii) and a number have died out despite being in the care of zoos. Of 48 zoo conservation plans, only 19 have strategies for reintroducing the species to the wild (Baratay & Hardouin-Fugier, 2002: 277). Of 10,000 zoos around the world, only 1,200 (12%) are registered for captive breeding and conservation; only 2% of the world's threatened species are in zoo conservation programmes and only 16 zoo projects have successfully returned animals to the wild (Shackley, 1996: 115).

The second problem is that a critical mass of surveys around the world have consistently shown that zoo visitors are mainly there for recreational or entertainment purposes – typically a pleasant day out with the family (De Courcey, 1995; Klenosky & Saunders, 2008; Mason, 2008; Moscardo, 2008; Mullan & Marvin, 1987; Ryan & Saward, 2004; Shackley, 1996; Tribe, 2004; Turley, 2001). Furthermore, these studies often found a contradiction in that visitors said they valued the zoo's conservation and education roles, but their behaviours and attitudes were mainly about their own entertainment.

The aim of this book is to revisit this issue of the role of zoos. As the title implies, the nexus between zoos and tourism is about conservation, education and entertainment. However, these three roles can conflict and the 'right' balance between them is a matter of ongoing debate. A revisiting is also appropriate given the highly dynamic nature of global tourism. While there was extensive discussion of the roles of zoos in the 1990s and early 2000s, the world has continued to change and the forces at play are different and dynamic. In turn, the debate about zoos and tourism is ongoing and ever-changing.

Changing trends in zoos and tourism

Consider some of the changes in the very short time since the 1990s. The pace of global environmental change has accelerated, through climate change, population growth, increasing pressure on natural resources and changing patterns of economic development. The rate of species extinction has increased and looks set to continue to grow. Species that looked relatively safe in the 1990s are now under threat. Habitat loss to farming and logging puts pressure on animals and also reduces the options for reintroduction. Such changes increase the potential importance of zoos in global conservation efforts. Sadly, they also mean that, in the future, tourists may only be able to see certain species in captivity.

Markets and fashions are changing. In 1987, Mullan and Marvin contrasted visitor responses to pandas at various zoos. Two were Asian (Beijing and Tokyo), where the locals were either indifferent or narrowly obsessed with photography. By contrast, at Washington DC Zoo, visitors were highly engaged and the pandas were named and anthropomorphised (Mullan & Marvin, 1987: xiii–xiv). This was one of their few references to non-Western zoos. Similarly, in the other works cited above, there were hardly any mentions of zoos or tourists outside the West. Little more than two decades on, we are acutely aware of the rapid rise and importance of Asian outbound tourism. Have the expectations and behaviours of these tourists changed? Has there been a convergence in urban Eastern and Western tastes and attitudes? If so, how does this affect the way zoos operate, including their marketing and interpretation programmes?

Ecotourism, once the *wunderkind*, has seemingly diminished. It is now seen as a niche market – important – but not attracting massive numbers. Other experiences are now seen as engaging and attractive. Indeed, there seems to have been a proliferation and fragmentation of all the things that tourists might be interested in. The concept of the 'experience' – memorable occurrences staged like a performance by a business (Pine & Gilmore, 1999) – has taken off and now dominates tourism marketing.

Perhaps most importantly, in this changing world, zoo managers have not been passive. They have taken note of the widespread criticism of their past efforts and of changing patterns in tourism and leisure. Responding to this changing world, they have reshaped the zoo experience.

Two trends stand out. The first has been to strongly emphasise that the primary role of zoos is conservation. This has been done through an increase in the number of specific conservation and reintroduction programmes *and* through sustained marketing/education campaigns concerning this role for zoos and the importance of conservation in general. It is now common to see major zoos devoting resources to convincing their visitors that the zoo they are visiting is a major conservation institution heavily involved in conservation. Such an approach positions these zoos as taking leadership in environmental issues. Ancillary to this are programmes to convince visitors that they are doing their part as well, simply by visiting that zoo, but even more if they change their behaviour as a result of the visit. Such changes have, not surprisingly, attracted criticism that they are little more than *Greenwash*, providing a 'feel good' experience with little substance (for an example of such criticism, see Millar & Houston, 2008a, 2008b).

The second trend has been for zoo managers to value add through experiences. Faced with the spectre of declining attendances, they have reshaped the zoo experience to increase revenue per head, encourage repeat visitation and attract new markets. In this, zoos have borrowed heavily from other attractions and leisure operations and learnt from their own past mistakes. The trend towards naturalistic enclosures has become the dominant one. Rather than having comprehensive collections, zoos have realised that it is better to have a lesser range with a focus on key star attractions. The appeal of these stars is bolstered by special programmes, such as 'Behind the Scenes' tours, offered at premium fees. This reshaping of the zoo visit has been integrated into marketing communication strategies that link the experience with the higher ideals of education and conservation.

The collection of chapters in this book explores and critiques these changes. Four broad patterns are discussed: conservation, new trends, experiences and the media. These are inter-related, certainly not black and white, but they provide a useful structure for considering the changes occurring in zoos and tourism.

Conservation, tourism and zoos

Modern zoos have striven to reposition themselves as leaders in conservation. Sinha (Chapter 2) examines a breakthrough programme involving the Philippines and a range of Western zoos. In the past, developing countries had practically no control over the zoo trade. Zoo collectors paid token fees for absolute ownership and even reintroduction programmes were largely under the control of Western zoos or agencies. Accordingly, developing countries and their peoples had little stake in conservation programmes. In a new institutional arrangement, the Philippines has negotiated with Western zoos so that the animals remain the property of the Philippines and co-operative reintroduction programmes are the highest priority.

However, any consideration of conservation in zoos has to take account of the attitudes and values of both zoo managers and visitors. Shani and Pizam (Chapter 3) argue that it is valuable to reconstruct a zoo typology in terms of the underlying values rather than more tangible factors, such as size or exhibit design. Their provocative typology ranges from zoos based on dominionistic or utilitarian values, through to those founded on moralistic or ecologistic principles.

One underlying value could be that animals exist for our commercial benefit. Wearing and Jobberns (Chapter 3) present the case that much of ecotourism is based on the commodification of nature and that this extends to zoos. While zoos are increasingly claiming to be ethical, Wearing and Jobberns contend that they still have a long way to go. Echoing other critics of zoos, they argue that wildlife tourism attractions and programmes in the home countries of animals are often more focused on animal welfare than zoos are.

This disconnection between rhetoric and reality is examined by Smith *et al.* (Chapter 5). Modern zoos increasingly contend that they enable people to make emotional connections with animals and that this experience may be so profound as to change values and attitudes – effectively transforming tourists into conservationists. Smith *et al.* argue that while this is influencing zoo practice and marketing, there is little evidence that this is actually occurring.

This lack of impact on visitors is also examined by Linke and Winter (Chapter 6). They undertook a detailed empirical study of visitors at two very different zoos in the same city – one open range with an African theme, the other an older, conventional, inner city zoo. Expecting to find significant differences in attitudes and values between visitors to the two zoos, instead they found very little difference. Furthermore, in line with other studies (e.g. Mason, 2008), they found that while those surveyed gave equal weighting to the importance of conservation, education and entertainment, they indicated that they were primarily there for entertainment.

The five chapters in this section are linked by the common banner of conservation. However, they also demonstrate that underlying any discussion of changes in conservation practices is the need to make changes in values and attitudes.

New Directions

Recent decades have seen the revival of aquaria as popular tourist attractions. Commercially minded (often privately owned) aquaria have come to characterise waterfront revitalisation tourism precincts. Furthermore, their success has encouraged many traditional zoos to develop their own aquarium-style exhibits. This dawning of the 'Age of Aquaria' has created new stars. What were once ignored or even feared are now seen as charismatic crowd pleasers. Dobson (Chapter 7) charts the changes in attitudes towards sharks and how they are presented and interpreted to tourists. His chapter parallels a later one by Cushing and Markwell (Chapter 14), which examines changing attitudes towards lizards and spiders.

Singapore Zoo has been very successful in developing a 'Night Safari' experience (Henderson, Chapter 8). Other zoos had experimented with special exhibits allowing viewing of nocturnal species, but Singapore had taken this concept much further, incorporating tour, food and beverage components. Henderson's exploration of this development also focuses on how Singapore Zoo and the Night Safari experience are an integral part of the tourism strategy for Singapore and how they complement other attractions and attributes of that destination.

Similar processes have been at work in Mumbai, though the result is uncertain. Hannam (Chapter 9) argues that Mumbai Zoo represents differing and changing views of what zoos should be. In the past, it appealed primarily to local people who were primarily interested in their own entertainment. Accordingly, animal welfare was a low priority. However, in recent years, there have been discussions about a major redevelopment of the zoo, mainly to make it more attractive to international tourists. Whether or not the redevelopment occurs, it is an instructive case study of potential change in non-Western countries.

Rounding off this section, Frost (Chapter 10) takes a historical view of the changes in zoos. He argues that we need to see zoos as one of a group of similar tourist attractions that, over time, have mutated and taken differing evolutionary paths. Zoos, national parks, theme parks and museums, he argues, share certain common characteristics and histories, and their current differences need to be understood in terms of their past.

The four chapters in this section provide insights into new directions being taken by zoos. These include the growth of aquaria, new experiences like Singapore's Night Safari and the need to reinvent older zoos for new markets. While perceived as new, these changes remind us of the historical evolution of zoos and connections with other tourist attractions. Looking back to the first section, the concept of conservation is still important, but in these new directions the entertaining of the visitor looms larger. The next section takes this focus on the visitor even further.

The Visitor Experience

Pine and Gilmore's (1999) *Experience Economy* was important in changing how zoos (and other tourist attractions) saw their visitors. It promised a bright new world where operators could 'value add', repackaging their product for a 'win-win' situation where visitors were more satisfied and zoos gained higher revenue. Introducing this section, Frost and Laing (Chapter 11) critique the application of the experience economy to zoos. First describing its growing application, they then argue that it also raises issues of sustainability, ethics and equity.

As with most tourist attractions, feeding visitors is an integral part of the zoo experience and as with most tourist attractions, it is also a common cause for complaint. Boksberger *et al.* (Chapter 12) investigate a zoo that has strategically chosen to redevelop its catering offerings, providing a higher standard and greater range and attempting to co-theme food outlets with zoo exhibits. This is an approach increasingly taken by major zoos in search of the benefits of the experience economy.

Volunteer programmes provide the means for some visitors to have richer and more extensive experiences at zoos. Holmes and Smith (Chapter 13) outline how many major zoos have large volunteer programmes, which enable them to provide visitor services within a constrained budget. These programmes work best when zoos understand the motivations of the volunteers, particularly the special experiences that the volunteers are seeking.

While experiences are often thought of as purely pleasurable, Cushing and Markwell (Chapter 14) argue that there is something deeply satisfying about more negative reactions, such as disgust. Examining a range of zoos specialising in reptiles, insects and spiders, they identify disgust as a major part of the appeal. This parallels the research by Dobson (Chapter 7) on sharks.

The final chapter in this section is by Crilley, whose research provides empirical data on the link between expectations and satisfaction among zoo visitors. He argues that a range of factors make up the zoo experience for visitors and that zoo managers need to understand this and incorporate them into their strategic plans. Such indicators could be collectively monitored over time and have the greatest value if they are consistently collected over a range of zoos and competing attractions.

The five chapters in this section delve deeply into the visitor experience at zoos. Taking the experience economy as a starting point, they go much further, demonstrating that the experience is much more than value adding. While focused primarily on the visitor, they also remind us that conservation remains in the background as an important influence on the experience and satisfaction.

The Media

The media is an important stakeholder for zoos (and indeed all tourist attractions). As Mason (Chapter 16) argues, the media may be both a promoter and a critic. Zoo managers would like to see the media as an important part of their marketing strategy, publicising new exhibits and animals. However, the media also resists too close a control and is always ready to pounce on a provocative story. Bad news sells newspapers and airtime and the ongoing controversy about the role of zoos often provides that big story. Mason's particular interest is in zoo reality shows, a growth area in modern times. He shows that while generally positive and promotional, they also regularly entertain deeper issues.

White (Chapter 17) provides a case study of the marketing strategy of Zoos Victoria, examining their branding and relationship with the external media. She particularly focuses on a number of campaigns to link the zoo's exhibits with conservation issues. Thus, for example, the opening of a new orangutan exhibit has coincided with a major multi-media campaign to change packaging laws regarding palm oil. The rapid growth of palm oil plantations in South East Asia threatens orangutan habitat. To protect these animals, consumers might like to choose not to purchase food and cosmetic products made with palm oil. However, labelling laws allow manufacturers to not disclose its use. Accordingly, Zoos Victoria has partnered with other conservation agencies to lobby to change the law and increase consumer awareness.

In Chapter 18, Frost looks at a selection of fictional media and how they portray zoos and their treatment of animals. His selection includes Winnie-the-Pooh and the films *Fierce Creatures*, *Jurassic Park* and *Madagascar*. He argues that while these are all primarily designed to be entertaining, there is also a common thread in this fictional media of promoting the debate over the role of zoos.

The three chapters in this section introduce the idea that the relationship between zoos and media is important and worthy of further consideration. While the media is an important ally in marketing zoos, it is also independent of zoo management. Whether it is news media, a reality show, fictional books or feature films, the makers of these media are trying to balance entertainment and information. In many ways, they are a valuable mirror on the concerns and attitudes of society regarding zoos.

Conclusions and Future Research

There have only been a few research studies on zoos and tourism and even less on aquaria and small wildlife parks (Frost & Roehl, 2008; Mason, 2000). Such a lack of enquiry is both curious and disappointing given their scale and importance. As modern zoos move to reposition themselves as conservation institutions, it is appropriate for us to consider them increasingly as an integral part of nature-based tourism. A great deal of research is undertaken on ecotourism, national parks, nature tours, wildlife watching and ecolodges, and we should be giving proportionate attention to zoos.

The aim of this book was to focus attention on the complex relationship between zoos and tourism. That relationship was framed in terms of multiple roles for zoos – that is – conservation, education or entertainment. Two qualifications need to be added to any consideration of these roles. First, zoos are dynamic institutions, and the balance between the different roles is constantly changing as society evolves. Second, the roles are not necessarily exclusive. Indeed, we might hope that the ideal zoo of the future will have a strong conservation focus and be educational and entertaining.

It is my hope that this volume provides signposts for future research. Many of the ideas contained here have been explored, but by no means completely covered. Hopefully this book is but a foundation for the future.

In these concluding comments, two specific research directions warrant emphasising. The first is that zoo managers are not passive; they have reacted to recent criticisms by implementing a wide range of changes. For zoos, the discussion about their multiple roles is not academic, but is driving their strategic thinking. Accordingly, there is value in taking a supply-side research approach, examining what zoos are doing and why. In taking that approach, there is further value in adopting comparative methodologies, contrasting zoos in different countries and those with differences in design, purpose and scale. The second direction is to consider the demand side. This incorporates issues of tourist choices, expectations and motivations. All these are also dynamic, and as societies continue to evolve, what we want zoos to be will also change.

References

ABS (Australian Bureau of Statistics) (1998) *Zoos, Parks and Gardens Industry, Australia, 1996–97*. Cat. No. 8699.0. Canberra: ABS.

ABS (2007) *Attendances at Selected Cultural Venues and Events*. Cat. No. 4114.0. Canberra: ABS.

ABS (2008) *Year Book Australia, 2008*. Cat. No. 1301. Canberra: ABS.

ACRES (2009) Campaigns. On WWW at http://www.acres.org.sg/campaigns. Accessed 22.8.09.

Adelman, L.M., Falk, J.H. and James, S. (2000) Impact of National Aquarium in Baltimore on visitors' conservation attitudes, behavior, and knowledge. *Curator* 43 (1), 33–61.

AES (2008) *The 2008 AES International Captive Elasmobranch Census*. On WWW at http://www.elasmo.org/census.php. Accessed 20.4.09.

African Impact (2008) *African Lion Rehabilitation, Zimbabwe*. On WWW at http://www.africanimpact.com/volunteers/lion-rehabilitation-zimbabwe. Accessed 24.10.08.

Agrawal, N., Menon, G. and Aaker, J. (2007) Getting emotional about health. *Journal of Marketing Research* 44 (1), 100–113.

Ajzen, I. (1991) The theory of planned behavior. *Organizational Behavior and Human Decision Processes* 50 (2), 179–211.

Ajzen, I. (2005) Laws of human behavior: Symmetry, compatibility, and attitude-behavior correspondence. In A. Beauducel, B. Biehl, M. Bosnjak, W. Conrad, G. Schönberger and D. Wagener (eds) *Multivariate Research Strategies* (pp. 3–19). Aachen: Shaker Verlag.

Ajzen, I. and Fishbein, M. (2005) The influence of attitudes on behavior. In D. Albarracín, B.T. Johnson and M.P. Zanna (eds) *The Handbook of Attitudes* (pp. 173–221). Mahwah, NJ: Erlbaum.

ALERT (African Lion Environmental Research Trust) (2009) *About ALERT*. On WWW at http://www.lionalert.org.

Alexander, E.P. (1979) *Museums in Motion: An Introduction to the History and Functions of Museums*. Nashville, TN: American Association for State and Local History.

Albert, A. and Bulcroft, K. (1988) Pets, families, and the life course. *Journal of Marriage and the Family* 50 (2), 543–552.

Almazan, R.R., Rubio, R.P. and Agoramoorthy, G. (2005) Welfare evaluations of nonhuman animals in selected zoos in the Philippines. *Journal of Applied Animal Welfare Science* 8 (1), 59–68.

Anathaswamy, A. (2004) Beware the ecotourist. *New Scientist* 181 (2437), 2.

Andersen, K. (1995) Culture and nature at Adelaide Zoo. *Transaction of the Institute of British Geographers* 20, 275–294.

Anderson, A.K. and Phelps, E.A. (2001) Lesions of the human amygdala impair enhanced perception of emotionally salient events. *Nature* 411 (6835), 305–309.

Animal Rights Coalition (2009) *Petting Zoos: An Educational Experience?* On WWW at http://www.animalright scoalition.com/doc/petting_zoo_factsheet.pdf. Accessed 16.2.09.

Anon. (1927) The snake park. *The Adelaide Register*, 23 March, p. 5.

AQWA (Aquarium of Western Australia) (2008) *AQWA Volunteer Information Sheet*. Perth: AQWA.

ARAZPA (2003) *ARAZPA Education Policy*. Department of Environment and Heritage, Commonwealth of Australia.

ARAZPA (2008) *Membership profile*. On WWW at http://www.arazpa.org.au/ Institutional-profile/default.aspx.

Armstrong, J., Gibson, N., Howe, F. and Porter, B. (1993) The role of ex-situ conservation. In C. Moritzand and J. Kikkawa (eds) *Conservation Biology in Australia and Oceania* (pp. 353–357). Norton: Surrey Beatty & Sons.

ATC (Australian Tourist Commission) (1998) *Sydney Australia Towards 2000: Facts and Contacts*. Sydney: ATC.

Australian Reptile Park (2005) *News and Events*. On WWW at http://www. reptilepark.com.au/news.asp?nID=17. Accessed 27.5.09.

AZA (Association of Zoos and Aquariums) (2003) *Standards for Elephant Management and Care*. On WWW at http://www.elephants.com/pdf/AZA%20 Elephant%20Standards%201.pdf.

AZA (2006) *Conservation Education Vision and Mission*. On WWW at http:// www.aza.org/ConEd/ConEdVisionMission/. Accessed 15.5.06.

AZA (2008) *Guidelines For Reintroduction of Animals Born or Held in Captivity*. Accessed 3.9.2010.

Bagarinao, T. (1998) Nature parks, museums, gardens, and zoos for biodiversity conservation and environmental education: The Philippines. *Ambio* 27 (3), 230–237.

Bailey, C. (2007) "Africa begins at the Pyrenees": Moral outrage, hypocrisy, and the Spanish bullfight. *Ethics and the Environment* 12 (1), 23–37.

Baillie, J., Hilton-Taylor, C. and Stuart, S.N. (2004) *2004 IUCN Red List of Threatened Species: A Global Species Assessment*. Gland: IUCN.

Baker, S. (2001) *Picturing the Beast*. Chicago, IL: University of Illinois Press.

Ballantyne, R. and Packer, J. (2005) Promoting environmentally sustainable attitudes and behaviour through free-choice learning experiences: What is the state of the game? *Environmental Education Research* 11 (3), 281–295.

Ballantyne, R., Packer, J. and Hughes, K. (2008) Environmental awareness, interests and motives of botanic gardens visitors: Implications for interpretive practice. *Tourism Management* 29 (3), 439–444.

Ballantyne, R., Packer, J. and Hughes, K. (2009) Tourists' support for conservation messages and sustainable management practices in wildlife tourism experiences. *Tourism Management* 30 (5), 658–664.

Balmford, A., Leader-Williams, N. and Green, M.J.B. (1995) Parks or arks: Where to conserve large threatened mammals? *Biodiversity and Conservation* 4, 595–607.

Balmford, A., Leader-Williams, N., Mace, G., Manica, A., Walter, O., West, C. and Zimmermann, A. (2007) Message received? Quantifying the impact of informal conservation education on adults visiting UK zoos. In A. Zimmermann, M. Hatchwell, L. Dickie and C. West (eds) *Catalysts for Conservation: A Direction for Zoos in the 21st Century* (pp. 120–136). Cambridge: Cambridge University Press.

Balmford, A., Mace, G.M. and Leader-Williams, N. (1996) Designing the ark: Setting priorities for captive breeding. *Conservation Biology* 10, 719–727.

Bandyopadhyay, R., Morais, D. and Chick, G. (2008) Religion and identity in India's heritage tourism. *Annals of Tourism Research* 35 (3), 790–808.

Banks, C.B. (2004) Overview and conservation priorities for the Philippine Crocodile. *Proceedings of 17th Working Meeting of the Crocodile Specialist Group* (pp. 129–135). Gland: IUCN.

Banks, C.B. (2005) *National Recovery Plan for the Philippine Crocodile, Crocodylus mindorensis, 2005–2008* (2nd edn). Quezon and Melbourne: Department of Environment & Natural Resources and the Royal Melbourne Zoological Gardens.

Baratay, E. and Hardouin-Fugier, E. (2002) *Zoo: A History of Zoological Gardens in the West*. London: Reaktion.

Barbieri, K. (2002) From petting zoos to stunt shows, free entertainment takes all forms. *Amusement Business* 114 (24), 1.

Barrows, C.W. and Giannapoulos, E. (2006) An exploratory study of outsourcing of foodservice operations in Canadian hotels. *Tourism* 54 (4), 375–383.

Bashaw, M., Bloomsmith, M., Marr, M. and Maple, T. (2003) To hunt or not to hunt? A feeding enrichment experiment with captive large felids. *Zoo Biology* 22 (2), 189–198.

BBC (2004) *Polar Bears turn Green in Singapore*. On WWW at http://www.news vote.bbc.co.uk. Accessed 22.8.09.

Beardsworth, A. and Bryman, A. (2001) The wild animal in late modernity: The case of the Disneyfication of zoos. *Tourist Studies* 1 (1), 83–104.

Becker, W.A. (1987) Theme restaurants, a unique dining experience. *Visions in Leisure and Business*, 6 (3), 51–55.

Beer, S. (2008) Authenticity and food experience – commercial and academic perspectives. *Journal of Foodservice* 19, 153–163.

Beeton, S. (2005) *Film-Induced Tourism*. Clevedon: Channel View Publications.

Benbow, S. (2000) Zoos: Public places to view private lives. *Journal of Popular Culture* 33 (4), 13–23.

Benntrupperbaumer, J. (1998) Reciprocal ecosystem impact and behavioural interactions between cassowaries and humans: Exploring the natural-human environment interface and its implications for endangered species recovery in North Queensland, Australia. Unpublished PhD thesis, James Cook University.

Bhardwaj, D. (ed.) (1998) *Domestic Tourism in India*. Indus: New Delhi.

Bhattacharyya. D. (1997) Mediating India: An analysis of a guidebook. *Annals of Tourism Research* 24 (2), 371–389.

Birney, B. (1988) Criteria for successful museum and zoo visits: Children offer guidance. *Curator* 31 (4) 292–316.

Bishop, R. (2004) Journeys to the urban exotic embodiment and the zoo-going gaze. *Humanities Research* 11 (1), 106–124.

Born Free Foundation (2008) *Romanian Zoo Crisis*. On WWW at http://www.bornfree.org.uk/campaigns/zoo-check/zoos/romanian-zoos. Accessed 14.3.08.

Bostock, S.St.C. (1993) *Zoos and Animal Rights: The Ethics of Keeping Animals*. London and New York: Routledge.

Botting, D. (1999) *Gerald Durrell: The Authorized Biography*. New York: Carroll & Graf.

Boyd, S. (2003) Marketing challenges and opportunities for heritage tourism. In A. Fyall, B. Garrod and A. Leask (eds) *Managing Visitor Attractions* (pp. 189–202). Oxford: Butterworth Heinemann.

Bowd, A.D. (1984) Development and validation of a scale of attitudes toward the treatment of animals. *Educational and Psychological Measurement* 44, 513–515.

Bradshaw, G.A., Schore, A.N., Brown, J.L., Poole, J.H. and Moss, C.J. (2005) Elephant breakdown. *Nature* 433, 807.

Bramwell, B. and Lane, B. (eds) (2000) *Tourism Collaboration and Partnerships: Politics, Practice and Sustainability.* Clevedon: Channel View Publications.

Broad, G. (1996) Visitor profile and evaluation of informal education at Jersey Zoo. *The Dodo: The Journal of the Wildlife Preservation Trusts* 32, 166–192.

Broad, S. and Jenkins, J. (2008) Gibbons in their midst? Conservation volunteers' motivations at the Gibbon Rehabilitation Project, Phuket, Thailand. In K. Lyons and S. Wearing (eds) *Journeys of Discovery in Volunteer Tourism* (pp. 72–85). Wallingford: CABI.

Broad, S. and Smith, L. (2004) Who educates the public about conservation issues? Examining the role of zoos and the media. In W. Frost, S. Beeton and G. Croy (eds) *Proceedings from the International Tourism and Media Conference* (pp. 15–23). Melbourne: Monash University Tourism Research Unit.

Broad, S. and Weiler, B. (1998) Captive animals and interpretation: A tale of two tiger exhibits. *Journal of Tourism Studies* 9 (1), 14–27.

Brooks, T.M., Abuel, M., Co, L., Coroza, O., Duya, L.V., Duya, A., Langhammer, P., Mallari, A., Morales, C., Palomar, N., Rodriguez, R., Tabaranza, B. and Trono, R. (2004) Targets and priorities for biodiversity conservation globally and in the Philippines. *Agham Mindanaw* 2, 1–10.

Buckley, R. (1996) Sustainable tourism: Technical issues and information needs. *Annals of Tourism Research* 23 (4), 925–928.

Bulbeck, C. (2005) *Facing the Wild: Ecotourism, Conservation and Animal Encounters.* London: Earthscan.

Butler, R.W. (ed.) (2006) *The Tourism Area Life Cycle*, 2 vols. Clevedon: Channel View Publications.

Cahill, L. and McGaugh, J.L. (1995) A novel demonstration of enhanced memory associated with emotional arousal. *Consciousness and Cognition* 4 (4), 410–421.

Cain, L. and Meritt, D. (1998) Zoos and aquariums. In B.A. Weisbrod (ed.) *To Profit or Not to Profit: The Commercial Transformation of the Nonprofit Sector* (pp. 217–232). Cambridge: Cambridge University Press.

Cain, L. and Meritt, D. (2008) The demand for zoos and aquariums. *Tourism Review International* 11 (3), 295–306.

Cairns Night Zoo (2009) A *great Australian night out!* On WWW at http://www.cairnsnightzoo.com/home.htm. Accessed 22.8.09.

Caldwell, L. and Andereck, K. (1994) Motives for initiating and continuing membership in a recreation-related voluntary association. *Leisure Sciences* 16 (1), 33–44.

Camhi, M., Fowler, S., Musick, J., Bräutigam, A. and Fordham, S. (1998) *Sharks and their Relatives: Ecology and Conservation.* Gland: IUCN/SSC Shark Specialist Group.

Cann, J. (2001) *Snakes Alive!: Snake Experts and Antidote Sellers of Australia* (2nd edn). Sydney: John Cann.

Carrell, S. (2004) Aquarium fish suffer abuse and ill-health. *The Independent*, 26 September.

Carwardine, M. (2001) *Killer Whales.* London: BBC.

Casamitjana, J. (2004) *Aquatic Zoos: A Critical Study of UK Public Aquaria in the Year 2004.* London: The Captive Animals Protection Society.

Cassidy, T. (1997) *Environmental Psychology: Behaviour and Experience in Context.* Hove: Psychology Press.

Cater, C. and Cater, E. (2007) *Marine Ecotourism: Between the Devil and the Deep Blue Sea*. Wallingford: CABI.

Catibog-Sinha, C.S. (2008a) Zoo tourism: Biodiversity conservation through tourism. *Journal of Ecotourism* 7 (2 & 3), 155–173.

Catibog-Sinha, C. (2008b) The role of urban green parks in promoting sustainable tourism and biodiversity conservation: Case study. In Y.H. Hwang (ed.) *Proceedings 14th Asia Pacific Tourism Association Conference, Tourism and Hospitality in Asia Pacific* (pp. 245–255). Bangkok: APTA.

Catibog-Sinha, C.S. and Heaney, L.R. (2006) *Philippine Biodiversity: Principles and Practice*. Quezon City: Haribon Foundation.

Cavanaugh, D. (2007) Fun food becomes food for thought at many zoos. *Tourism Attractions and Parks* April/May, 86–88.

Champ, J. (2002) A culturalist-qualitative investigation of wildlife media and value orientations. *Human Dimensions of Wildlife* 7, 273–286.

Chaudhary, M. (1996) India's tourism: A paradoxical product. *Tourism Management* 17 (8), 616–19.

Cheeta (2008) *Me Cheeta; The Autobiography*. London: Fourth Estate.

Chiang Mai Night Safari (2009) *About Chiang Mai Night Safari*. On WWW at http://www.chiangmainightsafari.com/en/home.htm. Accessed 20.8.09.

Christianson, S. and Loftus, E. (1987) Memory for traumatic events. *Applied Cognitive Psychology* 1 (4), 225–239.

Christie, S. (2007) Zoo-based fundraising for in-situ wildlife conservation. In A. Zimmermann, M. Hatchwell, L. Dickie and C. West (eds) *Zoos in the 21st Century: Catalysts for Conservation* (pp. 257–274). Cambridge: Cambridge University Press.

Chronis, A. (2005) Coconstructing heritage at the Gettysburg storyscape. *Annals of Tourism Research* 32 (2), 386–406.

Churchman, D. (1985) The educational impact of zoos and museums: A review of the literature. *Resources in Education* 20 (12), 133–161.

Churchman, D. and Bossler, C. (1990) Visitor behaviour at Singapore Zoo. *Resources in Education* 25 (8), 126.

Cialdini, R.B. (2001) *Influence: Science and Practice*. Boston, MA: Allyn and Bacon.

Cialdini, R.B., Petty, R.E. and Cacioppo, J.T. (1981) Attitude and attitude change. *Annual Review of Psychology* 32, 357–404.

CITES (2009) *Species database: CITES listed species*. On WWW at http://www.cites.org/eng/resources/species.html. Accessed 26.5.09.

Clubb, R. and Mason, G. (2003) Captivity effects on wide-ranging carnivores. *Nature* 425 (6957), 473–474.

Cobb, R. (2003) Chickenfighting for the soul of the heartland. *Text, Practice, Performance* 4, 69–83.

Coe, J.C. (2006) Mixed species rotation exhibits. *Proceedings of the 2006 ARAZPA Conference*. Christchurch, New Zealand.

Coe, J.C. and Lee, G.H. (1996) One-hundred years of evolution in Great Apes facilities in American zoos 1896–1996. *Proceedings of the AZA 1995 Western Regional Convention*. Bethesda, MD: American Zoo and Aquarium Association.

Coghlan, A. and Prideaux, B. (2008) Encounters with wildlife in Cairns, Australia: Where, what, who? *Journal of Ecotourism* 7 (1), 68–76.

Cohen, C. (2008) The Fish Tank That's So Big It Can Hold Four Whale Sharks. *Daily Mail*, 17 June.

Cohen, S.P. (2002) Can pets function as family members? *Western Journal of Nursing Research* 24 (6), 621–638.

Cole, S. (2006) Information and empowerment: The keys to achieving sustainable tourism. *Journal of Sustainable Tourism* 14 (6), 629–644.

Cole, S. (2007) Beyond authenticity and commodification. *Annals of Tourism Research* 34 (4), 943–960.

Compagno, L., Dando, M. and Fowler, S. (2005) *Sharks of the World*. London: Collins.

Conway, H. (1991) *People's Parks: The Design and Development of Victorian Parks in Britain*. Cambridge: Cambridge University Press.

Conway, W. (2007) Entering the 21st century. In A. Zimmermann, M. Hatchwell, L. Dickie and Ch. West (eds) *Zoos in the 21st Century: Catalysts for Conservation?* (pp. 12–21). Cambridge: Cambridge University Press.

Corkeron, P.J. (2004) Whale watching, iconography, and marine conservation. *Conservation Biology* 18, 3.

Correia, A., Moital, M., da Costa, C.F. and Peres, R. (2008) The determinants of gastronomic tourists' satisfaction: A second-order factor analysis. *Journal of Foodservice* 19, 164–176.

Crawford, D. (2008) *Shark*. London: Reaktion Books.

Crilley, G. (2005) A case for benchmarking customer service quality in tourism and leisure services. *Journal of Hospitality and Tourism Management* 12 (2), 97–107.

Crilley, G. (2008) Visitor service quality attributes at Australian gardens: Their use in predicting behavioural intentions. *Annals of Leisure Research* 11 (1 & 2), 20–40.

Crilley, G. and March, H. (2003) The Adelaide Zoo: Perceptions of service quality; establishing a baseline of the profile of adults and children customers, and how they engage with Adelaide Zoo. Unpublished report for Adelaide Zoo.

Crilley, G., March, H. and Whithouse, L. (2008) Bellwether or benchmark? Why you need to know what your visitors don't know about your zoo's roles, and what you can do about it. In G. Dick (ed.) *Proceedings of WAZA Conference* (pp. 20–24). Adelaide: WAZA.

Crocosaurus Cove (2009) On WWW at http://www.crocosauruscove.com. Accessed 1.8.09.

Crowcroft, P. (1978) *The Zoo*. Sydney: Philip Mathews.

Cunningham-Smith, P., Colbert, D.E., Wells, R.S. and Speakman, T. (2006) Evaluation of human interactions with a provisioned wild bottlenose dolphin (Tursiops truncatus) near Sarasota Bay, Florida, and efforts to curtail the interactions. *Aquatic Mammals* 32 (3), 11.

CZA (2009) *Central Zoo Authority of India – About Us*. On WWW at http://www.cza.nic.in. Accessed 15.7.09.

Dann, G. (1977) Anomie, ego-enhancement and tourism. *Annals of Tourism Research* 4 (4), 184–194.

Davey, G. (2007) Public perceptions in urban China toward zoos and their animal welfare. *Human Dimensions of Wildlife* 12 (5), 367–374.

Davis, B., Lockwood, A. and Stone, S. (1998) *Food and Beverage Management*. Oxford: Butterworth Heinemann.

Dean, A. (2009) Animal Business. *Melbourne Weekly Eastern*, 9 June, pp. 14–15.

DeBergerac, O. (1998) *The Dolphin Within*. Australia: Simon and Schuster.

De Courcey, C. (1995) *The Zoo Story*. Melbourne: Penguin.

DeGrazia, D. (2002) *ANIMAL RIGHTS: A Very Short Introduction*. Oxford: Oxford University Press.

De Lange, P. (1998) *The Games Cities Play*. Monument Park: De Lange.

Dennis, C. (2008) *Village Roadshow Proposal for Werribee Open Range Zoo*. Letter from President of Friends of the Zoo to members, 15 May 2008.

Design for Life (2009) *Zoological exhibit design*. On WWW at http://www.designforlife.com.sg/mike_cv.html. Accessed 18.8.09.

Desmond, J.C. (1999) *Staging Tourism: Bodies on Display from Waikiki to Sea World*. Chicago, IL: University of Chicago Press.

de Rojas, C. and Camareo, C. (2008) Visitor's experience, mood and satisfaction in a heritage context: Evidence from an interpretation center. *Tourism Management* 29, 525–537.

DeSteno, D., Petty, R., Rucker, D., Wegener, D. and Baverman, J. (2004) Discrete emotions and persuasion: The role of emotion-induced expectancies. *Journal of Personality and Social Psychology* 86 (1), 43–56.

Detwiler, A. (2007) A bountiful harvest: How botanic gardens café serves up nature's bounty. *Tourism Attractions and Parks* August, 136–140.

DeVellis, R. (1991) *Scale Development: Theory and Applications*. Newbury Park, CA: Sage.

Diamond, J. (1991) *The Rise and Fall of the Third Chimpanzee*. London: Random House.

Dierking, L.D., Adelman, L., Odgen, J., Lehnhardt, K., Miller, L. and Mellen, J. (2004) Using a behavior change model to document the impact of visits to Disney's Animal Kingdom: A study of investigating intended conservation action. *Curator* 47 (3), 322–343.

Dirkx, J.M. (2001) The power of feeling: Emotion, imagination, and the construction of meaning in adult learning, In S.B. Merriam (ed.) *The New Update on Adult Learning Theory* (pp. 63–72). San Francisco, CA: Jossey-Bass.

DNA (2009) *Animal Rights Groups Seek Closure of Mumbai Zoo*. On WWW at http://www.dnaindia.com/mumbai/report_animal-rights-groups-seek-closure-of-mumbai-zoo_1252499. Accessed 15.7.09.

Dobson, F.S. and Yu, J. (1993) Rarity in neotropical forest mammals – Revisited. *Conservation Biology* 7 (3), 586–591.

Dobson, J. (2004) The Potential for Wildlife Tourism to Contribute Towards Elasmobranch Conservation: A Case Study of the South African Cage Diving Industry. Paper at the European Elasmobranch Society meeting.

Dobson, J. (2006) Sharks, wildlife tourism and state regulation. *Tourism in Marine Environments* 3, 25–34.

Dobson, J. (2007) Jaws or Jawesome? Exploring the Nature of the Shark Diving Experience. *Proceedings of the 5th Coastal and Marine Tourism Congress*. Auckland: AUT.

Dobson, J. (2008) Shark! A new frontier in tourist demand for marine wildlife. In J. Higham. and M. Luck (eds) *Marine Wildlife and Tourism Management* (pp. 49–65). Wallingford: CABI.

Downs, A. (1972) Up and down with ecology – the issue attention cycle. *Public Interest* (28) 38–50.

Drummond, S. (2001) Critical success factors for the organization. In S. Drummond and I. Yeoman (eds) *Quality Issues in Heritage Visitor Attractions* (pp. 16–27). Oxford: Butterworth Heinemann.

Durrell. G. (1990) *The Ark's Anniversary*. London: Collins.

Eagly, A.H. and Chaiken, S. (1993) *The Psychology of Attitudes*. Orlando, FL: Harcourt Brace Jovanovich.

Ebersole, R. (2003) How NWF is making a difference. *National Wildlife* 41 (2), 4.

Edensor, T. (1999) *Tourists at the Taj*. London: Routledge.

Edensor, T. (2001) Performing tourism, staging tourism: Re(producing) tourist space and practice. *Tourist Studies* 1 (1), 59–81.

Eder, K. (1996) *The Social Construction of Nature*. London: Sage.

Edinburgh Zoo (2009) *Volunteer*. On WWW at http://www.edinburghzoo. org.uk/working-at-the-zoo/volunteer.Edwards, D. (2005) It's mostly about me: Reasons why volunteers contribute their time to museums and art museums. *Tourism Review International* 9, 21–31.

Edwards, J.S.A. and Gustafsson, I-B. (2008) The five aspect meal model. *Journal of Foodservice* 19, 4–12.

Ellis, C. (2003) Participatory environmental research in tourism: A global view. *Tourism Recreation Research* 28, 45–55.

Ellis, S. and Seal, U.S. (1996), *Conservation Assessment and Management Plan (CAMP) Process: Reference Manual*. Apple Valley, MN: IUCN/SSC Conservation Breeding Specialist Group.

Engelbrecht, T. and Smith, J. (2004) Dying to entertain us. *The Ecologist*, 1 October, p. 6.

Euromonitor (2009) *Tourist Attractions: Singapore*. London: Euromonitor.

Evans, K.L. (1997) Aquaria and marine environmental education. *Aquarium Sciences and Conservation* 1 (4), 234–250.

Farber, M.E. and Hall, T.E. (2007) Emotion and environment: Visitor's extraordinary experiences along the Dalton Highway in Alaska. *Journal of Leisure Research* 39 (2), 248–170.

Faulkner, B. and Vikulov, S. (2001) Katherine: Washed out one day, back on track the next: A post mortem of a tourism disaster. *Tourism Management* 22 (4), 331–344.

Fazio, R.H., Zanna, M.P. and Cooper, J. (1978) Direct experience and attitude-behavior consistency: An information processing analysis. *Personality and Social Psychology Bulletin* 4 (1), 48–51.

Fennell, D. (1999) *Ecotourism; An Introduction*. London: Routledge

Fields, K. (2002) Demand for the gastronomy tourism product: Motivational factors. In A.M. Hjalager and G. Richards (eds) *Tourism and Gastronomy* (pp. 36–50). London: Routledge.

Figgis, P. (2002) The double-edged sword: Tourism and national parks. *Habitat Australia* 28 (5), 24.

Fishbein, M. and Ajzen, I. (1975) *Belief, Attitude, Intention & Behavior: An Introduction to Theory & Research*. Reading: Addison-Wesley.

Flad, P.O. (2002) *Dienstleistungsmanagement in Gastronomie und Foodservice-Industrie*. Frankfurt am Main: Deutscher Fachverlag.

Fleay-Thomson, R. (2007) *Animals First: The Story of Pioneer Australian Conservationist & Zoologist Dr David Fleay*. Nerang: Petaurus.

Fleischer, A. and Pizam, A. (1997) Rural tourism in Israel. *Tourism Management* 18 (6), 367–372.

Florida, R. (2002) *The Rise of the Creative Class: And How It's Transforming Work, Leisure, Community and Everyday Life*. New York: Basic Books.

Florida, R. (2005) *Cities and the Creative Classes*. London and New York: Routledge.

Ford, C. (2009) A summer fling: The rise and fall of aquariums and fun parks on Sydney's ocean coast 1885–1920. *Journal of Tourism History* 1 (2), 95–112.

Franklin, A. (1999) *Animals and Modern Culture*. London: Sage.

Fraser, J., Gruber, S. and Condon, K. (2008) Exposing the tourist value proposition of zoos and aquaria. *Tourism Review International* 11 (3), 279–293.

Fraser, J. and Wharton, D. (2007) The future of zoos: A new model for cultural institutions. *Curator* 50 (1), 41–54.

Fravel, L. (2003) Critics question zoos' commitment to conservation. *National Geographic News*, 13 November.

Fredline, L. (2007) *An Analysis of the Domestic Wildlife Tourism Market in Australia*. Brisbane: Sustainable Tourism Cooperative Research Centre.

Frost, W. (2003) The financial viability of heritage tourism attractions: Three cases from rural Australia. *Tourism Review International* 7 (1), 13–22.

Frost, W. and Hall, C.M. (2009) *Tourism and National Parks: International Perspectives on Development, Histories and Change*. London and New York: Routledge.

Frost, W. and Roehl, W.S. (2008) Zoos, Aquaria and tourism: Extending the research agenda. *Tourism Review International* 11 (3), 191–196.

Fyall, A., Garrod, B. and Leask, A (2003) *Managing Visitor Attractions: New Directions*. Oxford: Butterworth-Heinemann.

Gartner, W.C. (1994) Image formation process. *Journal of Travel & Tourism Marketing* 2 (2/3), 191–216.

Gaston, K.J. and Blackburn, T.M. (1995) Rarity and body size: Some cautionary remarks. *Conservation Biology* 9, 210–213.

Gendron, S.M. (2004) Education and elasmobranchs in public aquariums. In M. Smith, D. Warmolts, D. Thoney and R. Hueter (eds) *The Elasmobranch Husbandry Manual: Captive Care of Sharks, Rays and their Relatives* (pp. 521–531). Columbus, OH: Ohio Biological Survey.

Gerdes, A., Uhl, G. and Alpers, G. (2009) Spiders are special: Fear and disgust evoked by pictures of arthropods. *Evolution and Human Behavior* 30, 66–73.

Germano, J. M. and Bishop, P.J. (2009) Suitability of amphibians and reptiles for translocation. *Conservation Biology* 23 (1), 7–15.

Gillespie, A. (2003) Legitimating a whale ethic. *Environmental Ethics* 25 (4), 17.

Glaston, A.R. (2001) Relevance of studbook data to the successful captive management of grey mouse lemurs. *International Journal of Primatology* 22 (1), 57–69.

Gollwitzer, P.M. and Sheeran, P. (2006) Implementation intentions and goal achievement: A meta-analysis of effects and processes. *Advances in Experimental Social Psychology* 38, 69–119.

Goodman, B. (2007) Georgia aquarium mourns another of its whale sharks. *The New York Times*, 14 June.

Grayson, B. (2006) *Shark Draws Crowds, Criticism to Aquarium*. On WWW at http://www.montereyherald.com/mld/montereyherald/news/16106324.htm. Accessed 1.12.06.

Gross, D. (2006) *Aquarium Conducts Exam on Whale Sharks*. On WWW at http://www.examiner.com/a-89889 ~ Aquarium_Conducts_Exam_on_Whale_Sharks.html. Accessed 13.11.06.

Grove, R. (1996) *Green Imperialism*. Cambridge: Cambridge University Press.

Hall. C.M. (2002) Travel safety and the media: The significance of the issue-attention cycle. *Current Issues in Tourism* 5 (3) 458–466.

Hall, C.M. and Sharples, L. (2005) The consumption of experiences or the experience of consumption? An introduction to the tourism of taste. In C.M. Hall, L. Sharples, R. Mitchell, N. Macionis and B. Cambourne (eds) *Food Tourism Around the World* (pp. 1–24). Oxford: Elsevier.

Ham, S.H., Weiler, B., Hughes, M., Brown, T., Curtis, J. and Poll, M. (2007) *Promoting Persuasion in Protected Areas: A Guide for Managers. Developing Strategic Communication to Influence Visitor Behaviour*. Brisbane: Sustainable Tourism CRC.

Hancocks, D. (2001) *A Different Nature: The Paradoxical World Of Zoos and Their Uncertain Future.* Berkeley and London: University of California Press.

Hannam, K. (2005) Tourism Management Issues in India's National Parks: An analysis of the RajivGandhi (Nagarahole) National Park. *Current Issues in Tourism* 8 (2), 165–180.

Hanson, E. (2002) *Animal Attractions: Nature on Display in American Zoos.* Princeton, NJ: Princeton University Press.

Harland, P., Staats, H. and Wilke, H. (1999) Explaining proenvironmental intention and behavior by personal norms and the theory of planned behavior. *Journal of Applied Social Psychology* 29 (12), 2505–2528.

Harrison, B. (1992) Naturalistic exhibits in zoo design. In B.H. Chua and N. Edwards (eds) *Public Space: Design, Use and Management.* Singapore: Centre for Advanced Studies/Singapore University Press.

Hayes, D. and MacLeod, N. (2007) Packaging places: Designing heritage trails using an experience economy perspective to maximise visitor engagement. *Journal of Vacation Marketing* 13 (1), 45–58.

Hayward, J. and Rothenberg, M. (2004) Measuring success in the 'Congo Gorilla Forest' conservation exhibition. *Curator* 47 (3), 261–282.

Hediger, H. (1968) *Man and the Animal in the Zoo.* London: Routledge.

Help Elephants (2008) *Quick Facts about Elephants in Zoos.* On WWW at http://www.helpelephantsinzoos.org/pdf/quick_facts.pdf. Accessed 8.9.08.

Henderson, J.C. (2005) Planning, changing landscapes and tourism in Singapore. *Journal of Sustainable Tourism* 13 (2), 123–135.

Henry, B.C. (2004) The relationship between animal cruelty, delinquency, and attitudes toward the treatment of animals. *Society and Animals* 12 (3), 185–207.

Herald Sun (2009) Bite Size. On WWW at http://www.eservices.com.au/heraldsun/BiteSize/March2009no18. Accessed 16.8.09.

Herbert, D.T. (2001) Literary places, tourism and the heritage experience. *Annals of Tourism Research* 32, 312–333.

Herbert, S. (1994) A question of taste. *Leisure Management* 14 (6), 49–50.

Heuer, F. and Reisberg, D. (1990) Vivid memories of emotional events: The accuracy of remembered minutiae. *Memory and Cognition* 18 (5), 496–506.

Higginbottom, K., Rann, K., Moscardo, G., Davis, D. and Muloin, S. (2001) *Status Assessment of Wildlife Tourism in Australia: An Overview – Part II: Status Assessment.* Gold Coast: Sustainable Tourism CRC.

Hill, C.A. (1971) An analysis of the zoo visitor. *International Zoo Yearbook* 11 158–165.

Hitchcock, M. and Darma Putra, I. (2007) *Tourism, Development and Terrorism in Bali.* London: Ashgate.

Hjalager, A.M. and Richards, G. (eds) (2002) *Tourism and Gastronomy.* London: Routledge.

Hoage, R.J. and Deiss, W.A. (eds) (1996) *New Worlds, New Animals: From Menageries to Zoological Parks in the Nineteenth Century.* Baltimore, MD: John Hopkins Press.

Holden, A. (2003) In need of new environmental ethics for tourism. *Annals of Tourism Research* 30 (1), 15.

Holmes, K. (2003) Volunteers in the heritage sector: A neglected audience? *International Journal of Heritage Studies* 9, 341–355.

Holmes, K. (2009) The value of volunteering: The volunteer's story. *Australian Journal on Volunteering* 14 (1), 1–9.

Holmes, K. and Edwards, D. (2008) Volunteers as hosts and guests in museums. In K. Lyons and S. Wearing (eds) *Journeys of Discovery in Volunteer Tourism: International Case Study Perspectives* (pp. 155–165). Wallingford: CABI.

Holmes, K. and Smith, K.A. (2009) *Managing Volunteers within Tourism: Attractions, Destinations and Events*. Oxford: Butterworth-Heinemann.

Holst, B. and Dickie, L.A. (2007) How do national and international regulations and polices influence the role of zoos and aquariums in conservation. In A. Zimmermann, M. Hatchwell, L. Dickie and C. West (eds) *Zoos in the 21st Century: Catalysts for Conservation* (pp. 22–33). Cambridge: Cambridge University Press.

Holzer, D., Scott, D. and Bixler, R. (1998) Socialization influences on adult zoo visitation. *Journal of Applied Recreation Research* 23 (1), 43–62.

Hom Cary, S. (2004) The tourist moment. *Annals of Tourism Research* 31 (1), 61–77.

Hooi, D.H. and Wan, C.Y. (1999) Singapore Zoological Gardens: Opening the gates to an enchanting experience. In D.H. Hooi (ed.) *Cases in Singapore Hospitality and Tourism Management* (pp. 237–266). Singapore: Prentice Hall.

Horak, J-C. (2006) Wildlife documentaries: From classical forms to reality TV. *Film History* 18, 459–475.

Hottola, P. (2005) The metaspatialities of control management in tourism: Backpacking in India. *Tourism Geographies* 7 (1), 1–22.

Howat, G. and Crilley, G. (2007) Customer service quality, satisfaction, and operational performance: A proposed model for Australian public aquatic centres. *Annals of Leisure Research* 10 (2), 168–195.

Howat, G., Murray, D. and Crilley, G. (1999) The relationships between service problems and perceptions of service quality, satisfaction and behavioural intentions of Australian public sports and leisure centre customers. *Journal of Park and Recreation Administration* 17 (2), 42–64.

Hoyt, E. (1992) *The Performing Orca – Why the Show Must Stop. An In-Depth Review of the Captive Orca Industry*. Bath: Whale and Dolphin Conservation Society.

Hoyt, E. (2001) *Whale Watching 2001. Worldwide Tourism Numbers, Expenditures, and Expanding Socioeconomic Benefits*. London: International Fund for Animal Welfare.

Hughes, M. and Carlsen, J. (2008a) A pathway to minimal impact wildlife viewing. *Tourism Review International* 11 (3), 205–212.

Hughes, M. and Carlsen, J. (2008b) Human-wildlife interaction guidelines in Western Australia. *Journal of Ecotourism* 7 (2/3), 13.

Hughes, M., Newsome, D. and Macbeth, J. (2005) Case study: Visitor perceptions of captive wildlife tourism in a Western Australian natural setting. *Journal of Ecotourism* 4 (2), 73–91.

Hughes, P. (2001) Animals, values and tourism – structural shifts in UK dolphin tourism provision. *Tourism Management* 22 (4), 321–329.

Hunter-Jones, P. and Hayward, C. (1998) Leisure consumption and the United Kingdom zoo. In N. Ravenscroft, D. Philip and M. Bennett (eds) *Leisure, Culture and Commerce* (pp. 97–107). Brighton: LSA.

Hutchins, M., Smith, B. and Allard, R. (2003) In defense of zoos and aquariums: The ethical basis for keeping wild animals in captivity. *JAVMA* 223 (7) 958–966.

Huxley, E.S. (1981) *Whipsnade Zoo: Captive Breeding for Survival*. London: Collins.

Ings, R., Waran, N. and Young, R. (1997) Attitude of zoo visitors to the idea of feeding live prey to zoo animals. *Zoo Biology* 16 (4), 343.

IUCN (1995) *IUCN Guidelines for Reintroduction*. Gland: IUCN.

IUCN (2004) *Technical Guidelines on the Management of Ex-situ Populations for Conservation*. On WWW at http://www.iucn.org/webfiles/doc/SSC/SSCwebsite /Policy_statements/IUCN_Technical_Guidelines_on_the_Management_of_Ex_ situ_populations_for_Conservation. Accessed 26.5.09.

IUCN (2008) *The IUCN Redlist of Threatened Species.* On WWW at http://www.iucnredlist.org. Accessed 26.5.09.

IUCN SSG (2008) *IUCN Shark Specialist Group Red List.* On WWW at http://www.iucnssg.org/index.php/iucn-red-list-2008. Accessed 5.5.09.

IUDZG/CBSG (IUCN/SSC) (1993) *The World Zoo Conservation Strategy: The Role of Zoos and Aquaria of the World in Global Conservation.* On WWW at http://www.waza.org/conservation/wczs.php.

James, C.L.R. (1963) *Beyond a Boundary.* New York: Pantheon (1984 edn).

Jamieson, D. (1985) Against zoos. In P. Singer (ed.) *In Defence of Animals* (pp. 108–117). Oxford: Blackwell.

Jamieson, D. (1995) Zoos revisited. In B.G. Norton, M. Hutchins, E.F. Stevens and T.I. Maple (eds) *Ethics on the Ark: Zoos, Animal Welfare and Wildlife Conservation* (pp. 52–66). Washington, DC: Smithsonian Institution.

Jarvis, C.H. (2000) If Descartes swam with dolphins: The framing and consumption of marine animals in contemporary Australian tourism. PhD thesis, University of Melbourne.

Jelinski, D.E., Krueger, C.C. and Duffus, D.A. (2002) Geostatictical analyses of interactions between Killer Whales (Orcinus Orca) and recreational whale-watching boats. *Applied Geography* 22, 19.

Jensen, J.M. (2008) An empirical investigation of the relationships between hygiene factors, motivators, satisfaction, and response among visitors to zoos and aquaria. *Tourism Review International* 11 (3), 307–316.

Jones, P.J.S. and Burgess, J. (2005) Building partnership capacity for the collaborative management of marine protected areas in the UK: A preliminary analysis. *Journal of Environmental Management* 77 (3), 227–243.

Joseph, C. and Kavoori, A. (2001) Mediated resistance: Tourism and the host community. *Annals of Tourism Research* 28(4), 998–1009.

Judd, D. (1999) Constructing the tourist bubble. In D. Judd and S. Fainstein (eds) *The Tourist City* (pp. 35–53). New Haven, CT: Yale University Press.

Jurong Bird Park (2009) *About Us.* On WWW at http://www.birdpark.com.sg/corporate/abtus.html. Accessed 20.8.09.

Kellert, S.R. (1978) *Policy Implications of a National Study of American Attitudes and Behavioral Relations to Animals.* Washington, DC: US Department of the Interior, Fish and Wildlife Service.Kellert, S.R. (1980) American attitudes toward and knowledge of animals: An update. *International Journal of the Study of Animal Problems* 1 (2), 87–119.

Kellert, S.R. (1985) Attitudes toward animals: Age-related development among children. *The Journal of Environmental Education* 16, 29–39.

Kellert, S.R. (1991) Japanese perceptions of wildlife. *Conservation Biology* 5 (3), 297–308.

Kellert, S.R. (1993) Values and perceptions or invertebrates. *Conservation Biology* 7 (4), 845–855.

Kellert, S.R. (1996) *The Value of Life: Biological Diversity and Human Society.* Washington, DC: Island Press.

Kelly, J.D. (1997) Effective conservation in the twenty-first century: The need to be more than a zoo. An organization's approach. *International Zoo Yearbook* 35, 1–14.

Kerr, J. (1991) Making dollars and sense out of ecotourism/nature tourism. *First International Conference in Ecotourism, Brisbane.*

Kestin, S. (2004) Other Stories from Marine Attractions: Below the Surface. *Sun Sentinel,* 17 May.

Kim, S., Clemenz, C. and Weaver, P. (2002) Segmenting Golfers by their attitudes toward food and beverage service available during play. *Journal of Hospitality & Leisure Marketing* 9 (3/4), 67–82.

King, N. and Higginbottom, K. (2008) Using tourism to achieve positive conservation outcomes for reintroductions of threatened species. In D. Lunney, A. Munn and W. Meikle (eds) *Too Close for Comfort: Contentious Issues in Human-Wildlife Encounter* (pp. 271–279). Sydney: Royal Zoological Society of NSW.

Kisling, V.N. Jr. (2002) Ancient collection and menageries. In V.N. Kisling Jr. (ed.) *Zoo and Aquarium History: Ancient Collections to Zoological Gardens* (pp. 1–48). Boca Raton, FL: CRC Press.

Kivela, N. and Crotts, J. (2006) Tourism and gastronomy: Gastronomy's influence on how tourists experience a destination. *Journal of Hospitality & Tourism Research* 30 (3), 354–377.

Klenosky, D.B. and Saunders, C.D. (2008) Put me in the zoo! A laddering study of zoo visitor motives. *Tourism Review International* 11 (3), 317–327.

Knudson, D.M., Cable, T.T. and Beck, L. (2003) *Interpretation of Cultural and Natural Resources* (2nd edn). State College, PA: Venture Publishing.

Koehler, B. and Koontz, T.M. (2008) Citizen participation in collaborative watershed partnerships. *Environmental Management* 41 (2), 143–154.

Koh, G. and Ooi, G.I. (2000) *State-Society Relations in Singapore*. Oxford: Oxford University Press.

Koob, T.J. (2004) Elasmobranchs in public aquarium: 1860 to 1930. In M. Smith, D. Warmolts, D. Thoney and R. Hueter (eds) *The Elasmobranch Husbandry Manual: Captive Care of Sharks, Rays and their Relatives* (pp. 1–14). Columbus, OH: Ohio Biological Survey.

Kotler, P. (1994) *Marketing Management – Analysis, Planning, Implementation and Control*. Englewood Cliffs, NJ: Prentice Hall.

Kotler, N. and Kotler, P. (1998) *Museum Strategy and Marketing*. San Francisco, CA: Jossey-Bass.

Knaub-Hardy, C. (2008) Green practices at zoo and aquarium restaurants. *Tourism Attractions and Parks*, August, 98–101.

Knopf, R. (1987) Human behavior, cognition, and affect in the natural environment. In D. Siokols and I. Altman (eds) *Handbook of Environmental Psychology* (pp. 783–826). New York: Wiley.

Kraus, S.J. (1995) Attitudes and the prediction of behavior: A meta-analysis of the empirical literature. *Personality and Social Psychology Bulletin* 21 (1), 58–75.

Kruse, C.K. and Card, J. (2004) Effects of a conservation education camp program on campers' self-reported knowledge, attitude, and behavior. *Journal of Environmental Education* 35 (4), 33–45.

Lake, A., Hyland, R., Mather, J., Rugg-Gunn, A., Wood, C. and Adamson, A. (2006) Food shopping and preparation among the 30-somethings: Whose job is it? (The ASH30 study). *British Food Journal* 108 (6), 475–486.

Lang, A. (2000) The limited capacity model of mediated message processing. *Journal of Communication* 50 (1), 46–70.

Leiper, N. (1990) Tourist attraction systems. *Annals of Tourism Research* 17 (3), 367–384.

Lemelin, R.H. (2006) The gawk, the glance and the glaze: Ocular consumption and polar bear tourism in Churchill, Manitoba, Canada. *Current Issues in Tourism* 9 (6), 19.

Lindemann-Matthies, P. and Kamer, T. (2005) The influence of an interactive educational approach on visitors' learning in a Swiss zoo. *Science Education* 90, 296–315.

Linge, J. (1992) How to out-zoo the zoo. *Tourism Management* 13 (2), 114–117.

Lück, M. (2008a) Captive marine wildlife: Benefits and costs of aquaria and marine parks. In J. Higham and M. Lück (eds) *Marine Wildlife and Tourism Management* (pp. 130–144). Wallingford: CABI.

Lück, M. (2008b) Managing marine wildlife experiences: The role of visitor interpretation programmes. In J. Higham and M. Lück (eds) *Marine Wildlife and Tourism Management* (pp. 334–346). Wallingford: CABI.

Lück, M. and Jiang, Y. (2007) Keiko, Shamu and friends: Educating visitors in marine parks and aquaria? *Journal of Ecotourism* 6 (2), 127–138.

Lunney, D. and Moon, C. (2008) The portrayal of human-wildlife interactions in the print media. In D. Lunney, A. Munn and W. Meikle (eds) *Too Close for Comfort: Contentious Issues in Human-Wildlife Encounters* (pp. 52–64). Sydney: Royal Zoological Society of NSW.

MacCannell, D. (1976) *The Tourist: A New Theory of the Leisure Class*. New York: Schocken Books.

MacDonald, E. and Ham, S.H. (2007) Call a therapist! Using social psychology to maximise the visitor learning experience. In *Towards 2107: Meeting the Challenges of the Coming Century, ARAZPA Annual Conference*. Te Papa, Wellington, NZ.

MacDonald, R.K. (1988) *Dr Seuss*. Boston, MA: Twayne.

Mallapur, A., Waran, N. and Sinha, A. (2008) The captive audience: The educative influence of zoos on their visitors in India. *International Zoo Yearbook* 42 (1), 214–224.

Mallinson, J. (2001) A sustainable future for zoos and their role in wildlife conservation. *First National Convention on Wildlife Tourism in Australia*, Tasmania.

Mallinson, J. and Hartley, J.R.M. (2008) Partnerships in conservation. *Zoo Biology* 27 (6), 488–497.

Manfredo, M.J. and Driver, B. (2002) Benefits: The basis for action. In M.J. Manfredo (ed.) *Wildlife Viewing: A Management Handbook*. Corvallis, OR: Oregon State University Press.

Manubay, G., Dotzour, A., Schulz, K., Smith, J.C., Housten, C., De Young, R. and Saunders, C.D. (2002) Evaluating exhibits that promote conservation behavior: Developing a theoretical framework. Paper read at 31st Annual North American Association for Environmental Education Conference, Boston, MA.

Markwell, K. (2008) Aquaria. In M. Luck (ed.) *The Encyclopaedia of Tourism and Recreation in Marine Environments* (pp. 24–27). Wallingford: CABI.

Markwell, K. (2009) Under Sobek's watchful eye: An observational study of visitors in the Lost World of Reptiles exhibit, Australian Reptile Park. *Proceedings of the 2009 Australasian Region Association of Zoological Parks and Aquaria Conference, Sydney*.

Marling, K.A. (1997) *Designing Disney's Theme Parks: The Architecture of Reassurance*. New York and Paris: Flammarion.

Martin, B. and Mason, S. (1993) Future for attractions: Meeting the needs of the new consumers. *Tourism Management* 14 (1), 34–40.

Martin, L. (1993) Shark conservation – Educating the public. In S. Bransetter (ed.) *Conservation Biology of Elasmobranchs*, NOAA Technical Report NMFS115, US Department of Commerce.

Mason, P. (1999) Zoos as heritage attractions. *International Journal of Heritage Studies* 5 (3/4), 152–164.

Mason, P. (2000) Zoo tourism: The need for more research. *Journal of Sustainable Tourism* 8 (4), 333–339.

Mason, P. (2003) *Tourism Impacts, Planning and Management*. Oxford: Butterworth Heinemann.

Mason, P. (2008) Roles of the modern zoo: Conflicting or complementary? *Tourism Review International* 11 (3), 251–263.

Mason, P., Grabowski, P. and Du, W. (2005) Severe acute respiratory syndrome, tourism and the media. *International Journal of Tourism Research* 7 (1), 11–21.

Mather, M., Mitchell, K., Raye, C., Novak, D., Greene, E. and Johnson, M. (2006) Emotional arousal can impair feature binding in working memory. *Journal of Cognitive Neuroscience* 18 (4), 614–625.

Mau, R. (2008) Managing for conservation and recreation: The Ningaloo Whale Shark Experience. *Journal of Ecotourism* 7 (2/3), 13.

Mayes, G., Dyer, P. and Richins, H. (2004) Dolphin-human interaction: Pro-environmental attitudes, beliefs and intended behaviours and actions of participants in interpretation programs: A pilot study. *Annals of Leisure Research* 7 (1), 34–53.

Mazur, N. (2001) *After the Ark? Environmental Policy Making and the Zoo*. Melbourne: Melbourne University Press.

McDermott, N. (2006) *Live animals thrown to the tigers – for the amusement of the crowd*. On WWW at http://www.dailymail.co.uk/news/article-408053/Live-animals-thrown-tigers--amusement-crowd.html. Accessed 29.5.09.

McGehee, N.G. and Kim, K. (2004) Motivation for agri-tourism entrepreneurship. *Journal of Travel Research* 43 (2), 161–170.

McIntyre, C. (2008) Museum foodservice offers – experience design dimensions. *Journal of Foodservice* 19, 177–188.

McKenzie-Mohr, D. and Smith, W. (1999) *Fostering Sustainable Behaviour: An Introduction to Community-based Social Marketing*. Vancouver: New Society.

Mee, B (2008) *We Bought a Zoo*. London: Harper Collins.

Melfi, V.A. (2005) The appliance of science to zoo-housed primates. *Applied Animal Behaviour Science* 90, 97–106.

Mellen, J. and MacPhee, M.S. (2001) Philosophy of environmental enrichment: Past, present, and future. *Zoo Biology* 20 (3), 211–226.

Middelton, V. (1989) Visitor attractions: Marketing implications for attractions. *Tourism Management* 10 (3), 229–232.

Milius, S. (2004) Din among the Orcas. *Science News*, p. 2.

Millar, R. and Houston, C. (2008a) Zoo rocked by abuse allegations. *The Age*, News Section, 19 January, pp. 1–2.

Millar, R. and Houston, C. (2008b) Animal rights & wrongs. *The Age*, Insight Section, 19 January, pp. 1–2.

Millennium Ecosystem Assessment (2005) *Ecosystems and Human Well-being: Biodiversity Synthesis*. Washington, DC: World Resources Institute.

Miller, P. and Lacy, R. (2003) Integrating the human dimension into endangered species risk assessment. In F. Westley and P. Miller (eds) *Experiments in Consilience: Integrating Social and Scientific Responses to Save Endangered Species* (pp. 41–63). Washington, DC: Island.

Miller, W.I. (1997) *The Anatomy of Disgust*. London: Harvard University Press.

Milman, A. (2008) Theme park tourism and management strategy. In A. Woodside and D. Martin (eds) *Tourism Management: Analysis, Behavior, and Strategy* (pp. 218–231). Cambridge, MA: CABI.

Milne, A.A. (1924) *When We were very Young*. London: Methuen (1984 edn).

Mittermeier, R.A., Robles, G.P., Hoffmann, M., Pilgrim, J., Brooks, T., Mittermeier, C.G., Lamoreux, J. and da Fonseca, G.A.B. (2004) *Hotspots: Revisited*. Mexico City: CEMEX.

Mony, P. and Heimlich, J. (2008) Talking to visitors about conservation: Exploring message communication through docent-visitor interactions at zoos. *Visitor Studies* 11 (2), 151–162.

Monterey Bay Aquarium (2007) *Monterey Bay Aquarium Annual Review*. Monterey: Monterey Bay Aquarium.

Moran, D. (2006) PETA takes bite out of Six Flags cockroach munch. *Herald News*, 29 September.

Morgan, J.M. and Hodgkinson, M. (1999) The motivation and social orientation of visitors attending a contemporary zoological park. *Environment and Behavior* 31 (2), 227–239.

Morgan, M., Elbe, J. and de Esteban Curiel, J. (2009) Has the experience economy arrived? The views of destination managers in three visitor-dependent areas. *International Journal of Tourism Research* 11, 201–216.

Morgan, N., Pritchard, A. and Pride, R. (2004) *Destination Branding: Creating the Unique Destination Proposition*. Oxford: Elsevier.

Morse, S. (2008) Post sustainable development. *Sustainable Development* 16 (5), 341–352.

Morton, A.B. and Symonds, H.K. (2002) Displacement of Orcinius orca (L.) by high amplitude sound in British Columbia, Canada. *Journal of Marine Science* 59: 10.

Moscardo, G. (1996) Mindful visitors: Heritage and tourism. *Annals of Tourism Research* 23 (2), 376–397.

Moscardo, G. (2008) Understanding visitor experiences in captive, controlled, and noncaptive wildlife-based tourism settings. *Tourism Review International* 11 (3), 213–223.

Moss, A.W. (1961) *Aliant Crusade: The History of the RSPCA*. London: Cassell.

Moss, A., Francis, D. and Esson, M. (2008) The relationship between viewing area size and visitor behavior in an immersive Asian elephant exhibit. *Visitor Studies* 11 (1), 26–40.

Mowforth, M. and Munt, I. (2008) *Tourism and Sustainability: Development, Globalization and New Tourism in the Third World* (3rd edn). London: Routledge.

Mullan, B. and Marvin, G. (1987) *Zoo Culture*. London: Weidenfeld and Nicolson.

Mullin, M.H. (1999) Mirrors and windows: Sociocultural studies of human-animal relationships. *Annual Review of Anthropology* 28, 24.

Muris, P., Mayer, B., Huijding, J. and Konings, T. (2008) A dirty animal is a scary animal! Effects of disgust-related information on fear beliefs in children. *Behaviour Research and Therapy* 46, 137–144.

Musick, M.A. and Wilson, J. (2008) *Volunteers: A Social Profile*. Bloomington & Indianapolis: Indiana University Press.

Myers, N., Mittermeier, R., Mittermeier, C., da Fonseca, G. and Kent, J. (2000) Biodiversity hotspots for conservation priorities. *Nature* 368, 734–737.

Myers, O.E., Saunders, C. and Birjulin, A. (2004) Emotional dimensions of watching zoo animals. *Curator* 47 (3), 299–321.

Nakamichi, M. (2007) Assessing the effects of new primate exhibits on zoo visitors' attitudes and perceptions by using three different assessment methods. *Anthrozoos* 20 (2), 155–165.

Newkirk, I. (1999) *You Can Save the Animals: 251 Ways to Stop Thoughtless Cruelty*. Roseville, CA: Prima.

Newsome, D., Dowling, R. and Moore, S. (2005) *Wildlife Tourism*. Clevedon: Channel View Publications.

Nightingale, J., Dickens, M. and Vincent, D. (2001) Aquariums: Some of the reasons they work so well. *Marine Technology Journal* 35 (1), 18–29.

Night Safari (2009) *About Night Safari*. On WWW at http://www.nightsafari.com.sg/about/welcomenote.htm. Accessed 20.8.09.

Nijman, J. (2006) Mumbai's mysterious middle class. *International Journal of Urban and Regional Research* 30 (4), 758–775.

Nimon, A.J. (1990) Making the zoo a positive educational experience. *Bulletin of Zoo Management* 28, 17–20.

Nussbaum, M.C. (2004) *Hiding from Humanity: Disgust, Shame and the Law*. Oxford: Princeton University Press.

O'Brien, T. (2002) Columbus Zoo officials say branded approach works best in food service. *Amusement Business* 114 (11), 32–34.

O'Dell, T. (2005) Experiencescapes: Blurring borders and testing connections. In T. O'Dell and P. Billing (eds) *Experiencescapes: Tourism, Culture and Economy* (pp. 11–33). Copenhagen: Copenhagen Business School Press.

Oduro, C., Antwi-Boasiako, C. and Yao, F. (2000) Visitor Assessment of the Accra Zoo from 1987–1997. *Ghana Journal of Forestry* 10 (1), 27–33

Oh, H., Fiore, A.M. and Jeoung, M. (2007) Measuring experience economy concepts: Tourism applications. *Journal of Travel Research* 46, 119–132.

Ohman, A., Flykt, A. and Esteves, F. (2001) Emotion drives attention: Detecting the snake in the grass. *Journal of Experimental Psychology: General* 130 (3), 466–478.

O'Mahony, B. and Hall, J. (2007) The influence of perceived body image, vanity and personal values on food consumption and related behaviour. *Journal of Hospitality Management* 14 (1), 57–69.

Ooi, C-S. (2005) A theory of tourist experiences: The management of attention. In T. O'Dell and P. Billing (eds) *Experiencescapes: Tourism, Culture and Economy* (pp. 51–68). Copenhagen: Copenhagen Business School Press.

Orams, M.B. (1996) A conceptual model of tourist–wildlife interaction: The case for education as a management strategy. *Australian Geographer* 27 (1), 39–51.

Orams, M.B. (1997) The effectiveness of environmental education: Can we turn tourists into 'greenies'? *Progress in Tourism and Hospitality Research* 3 (4), 295–306.

Orams, M.B. (2002) Feeding wildlife as a tourism attraction: A review of issues and impacts. *Tourism Management* 23 (3), 281–293.

Orbell, S. and Sheeran, P. (1998) 'Inclined abstainers': A problem for predicting health-related behavior. *British Journal of Social Psychology* 37 (2), 151–165.

Orr, N. (2006) Museum volunteering: Heritage as 'serious leisure'. *International Journal of Heritage Studies* 12, 194–210.

Paddle, R. (2000) *The Last Tasmanian Tiger: The History and Extinction of the Thylacine*. Cambridge: Cambridge University Press.

Parung, J. and Bititci, U.S. (2008) A metric for collaborative networks. *Business Process Management Journal* 14 (5), 654–674.

Patrick, P.G., Matthews, C., Ayers, D. and Tunnicliffe, S. (2007) Conservation and education: Prominent themes in zoo mission statements. *Journal of Environmental Education* 38 (3), 53–59.

PAWB (2008) Accomplishment Reports: MOA zoo partners. Manila: PAWB-DENR.

PAWS (2006) *Inspection Report on Mumbai Zoo*. On WWW at http://www.aapn.org/mumbaizoo.html Accessed 15.7.09.

Pearce, P.L. (1988) *The Ulysses Factor: Evaluating Visitors in Tourist Settings.* New York: Springer-Verlag.

PETA (2006) *Marine Mammal Parks: Chlorinated Prisons.* On WWW at http://www.peta.org/mc/factsheet_display.asp?ID=63. Accessed 8.10.06.

PETA (2009) *Zoos: Pitiful Prisons.* On WWW at http://www.peta.org/factsheet/files/FactsheetDisplay.asp?ID=67. Accessed 21.2.09.

Petty, R.E., Fabrigar, L. and Wegener, D. (2003) Emotional factors in attitudes and persuasion. In R. Davidson, K. Scherer and H. Goldsmith (eds) *Handbook of Affective Sciences.* Oxford: Oxford University Press.

Petty, R.E. and Cacioppo, J. (1986) *Communication and Persuasion: Central and Peripheral Routes to Attitude Change.* New York: Springer-Verlag.

Peyton, R.B. and Langenau Jr., E.E. (1985) A comparison of attitudes held by BLM biologists and the general public towards animals. *Wildlife Society Bulletin* 13, 117–120.

Phillips, C.J.C. and McCulloch, S. (2005) Student attitudes on animal sentience and use of animals in society. *Journal of Biological Education* 40 (1), 17–24.

Pickersgill, S. (1996) Does the traditional zoo have a future in the UK? In M. Robinson, N. Evans and P. Callaghan (eds) *Culture as the Tourist Product* (pp. 345–360). Sunderland: Centre for Travel and Tourism.

Pikkemaat, B. and Schuckert, M. (2007) critical success factors of theme parks – an exploration study. *Tourism* 55 (2), 197–208.

Pine, J.P. and Gilmore, J.H. (1999) *The Experience Economy: Work is Theatre & Every Business a Stage.* Boston, MA: Harvard Business School Press.

Pitchford, S. (2008) *Identity Tourism: Imaging and Imagining the Nation.* Bingley: Emerald.

Plummer, R., Kulczycki, C. and Stacey, C. (2006) How are we working together? A framework to assess collaborative arrangements in nature-based tourism. *Current Issues in Tourism* 9 (6), 499–516.

Polidoro, B.A., Livingstone, S.R., Carpenter, K.E., Hutchinson, B., Mast, R.B., Pilcher, N., Sadovy de Mitchenson, Y. and Valenti, S. (2008) Status of the world's marine species. In J.C. Vie, C. Hilton Taylor and S.N. Stuart (eds) *The 2008 Review of The IUCN Red List of Threatened Species.* Gland: IUCN.

Prance, G. (1997) A partnership agreement to generate innovative and practical responses to the problems of habitat destruction and species extinction. *Dodo* 33, 14–19.

Preece, R. (1993) Zoos, aquaria and circuses. In R. Preece and L. Chamberlain (eds) *Animal Welfare and Human Values* (pp. 185–210). Ontario: Wilfred Laurier University.

Prochaska, J.O. and Velicer, W. (1997) Behavior change: The transtheoretical model of health behavior change. *American Journal of Health Promotion* 12 (1), 38–48.

Puan, C.L. and Zakaria, M. (2007) Perception of visitors towards the role of zoos: A Malaysian perspective. *International Zoo Yearbook* 41 (1), 226–232.

Putnam, D. (2000) *Bowling Alone: The Collapse and Revival of American Community.* New York: Simon Schuster.

Quan, S. and Wang, N. (2004) Towards a structural model of the tourist experience: An illustration from food experiences in tourism. *Tourism Management* 25, 297–305.

Rabb, G.B. (1996) The changing roles of zoological parks in conserving biological diversity. *Biological Conservation* 76, 210.

Raguraman, K. (1998) Troubled passage to India. *Tourism Management* 19 (6), 533–43.

Rao, N. and Suresh, K. (2001) Domestic tourism in India. In K. Ghimire (ed.) *The Native Tourist* (pp. 198–228). London: Earthscan.

Reade, L.S. and Waran, N.K. (1996) The modern zoo: How do people perceive zoo animals? *Applied Animal Behaviour Science* 47, 109–118.

Reading, R. and Miller, A. (2007) Attitudes and attitude change among visitors. In A. Zimmermann, M. Hatchwell, L. Dickie and C. West (eds) *Zoos in the 21st Century: Catalysts for Conservation* (pp. 63–91). Cambridge: Cambridge University Press.

Reed, M.S., Fraser, E.D. and Dougill, A.J. (2006) An adaptive learning process for developing and applying sustainability indicators with local communities. *Ecological Economics* 59 (4), 406–418.

Regan, T. (1995) Are zoos morally defensible? In B.G. Norton, M. Hutchins, E.F. Stevens and T.L. Maple (eds) *Ethics on the Ark: Zoos, Animal Welfare and Wildlife Conservation* (pp. 38–51). Washington, DC: Smithsonian Institution Press.

Reser, J. and Bentrupperbaumer, J. (2000) Unpacking the nature and management implications of environmental concern. Paper presented at the International Symposium on Society and Resource Management. Western Washington University, Washington, DC.

Reuters (2006) No more polar bears for tropical Singapore Zoo. On WWW at http://www.planetark.com. Accessed 23.8.09.

Rey, N. (1939) *Raffy and the 9 Monkeys*. London: Chatto & Windus.

Rhoads, D.L. and Goldsworthy, R.J. (1979) The effects of zoo environments on public attitudes toward endangered wildlife. *International Journal for Environmental Studies* 13, 283–287.

Richards, G. (2001) The experience industry and the creation of attractions. In G. Richards (ed.) *Cultural Attractions and European Tourism* (pp. 55–69). Oxford: CABI.

Ritchie, B., Dorrell, H., Millar, D. and Miller G. (2004) Crisis communication and recovery of the tourism industry: Lessons from the 2001 UK foot and mouth disease outbreak. *Journal of Travel and Tourism Marketing* 15 (2&3), 199–216.

Ritchie, B. and Hudson, S. (2009) Understanding and meeting the challenges of consumer/tourist experience research. *International Journal of Tourism Research* 11, 111–126.

Rivenburgh, N., Louw, E., Loo, E. and Mersham, G. (2004) *The Sydney Olympics and Foreign Attitudes Towards Australia*. Gold Coast: Sustainable Tourism CRC.

Robinson, M. (1989) The zoo that is 'Not': Education for conservation. *Conservation Biology* 13 (3), 213–215.

Rockloff, S.F. and Moore, S.A. (2006) Assessing representation at different scales of decision making: Rethinking local is better. *Policy Studies Journal* 34 (4), 649–670.

Rogers, R.W. (1975) A protection motivation theory of fear appeals and attitude change. *Journal of Psychology* 91 (1), 93–114.

Rojek, C. (1997) Indexing, dragging, and social construction. In C. Rojek and J. Urry (eds) *Touring Cultures: Transformations of Travel and Theory* (pp. 52–74). London: Routledge.

Rosenfeld, S. and Terkel, A. (1982) A naturalistic study of visitors at an interactive mini-zoo. *Curator* 25 (3), 187–212.

Rothfels, N. (2002) *Savages and Beasts: The Birth of the Modern Zoo*. Baltimore, MD: John Hopkins University Press.

Ruhanen, L. (2008) Progressing the sustainability debate: A knowledge management approach to sustainable tourism planning. *Current Issues in Tourism* 11 (5), 429–455.

Runte, A. (1990) *Yosemite: The Embattled Wilderness*. Lincoln and London: University of Nebraska Press.

Russello, M.A. and Amato, G. (2004) Ex situ population management in the absence of pedigree information. *Molecular Ecology* 13 (9), 2829–2840.

Rützler, H. (2005) *Was essen wir morgen? 13 Food Trends der Zukunft*. Wien: Springer-Verlag.

Ryan, C. and Saward, J. (2004) The zoo as ecotourism attraction – visitor reactions, perceptions and management implications: The case of Hamilton Zoo, New Zealand. *Journal of Sustainable Tourism* 12 (3), 245–266.

Ryder, O.A. and Feistner, A.T.C. (1995) Research in zoos: A growth area in conservation. *Review of Industrial Organization* 4 (6), 671–677.

Saldanha, A. (2002) Music tourism and factions of bodies in Goa. *Tourist Studies* 2 (1), 43–62.

Schneider, M. (2005) Conference report: Exploring human-animal relationship. The 14th annual conference of the International Society for Anthrozoology. *Society and Animals* 13 (4), 355–357.

Shackley, M. (1996) *Wildlife Tourism*. London: International Thomson Business Press.

Shani, A. and Pizam, A. (2008) Towards an ethical framework for animal-based attractions. *International Journal of Contemporary Hospitality Management* 20 (6), 679–693.

Sharp, I. (1994) *The First 21 Years: The Singapore Zoological Gardens Story*. Singapore: Singapore Zoological Gardens.

Sheeran, P. (2002) Intention–behavior relations: A conceptual and empirical review. *European Review of Social Psychology* 12 (1), 1–36.

Shelton, E.J. and Tucker, H. (2007) Managed to be wild: Species recovery, island restoration, and nature-based tourism in New Zealand. *Tourism Review International* 11 (3), 197–204.

Sheridan, J. (2009) Zoo Goes Ape to Preserve Precious Forests. *The Sunday Age*, News section, August 9, p. 7.

Singapore Zoo (2009a) *About the Zoo*. On WWW at http://www.zoo.com.sg/about/abtwildlife.htm. Accessed 20.8.09.

Singapore Zoo (2009b) Record year for tourism receipts in 2008. Singapore Tourism Board Press Release, 10 January.

Singer, P. (1977) *Animal Liberation: Towards an End to Man's Inhumanity to Animals*. London: Granada.

Smith, A.J., Lee, D., Newsome, D. and Stoeckl, N. (2006) Production and consumption of wildlife icons: Dolphin tourism at Monkey Mia, Western Australia. In K. Meethan, A. Anderson and S. Miles (eds) *Tourism Consumption and Representation* (pp. 113–139). Wallingford: CABI.

Smith, J. (2003) Captive killer whales. *The Ecologist* 33 (10), 2.

Smith, K.A. (2003) Literary enthusiasts as visitors and volunteers. *International Journal of Tourism Research* 5, 83–95.

Smith, K.N., Shaw, J.H., Bettinger, T., Caniglia, B. and Carter, T. (2007) Conservation partnerships between zoos and aquariums, federal and state agencies, and nongovernmental organizations. *Zoo Biology* 26 (6), 471–486.

Smith, L. (2007) A qualitative analysis of profound wildlife encounters. *Journal of Dissertation* 1 (1).

Smith, L. (2009) Identifying behaviors to target during zoo visits. *Curator: The Museum Journal* 52 (1), 101–115.

Smith, L. and Broad, S. (2008a) Comparing zoos and the media as conservation educators. *Visitor Studies* 11 (1), 16–25.

Smith, L. and Broad, S. (2008b) Do zoo visitors attend to conservation messages? A case study of an elephant exhibit. *Tourism Review International* 11 (3), 225–236.

Smith, L., Broad, S. and Weiler, B. (2008) A closer examination of the impact of zoo visits on visitor behaviour. *Journal of Sustainable Tourism* 16 (5), 544–562.

Spada, J. (1988) *Grace: The Secret Life of a Princess*. London: Penguin.

Spiegel, S. and Schubel, J.R. (2001) The evolution of experience. *Marine Technology Journal* 35 (1), 5–9.

Sreekumar, T. and Parayil, G. (2002) Contentions and contradictions of tourism as development option: The case of Kerala, India. *Third World Quarterly* 23 (3), 529–548.

SSP (2008) *Species Survival Plan Program*. On WWW at http://www.aza.org/species-survival-plan-program.

Staiff, R., Bushell, R. and Kennedy, P. (2002) Interpretation in national parks: Some critical questions. *Journal of Sustainable Tourism* 10 (2), 97–113.

Stebbins, R.A. (1996) Volunteering: A serious leisure perspective. *Nonprofit and Voluntary Sector Quarterly* 25, 211–224.

Sternberg, E. (1997) The iconography of the tourist experience. *Annals of Tourism Research* 24 (4), 951–969.

Stevens, T. (1988) Zoos, a walk on the wild side. *Leisure Management* 8 (4), 53–88.

Stoinski, T.S., Allen, M., Bloomsmith, M., Forthman, D. and Maple, T. (2002) Educating zoo visitors about complex environmental issues: Should we do it and how? *Curator* 45 (2), 129–143.

The Straits Times (2009) New wildlife draw: River safari ready in 2011. *The Straits Times*, 11 February.

The Straits Times (2008) Work on the wild side. *The Straits Times*, 24 November.

The Straits Times (2002) Call of the wild. *The Straits Times*, 19 April.

The Straits Times (2001) A boon for baboons. *The Straits Times*, 26 August.

Strehlow, H. (2002) Zoological gardens of Western Europe. In V.N. Kisling Jr. (ed.) *Zoo and Aquarium History: Ancient Collections to Zoological Gardens* (pp. 75–116). Boca Raton, FL: CRC Press.

Sundstrom, E., Bell, P.A., Busby, P.L. and Asmus, C. (1996) Environmental psychology: 1984–1994. *Annual Review of Psychology* 47, 485–512.

Sutton, S. (1998) Predicting and explaining intentions and behavior: How well are we doing? *Journal of Applied Social Psychology* 28 (15), 1317.

Swanagan, J.S. (2000) Factors influencing zoo visitors' conservation attitudes and behaviour. *Journal of Environmental Education* 31 (4), 26–31.

Swarbrooke, J. (1995) *The Development & Management of Visitor Attractions*. Oxford: Butterworth Heinemann.

Swarbrooke, J. (1999) *Sustainable Tourism Management*. Wallingford: CABI.

Swarbrooke, J. (2002) *Development and Management of Visitor Attractions* (2nd edn). Oxford: Butterworth-Heinemann.

Swarbrooke, J. and Horner, S. (1999) *Consumer Behaviour in Tourism*. Oxford: Butterworth Heinemann.

Szabo, L. (2006) Elephant Debate: Live in Zoo or Roam Free. *USA Today*, 1 November.

Talmi, D., Schimmack, U., Paterson, T. and Moscovitch, M. (2007) The role of attention and relatedness in emotionally enhanced memory. *Emotion* 7 (1), 89–102.

Tan, E., Yeoh, B. and Teo, P. (2001) *Tourism Management and Policy: Perspectives from Singapore*. Singapore: World Scientific.

Taronga Conservation Society (2008) *Beneath the surface…Taronga Conservation Society Annual Report*. Sydney: Taronga Conservation Society.

Tarpey, C. (1993) New Zoos – taking down the bars. *National Geographic*, July 1993 2–37.

Tarrant, M.A., Manfredo, M. and Driver, B. (1994) Recollections of outdoor recreation experiences: A psychophysiological perspective. *Journal of Leisure Research* 26 (4), 357–371.

Tasmanian Devil Conservation Park (2009) On WWW at http://www.tasmanian devilpark.com/wild.html. Accessed 19.5.09.

Taylor, N. and Signal, T.D. (2005) Empathy and attitudes to animals. *Anthrozoös* 18 (1), 18–27.

Taylor, R. and Shanka, T. (2008) Visitor value perception of a heritage tourism site development: A case study. *Tourism Analysis* 13 (2), 131–142.

Teo, P. and Chang, T.C. (2000) Singapore: Tourism development in a planned context. In C.M. Hall and S.J. Page (eds) *Tourism in South and Southeast Asia* (pp. 117–128). London: Routledge.

Thinkquest (2000) *Sydney 2000 Olympic Mascots*. On WWW at http://www.library.thinkquest.org/27850/library/sydney2000/ideal/mascots.shtml. Accessed 15.3.03.

Thwaite, A. (1992) *The Brilliant Career of Winnie-the-Pooh: The Story of A.A. Milne*. London: Methuen.

Tian-Cole, S., Crompton, J. and Willson, V. (2002) An empirical investigation of the relationships between service quality, satisfaction and behavioural intentions among visitors to a wildlife refuge. *Journal of Leisure Research* 34 (1), 1–24.

Tilden, F. (1957) *Interpreting Our Heritage*. Chapel Hill, NC: University of North Carolina Press.

Times of India (2009) *Mumbai Zoo to Don New Look by 2012*. On WWW at http://www.timesofindia.indiatimes.com/Cities/Mumbai/Mumbai-zoo-to-don-new-look-by-2012/articleshow/4674595.cms. Accessed 15.7.09.

Tisdell, C. and Wilson, C. (2001) Wildlife-based tourism and increased support for nature conservation financially and otherwise: Evidence from sea turtle ecotourism at Mon Repos. *Tourism Economics* 7 (3), 233–250.

Tomas, S., Crompton, J. and Scott, D. (2003) Assessing service quality and benefits sought among zoological park visitors. *Journal of Park and Recreation Administration* 21 (2), 105–124.

Tomas, S.R., Scott, D. and Crompton, J.L. (2002) An investigation of the relationship between quality of service performance, benefits sought, satisfaction and future intention to visit among visitors to a zoo. *Managing Leisure* 7 (4), 239–250.

Tourism Australia (2009) *Activities Fact Sheet*. Canberra: Tourism Australia.

Tremblay, P. (2002) Tourism wildlife icons: Attractions or marketing symbols? *Journal of Hospitality and Tourism Management* 9, 164–181.

Tremblay, P. (2008) Wildlife in the landscape: A top end perspective on destination-level wildlife and tourism management. *Journal of Ecotourism* 7 (2/3), 18.

Triandis, H.C. (1971) *Attitude and Attitude Change*. New York: John Wiley.

Tribe, A. (2001) *Captive Wildlife Tourism in Australia*. Gold Coast: Sustainable Tourism CRC.

Tribe, A. (2004) Zoo tourism. In K. Higginbottom (ed.) *Wildlife Tourism: Impacts, Management and Planning* (pp. 35–56). Melbourne: Common Ground.

Tribe, A. (2006) Perceptions of zoos: Conservation and credibility. *Proceedings of the Wildlife Tourism Australia Third Annual Conference, August 13–15, 2006, Perth* (pp. 177–186).

Tribe, A. and Booth, R. (2003) Assessing the role of zoos in wildlife conservation. *Human Dimensions of Wildlife* 8, 65–74.

Tuan, Yi-Fu (1984) *Dominance and Affection: The Making of Pets.* New Haven, CT: Yale University Press.

Turley, S.K. (1999) Conservation and tourism in the traditional UK zoo. *The Journal of Tourism Studies* 10 (2), 2–13.

Turley, S. (2001) Children and the demand for recreational experiences: The case of zoos. *Leisure Studies* 20(1), 1–18.

UNEP (2006) *Marine and Coastal Ecosystems and Human Well-Being: A Synthesis Report based on the Findings of the Millennium Ecosystem Assessment.* Nairobi: UNEP.

Uriely, N. (2005) The tourist experience: Conceptual developments. *Annals of Tourism Research* 32 (1), 199–216.

Urry, J. (1990) *The Tourist Gaze: Leisure and Travel in Contemporary Societies.* London: Sage.

Uzzell, D. and Ballantyne, R. (1998) Heritage that hurts: Interpretation in a postmodern world. In D. Uzzell and R. Ballantyne (eds) *Contemporary Issues in Heritage and Environmental Interpretation* (pp. 152–171). London: The Stationery Office.

van der Berg, L., van der Borg, J. and van der Meer, J. (1995) *Urban Tourism.* Aldershot: Avebury.

van Linge, J.H. (1992) How to out-zoo the zoo. *Tourism Management* 13 (1), 115–117.

Vining, J. (2003) The connection to other animals and caring for nature. *Human Ecology Review* 10 (2), 87–99.

Virtual Tourist (2005) *London Dungeon: Blood! Gore! Disease!* On WWW at http://www.virtualtourist.com/travel/Europe/United_Kingdom/England/Greater_London/London-309228/Things_To_Do-London-London_Dungeon-BR-3. Accessed 25.5.09.

VisitBritain (2007) *The 2006 Survey of Visits to Visitor Attractions in England.* London: VisitBritain.

Volunteering Australia (2007) *What are the Real Costs of Volunteering.* Melbourne: Volunteering Australia.

Waldau, P. (2006) Religion and animals. In P. Singer (ed.) *In Defense of Animals: The Second Wave* (pp. 69–83). Oxford: Blackwell.

Waldron, J.L. (1998) The life impact of transcendent experiences with a pronounced quality of noesis. *Journal of Transpersonal Psychology* 30 (2), 103–134.

Walker, S. (2001) Zoological gardens of India. In V. Kisling (ed.) *Zoo and Aquarium History.* London: CRC.

Wall, G. (1997) Is ecotourism sustainable? *Environmental Management* 21 (4), 9.

Walpole, M.J. and Leader-Williams, N. (2002) Tourism and flagship species in conservation. *Biodiversity and Conservation* 11, 543–547.

Wanhill, S. (2003) Interpreting the development of the visitor attraction product. In A. Fyall, B. Garrod and A. Leask (eds) *Managing Visitor Attractions: New Directions* (pp. 16–35). Oxford: Butterworth-Heinemann.

Ward, P.I., Mosberger, N., Kistler, C. and Fischer, O. (1998) The relationship between popularity and body size in zoo animals. *Conservation Biology* 12 (6), 1408–1411.

Watson, S. and McCracken, M. (2002) No attraction in strategic thinking: Perceptions on current and future skills needs for visitor attraction managers. *International Journal of Tourism Research* 4, 367–378.

Watters, J.V. and Meehan, C.L. (2007) Different strokes: Can managing behavioral types increase post-release success? *Applied Animal Behaviour Science* 102 (3–4), 364–379.

Watts, S. (2001) *The End of the Line? Global Threats to Sharks*. San Francisco, CA: WildAid.

Watts, S. (2003) *Shark Finning: Unrecorded Wastage on a Global Scale*. San Francisco, CA: WildAid.

WAZA (2005) *Building a Future for Wildlife – The World Zoo and Aquarium Conservation Strategy*. Bern: WAZA.

WCMC (1992) *Global Biodiversity: Status of the Earth's Living Resources*. World Conservation Monitoring Center. London: Chapman and Hall.

Wearing, S.L. and Neil, J. (1998) From home to identity: Refiguring self and identity through ecotourism connections. *14th World Congress of Sociology*. Universte de Montreal, Canada.

Wearing, S.L. and Neil, J. (1999) Ecotourism: Impacts, potential and possibilities. Oxford: Butterworth-Heinemann.

Weiler, B. and Smith, L. (2009) Does more interpretation lead to greater outcomes? An assessment of the impacts of multiple layers of interpretation in a zoo context. *Journal of Sustainable Tourism* 17 (1), 91–105.

Weller, R. (1998) The garden of intelligence: Re-forming the denatured. *Transition* 59–60, 114–131.

Westley, F. and Miller, P. (eds) (2003) *Experiments in Consilience: Integrating Social and Scientific Responses to Save Endangered Species*. Washington, DC: Island.

Whatmore, S. (2002) *Hybrid Geographies: Natures, Cultures, Spaces*. London: Sage.

Wight, P. (1994) Environmentally responsible marketing of tourism. In E. Cater and G. Lowman (eds) *Ecotourism: A Sustainable Option?* (pp. 39–55). New York: Wiley.

Williams, J. (1997) We never eat like this at home: Food on holiday. In P. Caplan (ed.) *Food, Health and Identity* (pp. 151–171). London: Routledge.

Williams, V. (2001) *Captive Orcas 'Dying to Entertain You' The Full Story*. Chippenham:Whale and Dolphin Conservation Society.

Wilson, A. (1992) *The Culture of Nature: North American Landscapes from Disney to the Exxon Valdez*. Cambridge: Blackwell.

Wilson, L.A. (2007) The family farm business? Insights into family, business and ownership dimensions in open-farms. *Leisure Studies* 26 (3), 357–374.

Woods, B. (1998) Animals on display: Principles for interpreting captive wildlife. *Journal of Tourism Studies* 9 (1), 28–39.

Woods, B. (2002) Good zoo/bad zoo: Visitor experiences in captive settings. *Anthrozoos* 15 (4), 343–360.

Wood, B. and Peake, J. (1998) The dynamics of foreign policy agenda setting. *American Political Science Review* 92, 173–184.

Woody, S., McLean, C. and Klassen, T. (2005) Disgust as a motivator of avoidance of spiders. *Journal of Anxiety Disorders* 19 (4), 461–475.

WRS (2009a) *Wildlife Reserves Singapore Policy and Guidelines on Animal Welfare and Ethics*. Singapore: WRS.

WRS (2009b) Recommendation for polar bear Inuka to stay in Singapore, 27 January 2007. On WWW at http://www.zoo.com.sg/whatsnew/awec.htm. Accessed 22.8.09.

WRS (2008) *Wildlife Reserves Singapore Yearbook 2007–2008*. Singapore: WRS.

WRS (2007) *Wildlife Reserves Singapore Yearbook 2006–2007*. Singapore: WRS.

WRS (2006) *Wildlife Reserves Singapore Yearbook 2005–2006*. Singapore: WRS.

Yollin, P. (2006) Not your mama's 'birds and bees', the Zoo's x-rated sex tour is graphic, kinky. *San Francisco Chronicle*, February 15.

Young, R.J. (2003) *Environmental Enrichment for Captive Animals*. Oxford: Blackwell.

Zajonic, R.B. (1968) Attitudinal effects of mere exposure. *Journal of Personality and Psychology* 9, 1–29.

Zeithaml, V., Berry, L. and Parasuraman, A. (1996) The behavioral consequences of service quality. *Journal of Marketing* 60 (2), 31–46.

Zeppel, H. and Muloin, S. (2008) Conservation benefits of interpretation on marine wildlife tours. *Human Dimensions of Wildlife* 13 (4), 280–294.

Zerah, M-H. (2007) Conflict between green space preservation and housing needs: The case of the Sanjay Gandhi National Park in Mumbai. *Cities* 24 (2), 122–132.

Zimmermann, A., Hatchwell, M., Dickie, L. and West, C. (eds) (2007) *Zoos in the 21st Century: Catalysts for Conservation*. Cambridge: Cambridge University Press.

Zoltak, J. (2005) Owners of petting zoos brace for fallout. *Amusement Business* 117 (4), 25.

Zoological Parks Authority (2007) *Zoological Parks Authority Annual Report*. Perth: Zoological Parks Authority.

Zoological Parks and Gardens Board (1997) *Zoological Parks and Gardens Board Victoria, Australia – Annual Report 1996/97*. Zooligical Park and Gardens Board.

Zoos Victoria (2008a) *About Werribee Open Range Zoo*. On WWW at http://www.zoo.org.au/About_Werribee_Open_Range_Zoo.

Zoos Victoria (2008b) *Friends Of The Zoo*. On WWW at http://www.zoo.org.au/fotz.

Zoos Victoria (2008c) *Zoos Victoria Annual Report 2007–2008*. On WWW at http://www.zoo.org.au/zpgb/annual_reports.

Zoos Victoria (2008d) *Looking for a Way to get Closer? Book a behind the Scenes Experience*. Melbourne: Zoos Victoria.

Zoos Victoria (2009) Vision and Mission. On WWW at http://www.zoo.org.au/About_ZV/Vision_and_Mission. Accessed 17.8..09.

Zoo Zurich (2009) *Zoo Zurich – Facts and Figures*. On WWW at http://www.zoo.ch.

Index